THE CURRICULUM

D0263461

THE CURRICULUM

Theory and Practice

FOURTH EDITION

A. V. Kelly

P·C·P
Paul Chapman
Publishing Ltd

Paul Chapman Publishing Ltd
A SAGE Publications Company
6 Bonhill Street
London EC2A 4PU

SAGE Publications Inc.
2455 Teller Road
Thousand Oaks, California 91320

SAGE Publications India Pvt Ltd
32, M-Block Market
Greater Kailash-I
New Delhi 110 048

British Library Cataloguing in Publication Data
A catalogue record for this book is available from the British Library

ISBN 1 85396 430 1
ISBN 1 85396 384 4 (pbk)

Library of Congress catalog card number available

Typeset by Dorwyn Ltd, Rowlands Castle
Printed in Great Britain by Athenaeum Press, Gateshead

D E F G H   3

Contents

_____

The teacher, like the artist, the philosopher and the man of letters, can only perform his work adequately if he feels himself to be an individual directed by an inner creative impulse, not dominated and fettered by an outside authority.

Bertrand Russell, *Unpopular Essays* (1950:159)

Introduction

The first edition of this book was published at a time when an understanding of the complexities of the curriculum and of curriculum planning was evolving at a quite rapid rate. That evolution was due to two interrelated factors. First, significant changes were occurring in the curricula of schools, both in the UK and elsewhere, especially in the USA, as educationists and teachers sought to develop forms of curricular provision which would be more appropriate to the economic, social and, indeed, political conditions of the twentieth century. And, second, there was inevitably extensive theoretical reflection on these changes; indeed, the value of the work of bodies such as the Schools Council in England and Wales at that time may be said to lie more in the theoretical insights it generated than in any changes in the practices of schools and teachers which it brought about.

In 1977, then, our first edition set out to draw together some of these many insights for the benefit both of practitioners and of students of curriculum. In particular, it was offered in the hope that it might contribute in some small way to a bridging of the gap between the theory and practice of education by convincing teachers of the importance of developing a theoretical underpinning to their work. For a crucial premise of the book was a conviction that without this, as the Foreword to the first edition said, 'there can be no effective curriculum development no matter how hard people try from outside the school to promote it'.

Only five years later, in 1982, the second edition began by acknowledging that it was being offered in a significantly different climate, that 'shades of the prison house' were beginning to close in around pupils and teachers. There was still sufficient optimism, however, for the same fundamental positions to be taken – the importance of sound theoretical reflection on practice and the justification of this in terms of the centrality of the teacher to effective curriculum development. However, a further, and perhaps prophetic, argument was advanced in support of these positions – the need for teachers to have a sound theoretical perspective as a defence against the imposition on them of policies framed by amateurs, as we expressed it in the Introduction to the second edition, the placing of curriculum control 'in the hands of others who are in no position to exercise it effectively'.

By 1989, when the third edition was published, a number of battles had been lost, and the Introduction to that edition described the extent to which the social and political climate of curriculum planning had changed. 'The background constraints on curriculum planning have moved into the foreground; indeed, constraints have become directives; concern with curriculum evaluation has grown into demands for teacher appraisal and accountability; the role of the teacher in curriculum planning and development, whose centrality both earlier editions were concerned to stress, has been rapidly eroded and dramatically reduced in scope; the evolutionary process of curriculum development has been effectively halted; and, in general, the "secret garden" of the curriculum has been thrown open to the public – an event which, as in many other stately homes, has led to ossification as well as preservation and to much trampling on the flower-beds.'

Clearly, in writing that, one had in mind the dramatic change in policy in England and Wales which culminated in the 1988 Education Act and the establishment of the National Curriculum and its paraphernalia of regular assessment and Ofsted inspections. But, while perhaps this development was particularly extreme in its scope and its effects, similar changes were to be seen occurring elsewhere, so that the problems identified there had to be seen as not merely of parochial concern in England and Wales, or even in the UK as a whole, but as problems which could be seen in one shape or another besetting educational provision throughout the 'free' world.

In that context, the third edition reiterated the fundamental principles which had been the underpinning of its two predecessors. To these it added, however, that there was an obligation on politicians and their advisers (a category which, according to well substantiated rumour, included hairdressers and cleaners), since they had taken on the role of curriculum planners, to develop a proper understanding that 'the planning of an educational programme is a far more sophisticated activity than most of the present amateur planners seem able, or willing, to recognize, and that it necessitates an intellectual depth of understanding which they manifestly lack', since 'the over-simplification of curricular issues puts education itself at risk and must lead to a lowering of educational standards rather than that raising of standards which current policies purport to be seeking'.

Of particular interest, then, in the context of this book and its history, are two developments which can be observed to have occurred in the intervening years. First, there has been that inevitable loss of those many insights the first edition attempted to summarize and collate, which is the corollary of the loss of independence of judgement for teachers. The school curriculum has ceased to evolve, indeed in many places (most notably in provision for Primary education, and especially the early years) has been forced back to an earlier and more primitive form. And those insights which had emerged from the attempts at curriculum change and evolution of the 1960s and 1970s have been ignored and in fact stifled. In the face of political dictation on the scale we have witnessed, therefore, the curriculum debate has come to seem increasingly pointless and the evolution of curricular understandings has been severely retarded if not halted altogether. Perhaps the best evidence of this is that this edition has had to continue to rely on illustrations drawn from earlier experimentation and practice and from the theoretical debates which these fuelled, since little that is more recent has been able to emerge.

Second, however, there has arisen a new debate, focused on the politicization of education and its implications not only for the curriculum itself but also for the very notion of democracy and the concept of the 'free' society. There has been a significant shift of focus onto the political processes themselves and an increased interest in concepts of democracy, their implications for educational provision, the impact of competing ideologies, the use of testing, inspection and the legitimation of discourse as a strategy of political control and a long list of similar issues arising from reflection on the process of politicization itself.

In the current context, therefore, the two central tasks of this revision are to identify the major implications of the process of politicization which the intervening years have seen, and to reaffirm the open debate about curriculum which that process has largely stifled. The concern must be to maintain the understandings and insights which were the fruits of that wide ranging debate of earlier times and to view the politicization process from the perspective they provide.

This fourth edition, then, while yielding no ground in relation to the values and principles which have been consistently advocated since 1977 by all three of its antecedents, must recognize these shifts of focus and the resultant need not only for changes in emphasis but for discussion of a number of newly emergent aspects of curriculum studies.

These two perspectives, then, provide the key questions which the student of curriculum and the responsible professional educator must address in the current social and political context. And it is encouraging to know that the number of people who are still interested in addressing them is sufficient to warrant a fourth edition of a book which, unlike many others, will continue to affirm the values and principles which prompted its first publication twenty years ago.

1

The curriculum and the study of the curriculum

It is stating the obvious to assert that education has changed drastically in the last twenty or thirty years. Both in the United Kingdom and elsewhere many important modifications have been made to all aspects of the education system. Nor is it surprising that the nature and structure of our education system should have been changing so extensively at a time when we have been experiencing social change of an equally dramatic kind, much of it prompted by rapid technological advance. The education system is a social institution which should be expected to change along with other such institutions. It would be more surprising, not to say disturbing, if the education system were to stand still while all else changed. And it is the need to ensure that it continues to develop, and that it responds appropriately not only to other changes in society but also to our increasing understanding of the educational process itself, which is, or should be, the central concern of educational studies and especially of curriculum studies.

One feature that has characterized the curriculum change of recent years is the increased incidence of planning in curriculum development. Most of the curriculum change that we saw before this was of a kind best described as unplanned 'drift' (Hoyle, 1969a). From the 1960s on, however, educationists began to see the need for planned innovation, to recognize that if educational change is to keep pace with and match changes in society, if it is at the same time to maintain also those standards and values which may be seen as transcending particular times and particular societies, and if it is to respond to that increased understanding of education and curriculum which has come from extensive work in the field of curriculum studies, it must be deliberately managed rather than merely left to happen. To recognize this is not, of course, to be committed to a totally revolutionary approach to curriculum development. The advantages of evolution over revolution are at least as evident in education as elsewhere. It is, however, to acknowledge that the process of evolution can be smoother, quicker and more effective, if it is not left to chance but implemented according to carefully thought-out strategies.

Recent experience, especially in England and Wales, has reinforced the case for curriculum evolution rather than revolution. For the shift we have seen towards central political control of the school curriculum has sometimes been revolutionary in its effect, so that it has often been far from smooth and thus less effective than it might have been.

One reason for this has been a failure to recognize that the changes which have occurred in society have been social, moral and political as well as, indeed as a consequence of, technological and economic developments. The natural evolution of the curriculum was reflecting this, especially in terms of attempts to overcome privilege and inequality and to move towards a more truly egalitarian system. Direct political intervention, by concentrating on the economic functions of the educational system, has largely ignored that dimension of educational provision along with its responsibility for promoting the personal development of the young, thus activating all of the consequences which that omission has for the quality of life in society.

It has also led to a technicist approach to the study of education by ignoring all or most of the insights which had been derived from explorations which had sought to go beyond concerns of mere methodology, to ask the 'why' questions concerning educational provision as well as those restricted to the 'how'. These insights have thus been placed at risk, and it is the central concern of this book, as has already been pointed out, to regain those insights and to reaffirm this kind of study of education and curriculum.

It is the aim of this chapter, then, to identify what is involved in this, to outline some of the essential ingredients both of the practice of curriculum planning and development and the study of curriculum. All or most of these points will be examined in greater detail in the chapters that follow, but an overall framework, a rationale, a cognitive map offered at the outset may help to establish and maintain the interrelationship of the many factors involved in curriculum planning.

What is the curriculum?

The first need is to achieve some clarity over what we are to understand by the term 'curriculum'. It is a term which is used with several meanings and a number of different definitions of it have been offered, so that it is important that we establish at the beginning what it should be taken to signify throughout this book, and, perhaps more importantly, what it should *not* be taken to mean.

The total curriculum

To begin with, it will be helpful if we distinguish the use of the word to denote the content of a particular subject or area of study from the use of it to refer to the total programme of an educational institution. Many people still equate a curriculum with a syllabus and thus limit their planning to a consideration of the content or the body of knowledge they wish to transmit or a list of the subjects to be taught or both. The inadequacies of this view of curriculum as content will be explored more fully in Chapter 3. It will be immediately clear, however, that this kind of definition of curriculum is limiting in more than one way and that it is likely to hamper rather than to assist the planning of curriculum change and development. Indeed, some of the inadequacies of previous and current attempts at curriculum planning can be attributed to the fact that they have tended to proceed in a rather piecemeal way within subjects rather than according to any overall rationale.

This dimension of curriculum development is, of course, important, but it is the rationale of the total curriculum that must have priority. 'Schools should plan their curriculum as a whole. The curriculum offered by a school, and the curriculum received by individual pupils, should not be simply a collection of separate subjects' (DES, 1981:12). At the very least, the total curriculum must be accorded prior consideration, and a major task that currently faces teachers and curriculum planners is to work out a basis and develop a rationale on which some total scheme can be built.

Any definition of curriculum, if it is to be practically effective and productive, must offer much more than a statement about the knowledge-content or merely the subjects which schooling is to 'teach' or transmit. It must go far beyond this to an explanation, and indeed a justification, of the purposes of such transmission and an exploration of the effects that exposure to such knowledge and such subjects is likely to have, or is intended to have, on its recipients – indeed it is from these deeper concerns, as we shall see later, that any curriculum planning worthy of the name must start.

These wider concerns will be the focus of our discussions in this book, and we will understand by the term 'curriculum' the overall rationale for any educational programme, including those more subtle features of curriculum change and development and especially those underlying principles which we have just suggested are the most crucial element in curriculum studies. Much of what is said about curriculum development in this sense will, of course, be of relevance to the problems of developments within individual subject areas, but the prime concern must be with the totality.

The 'hidden' curriculum

A further question that needs to be resolved is whether we are to place any limit on the kinds of school activity that we will allow to count as part of the curriculum when it is defined in this way.

For example, some educationists speak of the 'hidden curriculum', by which they mean those things which pupils learn at school because of the way in which the work of the school is planned and organized, and through the materials provided, but which are not in themselves overtly included in the planning or even in the consciousness of those responsible for the school arrangements. Social roles, for example, are learnt in this way, it is claimed, as are sex roles and attitudes to many other aspects of living. Implicit in any set of arrangements are the attitudes and values of those who create them, and these will be communicated to pupils in this accidental and perhaps even sinister way. This factor is of course of particular significance when the curriculum is planned and imposed by government.

Some would argue of course that the values implicit in the arrangements made by schools for their pupils are quite clearly in the consciousness of teachers and planners, again especially when the planners are politicians, and are equally clearly accepted by them as part of what pupils should learn in school, even though they are not overtly recognized by the pupils themselves. If this is the case, then, the curriculum is 'hidden' only to or from the pupils, and the values to be learnt clearly form a part of what is planned for pupils. They must, therefore, be accepted as fully a part of the curriculum, and most especially as an important focus for the kind of study of curriculum with which we are concerned here, not least because important questions must be asked concerning the legitimacy of such practices.

Others, however, take a less definite and perhaps less cynical line on this but wish nevertheless to insist that teachers do have a responsibility here. They accept that some of the values and attitudes learnt via the hidden curriculum are not directly intended by teachers, but believe that, since these things are being learnt as a by-product of what is planned and of the materials provided, teachers should be aware of and accept responsibility for what is going on, for what their pupils are learning in this unplanned way. It is this view which is at the heart of attempts to eliminate implicit racism and sexism from the experiences children receive at school.

It is because of the all-pervasive nature of such experiences and hidden forms of learning, and also because of the assumed impossibility of eliminating such unplanned, and thus uncontrolled, learning, that some theorists, such as Ivan Illich (1971), have recommended a 'deschooling' of society and have claimed that all forms of organized schooling must involve the imposition of the values implicit in the selection of the content of such schooling on its recipients, and thus constitute an invidious form of social and political control through the distribution of knowledge. This is an important point and one to which we shall return in Chapter 2. What it suggests which is of importance here, however, is that, if we are not to go to the lengths of abolishing schooling altogether, we cannot merely ignore these hidden aspects of the school curriculum, and certainly must not adopt a definition of curriculum which excludes them from all critical consideration. Rather our definition must embrace all the learning that goes on in schools whether it is expressly planned and intended or is a by-product of our planning and/or practice. For it is difficult to exonerate teachers completely from responsibility for these implicit forms of learning. Rather they need to be sensitized to them and helped to recognize and identify the hidden implications of some of the materials and the experiences they offer their pupils.

The planned curriculum and the received curriculum

Much the same point emerges when we consider the distinction which has sometimes been made between the official curriculum and the actual curriculum, or between the planned curriculum and the received curriculum. By the official or planned curriculum is meant what is laid down in syllabuses, prospectuses and so on; the actual or received curriculum is the reality of the pupils' experience. The difference between them may be conscious or unconscious, the cause of any mismatch being either a deliberate attempt by the teachers or others to deceive, to make what they offer appear more attractive than it really is, as with the National Curriculum for England and Wales, or merely the fact that, since teachers and pupils are human, the realities of any course will never fully match up to the hopes and intentions of those who have planned it.

Both of these distinctions are important and we would be foolish to go very far in our examination of the curriculum without acknowledging both the gaps that must inevitably exist between theory and practice and the predilection of some teachers, and more especially national planners, for elaborate 'packaging' of their wares.

It becomes even more important, then, that we should not adopt a definition of curriculum which confines or restricts us to considerations only of that which is planned. What is actually received by pupils must be an equally important, or even more important concern, so that the actual or received curriculum must be seen as the teacher's or planner's responsibility every bit as much as the 'hidden' curriculum.

Furthermore, we must not lose sight of the fact that curriculum studies must ultimately be concerned with the relationship between these two views of the curriculum, between intention and reality, and, indeed, with closing the gap between them, if it is to succeed in linking the theory and the practice of the curriculum (Stenhouse, 1975).

The formal curriculum and the informal curriculum

Lastly, we must also recognize the distinction that is often drawn between the 'formal' curriculum and the 'informal' curriculum, between the formal activities for which the timetable of the school allocates specific periods of teaching time and those many informal activities that go on, usually on a voluntary basis, at lunch-times, after school hours, at weekends or during holidays. These latter activities – sports, clubs, societies, school journeys and the like – are often called 'extracurricular' activities and this suggests that they should be seen as separate from, as over and above the curriculum itself.

The reasons for this, however, are difficult to discern. For activities of this kind are usually regarded as having as much educational validity and point as any of the formal arrangements of the school. Indeed, some would even argue that in certain cases they have more point than many such arrangements. It was for this reason that the Newsom Report (CACE, 1963:para.135)) recommended that they 'ought to be recognized as an integral part of the total educational programme' and that to this end they be included in the formal timetable of an extended day. And the inclusion of this kind of activity in the formal provision made by the school has also been a major feature of the philosophy of many of those concerned with the development of community schools (Cooksey, 1972, 1976a, 1976b).

Again, it would seem that, if we are concerned with curriculum planning, it would be foolish to omit by our definition of the curriculum a whole range of activities which teachers plan and execute with deliberate reasons and intentions. In looking at curriculum planning, therefore, there would appear to be nothing to be gained from leaving out of consideration any planned activity. It is for this reason that John Kerr (1968:16) defined the curriculum as 'all the learning which is planned and guided by the school, whether it is carried on in groups or individually, inside or outside the school'. Such a definition provides us with a basis for planning all the organized activities of a school.

However, there are real difficulties in attempting to operate with a definition of curriculum which excludes from consideration the unplanned effects of teacher activity, as the notions of the 'hidden' and the 'actual' or 'received' curriculum indicate. There are more aspects to curriculum than are dreamed of in the philosophy of most teachers, and certainly of most politicians, and a definition of curriculum which confines its scope to what teachers, or politicians, actually plan will omit many of those important dimensions of curriculum studies we identified earlier. We need a definition which will embrace at least four major dimensions of educational planning and practice: the intentions of the planners, the procedures adopted for the implementation of those intentions, the actual experiences of the pupils resulting from the teachers' direct attempts to carry out their or the planners' intentions, and the 'hidden' learning that occurs as a by-product of the organization of the curriculum, and, indeed, of the school.

The problems of definition are thus serious and complex and the chapters which follow will reveal that in planning for curriculum change and development we need to be aware of all aspects and dimensions of the educational experiences which pupils have during any period of formal education, and with their underlying principles and rationale. The definition adopted here, therefore, is that the curriculum is the totality of the experiences the pupil has as a result of the provision made.

If we take this broad definition of curriculum as our starting point, then, it becomes possible to identify the kinds of issue which the study of curriculum must address – the issues which subsequent chapters will explore in greater detail.

Before we do that, however, there is a further preliminary point which must be made. For a major premise of what follows is that in all successful curriculum development and implementation the teacher is the crucial element. And we must pause for an explanation of why this stance has been adopted.

The centrality of the teacher

It must first be stressed that all that is said about curriculum planning and development in this book applies as much to the individual teacher in the preparation of his or her individual 'lessons' or other programmes of work with children as it does to those who find themselves charged with curriculum development at school, local authority or even national level.

A major reason for stressing this is not merely to remind teachers of the degree of responsibility they must accept for their own professional work, nor only to emphasize their consequent need for the kinds of understanding of curriculum which this book is seeking to provide; it is, perhaps more importantly, because of the 'make or break' role that teachers have in all curricular activities, even in relation to those which originate outside their schools.

There have been many attempts over the last two or three decades to bring about curriculum change, most notably those sponsored by the Schools Council during its lifetime, some of the later work of the Assessment of Performance Unit and, most recently, the decision to change the curricula of all schools to fit the demands of the new National Curriculum. These strategies for external manipulation of the curriculum we shall explore in greater detail in later chapters.

The most important point to be noted here, however, is what we have learned from the experience of these projects and activities about the role of the individual teacher in curriculum change and development. We must especially note the failure of early attempts by the Schools Council to produce 'teacher-proof' packages – schemes of work, versions of curriculum, supporting materials and so on of a kind which teachers would accept, use and apply in the precise form that the central planners had in mind. In every case, teachers have adapted and used what they have been offered in their own ways and for their own purposes. Some project directors were inclined to throw up their hands in despair at this phenomenon, at what they saw, and sometimes described, as 'cannibalism'. Others went along with it eventually and built into their schemes proper forms of allowance for this kind of personal and local adaptation by teachers. The Schools Council itself, just before its demise, adopted a policy of supporting school-based curriculum developments, assisting teachers and groups of teachers with the process of developing their own curricula rather than attempting to 'sell' them prepackaged programmes which might not be geared appropriately to the specific needs of the individual school. And some of the later work of the Assessment of Performance Unit was concerned much more with offering its findings to teachers, while leaving it to them to decide whether and how they might use these in their own contexts, than with attempts at imposing the same solutions to teaching problems on all (Kelly, 1987). In short, there has come a growing awareness that each school is unique and that its curricular needs are thus largely idiosyncratic.

The implications of this kind of experience for the implementation of forms of centralized control such as the National Curriculum are interesting and will be explored more fully later. We have here another example of the failure or the refusal of the architects of these policies to take any account or cognizance of the substantial experience and findings of earlier research and practice.

What we must note here, however, is that the teachers have a 'make or break' role in any curriculum innovation. Teachers have been known to sabotage attempts at change; certainly it is clear that such attempts can succeed only when the teachers concerned are committed to them and, especially, when they understand, as well as accept, their underlying principles. The practice of education cannot be a mechanical, largely mindless activity; it requires constant decisions and judgements by the teacher, and these he or she cannot make properly without fully appreciating and accepting the underlying rationale of any activity. Teaching, interpreted in a purely technicist sense, may be undertaken in a mechanistic manner. If, however, our concern is with *education*, in the full sense, much more than this is required, since education is essentially an interactive process. 'The building block is the moral purpose of the *individual* teacher. Scratch a good teacher and you will find a moral purpose' (Fullan, 1993:10).

The quality of any *educational* experience, then, will depend to a very large extent on the individual teacher responsible for it; and any attempt at controlling the curriculum from the outside which does not recognize that must be doomed to failure, or at best to triviality. An alternative strategy for ensuring compliance to external requirements is of course to introduce stringent measures for controlling the activities of teachers, through schemes of pupil assessment, regular inspections, teacher appraisal and accountability, and this aspect of current policies we must also consider later. Such a strategy, however, cannot ensure commitment or understanding; and obedience to authority on the part of teachers may not be the best basis for the practice of education as we are viewing it here, although it may well be adequate if the concern goes no further than teaching or instruction.

The corollary of this is that it becomes even more important for teachers to work at developing the kind of broader understanding of curricular provision which a study of the curriculum at the level we are advocating should bring. Indeed, it might be argued that there is a major professional obligation on them to do so, since this is the only route to effective practice. Hence, recent years have seen the emergence of concepts such as that of 'the teacher as researcher' (Stenhouse, 1975) and of 'action research' as a key element in continous professional development.

On the other hand, increased centralized control of teachers' work has had the effect of discouraging this kind of professional activity on the part of teachers. It has always been important, even when we acknowledge the central role of the teacher in education, not to lose sight of the fact that he or she is operating in a context hedged about with many constraints and pressures, social and political as well as physical and organizational. No curriculum planning of any kind can go on in a vacuum; it must take place in an environment which is subject to pressures and constraints of many kinds.

Recent developments, however, most notably the constraints imposed on teachers in England and Wales by the statutory requirements of the 1988 Education Act, have converted these indirect constraints into direct control. The more direct influences of central government on the school curriculum have been slowly converted from influence to intervention and from intervention to direct control. The most important effect of this is that teachers now have little or no say in the official curriculum of the nation's schools, so that they are now expected to operate a curriculum which has been imposed upon them from without and to implement curricular policies over whose framing they have had little or no influence.

This latter point raises some interesting issues in the light of what we said earlier about the need for teachers to be committed to the curricular provision they are making if they are to make it properly and effectively. One of the strengths of the previous system was that most teachers did believe in what they were doing, or at least enjoyed a good deal of scope to make of it something they could believe in. No doubt there will be many who will believe in what they are now required to do. But for those who do not there are clearly important problems to be faced. At a more theoretical level, these are problems which highlight the distinction we referred to earlier in this chapter between the official and the actual curriculum, between the intention and the reality, between theory and practice. They also resurrect those difficulties we have also noted which arise from earlier attempts to manipulate teachers by remote control or to create teacher-proof curricula.

There is thus every discouragement in the present political climate for teachers who wish to view their professionalism in 'extended' terms and to pursue a study of curricular issues at levels beyond that of the mere 'delivery' of their subject knowledge. Indeed, the processes they are subject to have been described by many commentators as processes of deprofessionalisation. If, however, their role is central, and if, further, the effective fulfilment of that role is · dependent on a breadth of understanding of curriculum, the implications of the loss, or the suppression, of these insights are extremely serious for the long-term quality of educational provision.

Key aspects of curriculum studies

Now that we have established and explained the definition of 'curriculum' and the view of the role of the teacher within it which provide the major premises of the discussion which follows, we can identify briefly the broad issues which the rest of the book will seek to address in greater detail. All of these will be seen to reflect insights which have been gained from curriculum change, taken in its broadest sense, and reflection on that change. And all of them will be seen to be at risk in the current political climate.

Strategies for curriculum change and control

One family of issues we must concern ourselves with is that of the lessons which have been learned from the many attempts which have been made to change the curriculum.

We have just noted that one of those lessons has been that the teacher's role is central to the effectiveness of any attempt at curriculum change or development. The converse of this is what we have also learned concerning the role, effectiveness and, indeed, the value of national agencies for curriculum development and change. In particular, as we have seen, the work of the Schools Council and other national agencies of change in England and Wales taught us much about how such bodies, external to the schools themselves, might most effectively promote change and development within the schools – especially, as we have also seen, by supporting developments within rather than seeking to impose change from without. These are lessons which those responsible for the implementation of the National Curriculum have failed – or refused – to acknowledge. The notion that all curriculum development is teacher development was first promulgated several decades ago (Stenhouse, 1975), and, indeed, had become almost a truism until it was rejected in favour of more coercive methods.

Those coercive methods, in addition to including the application of sanctions of various kinds, have also embraced more subtle strategies of change. We will see, for example, how effectively rhetoric, metaphor and the control of discourse generally are being used to bring about the changes which government has sought to impose on the school curriculum. And, at a more readily discernible level, we can recognize how assessment and inspection are being employed as part of the same kind of coercive strategy.

This takes us to a second major family of issues the student of curriculum must address.

Assessment, evaluation, appraisal and accountability

Among the insights into the workings of curriculum which emerged from the research and studies of the 1970s and 1980s were many in the related areas of pupil assessment, curriculum evaluation and, perhaps to a lesser extent, teacher appraisal. There was significant development both in techniques (for example the introduction of some highly sophisticated forms of pupil assessment) and in our understanding of the effects and implications of the adoption of particular forms and approaches (for example the ideas of self-evaluation and action research).

However, that move towards direct political control of the school curriculum which we have just noted has been accompanied by a major shift in the view taken of the purposes of these related elements of educational policy and practice and, as a consequence, in the procedures adopted to achieve those purposes.

For pupil assessment, curriculum evaluation, teacher appraisal and, indeed, school inspections have come to be regarded, and used, as key instruments in the establishment of direct political control, of combating that centrality of the teacher we have also just noted and of imposing a narrow and bureaucratic form of teacher accountability. We have experienced an era of 'assessment-led educational reform' (Hargreaves, 1989:99).

Thus sophisticated forms of pupil assessment have given way to regular, and somewhat simplistic, testing, thus marking a shift from a formative and diagnostic function to a largely summative one, designed to provide figures for 'league tables' rather than to offer information about individual pupils which might guide the planning of their future provision, and to the use of graded tests rather than pupil profiling (Hargreaves, 1989). The focus of evaluation has moved from a concern with the value of what is being offered to a concentration on the effectiveness of its 'delivery'. And teachers and schools are appraised also in terms of the effectiveness of their 'delivery' of whatever is dictated rather than in relation to what might be seen as the wider concerns of education.

This does not, however, mean that there is no longer a need for teachers to familiarize themselves with the issues and the techniques of assessment and evaluation. Teachers will continue to wish to assess their pupils in order to make adequate provision for them and to evaluate their own work with the same purposes in mind; and they will still need quite sophisticated techniques and understandings in order to do so. The insights gained in this area too, therefore, need to be maintained. One hopes also that, even with little direct power to bring about change themselves, they will wish to continue to evaluate official policies and practices, if only to assert their professionalism and to maintain that curriculum debate we are suggesting is becoming more rather than less important in the new era.

This, then is another major area we will need to explore in greater detail later in this book.

The politicization of curriculum

The uses and abuses of assessment and evaluation which we have just touched upon alert us to a further major area which the student of curriculum cannot afford to ignore, especially in the current social and political climate. For, as we have already noted, the flavour of the curriculum debate, as it has been conducted over the two decades which have passed since the publication of the first edition of this book, has become increasingly and strongly political.

The placing of the school curriculum in the hands of a series of politically motivated quangos, which reconstruct themselves – or, at least, rename themselves – almost annually, along with their use and abuse of devices such as assessment and inspections to achieve what are fundamentally political goals, has not only reinforced the need for continued and careful study of all of these aspects of curriculum; it has also called for a focusing of attention on this process of politicization itself.

We have long been familiar with the importance of education in the achievement of political goals. Indeed, it was the first exponent of education theory, Plato himself, who drew our attention to this and recognized educational provision as the key to achieving the kind of society he wished to see established. His advice has not gone unheeded by those engaged in social engineering of many forms since that time, most notably those seeking to establish and maintain social control in totalitarian societies – fascist Spain, for example, Nazi Germany and communist Russia.

The appropriateness of employing similar techniques in societies which purport to be democratic, however, demands to be explored. And so, it is no surprise to discover that the last decade or so has seen the appearance of a plethora of books and articles which have set about precisely this kind of exploration.

Hence, no attempt to fuel the curriculum debate at the beginning of the third millennium can ignore this crucial dimension of that debate. Indeed, we shall see, as perhaps we have seen already, that it is an area of concern which now permeates discussion of all other aspects of the study of curriculum.

Knowledge, ideology and curriculum planning

Finally, we must note another crucial theme which underpins all of these issues – a series of fundamental questions about human knowledge and the implications of these for the ways in which we set about planning the school curriculum.

The content of what we expect children to learn during their schooling is clearly a crucial element in curriculum planning, whatever view we take of education, curriculum or, indeed, knowledge itself. There are important questions to be addressed, however, concerning how the knowledge content of a curriculum relates to its other dimensions. Indeed, an important first step in any study of curriculum is the recognition that other dimensions exist. For it has too often been assumed, again notably by the architects of the National Curriculum for England and Wales, that to plan a curriculum is merely to outline the knowledge content to be 'delivered' and imbibed.

It has been suggested (Tyler, 1949) that the curriculum has to be seen as consisting of four elements, and curriculum planning, therefore, as having four dimensions: objectives, content or subject matter, methods or pro-cedures and evaluation. In short, the claim is that we must distinguish in our curriculum planning what we are hoping to achieve, the ground we are planning to cover in order to achieve it, the kinds of activity and methods that we consider likely to be most effective in helping us towards our goals and the devices we will use to evaluate what we have done. Tyler's own way of putting this point is to suggest that there are 'four fundamental questions which must be answered in developing any curriculum and plan of instruction' (1949:i). These he lists as:

1. What educational purposes should the school seek to attain?
2. What educational experiences can be provided that are likely to attain these purposes?
3. How can these educational experiences be effectively organized?
4. How can we determine whether these purposes are being attained?

This analysis, then, if taken just as it stands, would give us a very simple model for curriculum planning, a linear model which requires us to specify our objectives, to plan the content and the methods which will lead us towards them and, finally, to endeavour to measure the extent of our success. It is, however, too simple a model for many reasons, as we shall see when we discuss the issue more fully later in this book.

What we must note here, however, is that rather than offering us a single, and simple, model for curriculum planning, Tyler's work can be seen as having alerted us to the possibility of adopting any of several planning models. For, if a curriculum can, or must, be viewed in terms of these four elements, different planning models will emerge according to the ways in which we might permutate those elements, the priorities we might give to them and the choice of focus we might adopt.

We have already noted that some planners see curriculum content as central, so that the acquisition of that content by pupils becomes the central purpose of the curriculum, the organization becomes a matter solely of effectiveness of 'delivery' and evaluation is focused on the degree of attainment achieved by the pupils.

Tyler's own concern, however, as we have just noted, was with the purposes of the curriculum, so that he is usually seen as one of the founding fathers of the 'aims-and-objectives' model of curriculum planning. Within that model, the educational purposes of the curriculum take pride of place, content is selected not for its own sake but for its presumed efficacy at enabling us to achieve those purposes, organization is similarly designed with these objectives in mind, and evaluation is framed so as to assess how far those objectives have been achieved.

Yet a third model has emerged more recently, as some have placed the emphasis on the organization of the educational experiences. This model has been described as a 'process' model (Stenhouse, 1975) or as a 'developmental' model (Blenkin and Kelly, 1987, 1996). With this model, the planner begins from a concept of education as a series of developmental processes which the curriculum should be designed to promote. The selection of both content and methods or procedures is made with the promotion of these developmental processes as the central concern. And evaluation is focused both on the suitability of the content and procedures selected and on an assessment of the development which may, or may not, have occurred.

Thus we can immediately see that curriculum planning is not the simple matter some would have us believe. For it must begin with the crucial choice of the most appropriate planning model for the work we have in mind. Furthermore, it must be accompanied by a justification of that choice. For it is not acceptable that we should plan something as important as a curriculum, at whatever level, by simply plucking a planning model out of the air without serious consideration of all possible alternatives.

This last point takes us into an additional complication. For it will already perhaps be clear that each of the three models which have been identified represents not only a distinctive conceptualization of curriculum but also an equally distinctive concept of what education is about, what its purposes and functions are. In other words, each reflects a different educational ideology, which can in turn be related to a particular intellectual ideology and, perhaps most seriously, a particular political ideology.

It is this which makes curriculum planners, especially those working on behalf of political agencies, reluctant to advertise the fact that different models for planning the school curriculum exist. For to do so raises an obligation for them to justify their own choice and thus to make public the ideology they are seeking to impose. It is this also, therefore, that makes this an important area of exploration for the student of curriculum, and, indeed, for any teacher who wishes to lay claim to the title of professional educator.

We must finally note that a major issue which lies behind this debate about models is the view taken of human knowledge. For, among the many insights which we are claiming are currently being lost from the educational debate are those which relate to questions about the nature of human knowledge and, in particular, the ways in which the distribution of knowledge can be, and is, manipulated in society for political ends. What has been called 'the politics of knowledge' has come to be seen as a major focus of consideration by the student of curriculum and its claims to importance have been much strengthened by official policies and practices in recent years.

This becomes especially sinister when one notes that nothing has characterized intellectual development in the twentieth century more than a growing appreciation of the problematic nature of human knowledge. That current movement known as postmodernism, while in itself problematic, has over the last two or three decades highlighted the dangers of dogmatism, raised important issues concerning the validity of knowledge claims and thus, above all, drawn our attention to the concept of ideology and the political dangers of ideological domination. Hence, there has arisen a recent emphasis on concepts of democracy and their implications for curriculum planning (Kelly, 1995).

It is with this fundamental debate concerning human knowledge that we will begin our deeper explorations of curriculum in Chapter 2.

First, however, we must conclude this introductory chapter by asking, given the definition of curriculum which we have adopted and the consequent areas of concern we have identified, what are the key features of the kind of study we are about to embark upon.

What is involved in the study of the curriculum?

It is important from the outset to be clear about the kind of study we are involved in when we begin to explore issues related to curriculum planning and development. And there are several points which can be made straight away as a contribution to the attainment of such clarity.

A study in its own right

The first is that the area of study which has come to be known as curriculum studies has emerged from the attempts, over the last two decades, of researchers and some of those who have been concerned to teach educational studies to develop an approach to the study of education which would not be limited by being conducted within the confines of other disciplines, such as philosophy, psychology and sociology. The traditional approach to the study of education through these 'contributory disciplines', as they were once and in some places still are called, has led to serious inadequacies not least because of the approach's consequent inability to handle issues in an interdisciplinary way, in spite of the fact that it would be very difficult to identify any single educational issue which does not require a contribution from all these disciplines and often several others too.

Quite serious and extensive problems have arisen when the solutions to educational questions have been sought, and accepted, from psychologists or philosophers or sociologists, since inevitably such experts have a limited, one-sided and thus distorted view of the educational issues or practices to which they are applying the techniques and the methodologies of their own disciplines. Thus, for example, major problems were created by the establishment of a differentiated system of secondary schooling on the basis of the psychologists' view of intelligence and intelligence testing without the complementary and modifying contributions of a philosophical analysis of the concept of intelligence or of a sociological comment on the implications of such a system for the nature of society. Many other examples could readily be found in the history of the development of the schooling system in the United Kingdom or, indeed, in any other country.

Curriculum studies, then, has emerged from an attempt to study education and to explore educational problems in their own right and not as philosophical problems or as psychological or sociological phenomena. The concern has been to end the practice of viewing the study of education as a sub-branch of any or all of these other disciplines.

Practice as well as theory

Allied to this has been a concern to study education as a practical activity and not merely as a body of theory, to get to grips with the realities of educational practice and to do so 'from the inside', in a manner that the philosopher, the psychologist or the sociologist can never do. Their studies have essentially and inevitably been conducted from the outside; their concern has been with the effects of educational practice rather than with its nature, with the realities of the classroom. If recently they have begun to turn their attention to these realities, they have in effect been developing as sub-branches of curriculum studies.

We must not of course lose sight of the value of such empirical research to the curriculum planner. For the evidence which emerges from such studies is of immense value to the student of curriculum, and especially to those engaged in curriculum planning at whatever level. We need to be made aware of the effects of our policies and practices in areas such as curriculum planning, approaches to teaching, the organization of schooling, the use of testing and other assessment techniques and so on. In particular, we need to be kept apprised of the **side**-effects of what we plan and do, since these are the essence of that 'hidden' dimension of curriculum which we are suggesting should not be permitted to remain hidden.

However, we must note a significant limitation on the value of empirical studies of this kind. For such studies must by definition be descriptive rather than prescriptive. It is not the part of any of those experts to tell us what we *ought* to be doing in education, any more than it is the part of the scientist or the technologist to tell us what we ought to do with his or her findings or inventions. Yet educational practice must essentially be concerned with questions of what *ought* to be done. Teachers in their practice must make such decisions – by the day and sometimes by the minute; they must be prescriptive. And so, if they, and curriculum planners generally, are to be assisted in this quite crucial aspect of their task, they need the support of studies which can and do take full account of the value dimension of education.

Not an applied science

In general, these difficulties illustrate the problems and the inadequacies of all attempts to adopt a 'scientific' approach to the study or the planning of education and/or curriculum. Curriculum studies cannot be seen as a science, and especially not as an applied science. The history of attempts to theorize about education is littered with examples of this kind of scientist approach, and all of them have been theoretically misleading and practically harmful. Human beings seem to need the security of certainty in all areas of experience, and thus they are prey to all illusory forms of such certainty. This tendency is particularly odd, since it is the case that the more specifically human an activity is, the less susceptible it is to understanding through a search for objective 'truths'. Education is one such human activity, and thus does not lend itself to study of a narrowly scientific kind. It is what Maurice Holt (1981:80) has described as 'a complex and ultimately impenetrable process'. And a major reason for this is that there are many areas, most notably those of values – moral and aesthetic (and thus educational) – in which knowledge with claims to some kind of scientific certainty cannot be attained. Indeed, when we come to look at the significance for the curriculum of that movement which has come to be called postmodernism, we will see that there are good grounds for questioning and challenging knowledge claims in all fields.

Unfortunately, attempts to make the curriculum the object of scientific exploration, and, more seriously, the practice of offering educational prescriptions as if they are indisputable deductions from, or conclusions of, such scientific study, continue to be made. Nor are these confined to those working in the 'contributory disciplines'. This kind of not-to-be-questioned assertion is all too prevalent, as we shall see later, in those many pronouncements we are now offered from official sources. S. J. Curtis (1948:255) quotes a story about Robert Lowe: 'There is a story that when an HMI went to consult him, Lowe said, "I know what you've come about, the science of education. There is none. Good Morning."' Whether or not Lowe himself was fully aware of the significance of that assertion – or, indeed, meant it in the sense in which we are taking it here – it is a pity that the said HMI did not pass this pearl of wisdom down to his descendants. For we are still beset by government officials, with little or no understanding of the realities of teaching, pressing on us the notion of teaching as an applied science and seeking to rubbish the 'quaint old-fashioned and ultimately highly damaging British view that teaching is an art' (Reynolds, quoted in the *Times Educational Supplement*, 22 May, 1998:2) – an assertion which could only be made by someone intellectually incapable, or more likely, unwilling, to recognize the important conceptual distinction between education and teaching.

If, however, there is no science of education (as opposed to teaching), and thus no scientific and indisputable base for educational prescriptions, it must follow that all such prescriptions will reflect nothing more solid than the preferences, the values, the ideology of those who are offering them. And so, there is an obligation on such persons, first, not to behave as though this were not the case or as though their prescriptions enjoyed some kind of scientific objectivity that those of others do not, and, second, having recognized that, to see also the necessity of offering some justification of their views. To offer them as views without justification is to risk being totally ignored; to use a position of power to impose them without justification is to stand convicted of indoctrination and the abuse of authority.

Again we see, therefore, that the concept of ideology is an important one in curriculum studies, as is the concept of ideologies competing for dominance and of the curriculum as a battle ground for these competing ideologies. A study of curriculum, while not offering us spurious answers to questions of values, will, like Socrates of old, draw our attention to important questions which need to be asked about policies and practices and help us to achieve the kind of clarity which will enable us to see their underlying ideologies more clearly.

Beyond methodology

Curriculum studies as it is being defined here, then, goes far beyond what is now often called by that name in many courses of teacher education. For the term is often now used to denote those courses which once were known as professional studies. The added ingredient of curriculum studies is the requirement it places on the student of curriculum to be critical and questioning in his or her approach, to face the value issues central to such studies and, in short, to recognize that the concern is not with mere methodology, with the *how* of educational practice, but much more with questions of the justification of such practice, with the *why* as well as the how. It is this critical dimension that is crucial to curriculum studies, at least as it is conceived throughout this book. Curriculum studies must be seen as a form of professional studies which takes full account of the need for teachers to adopt what has been called an 'extended' professionalism, that attitude to their work which makes them professionals in the full sense rather than mere practitioners.

We can take this further. At one level, curriculum studies can be seen, and is seen by many, as concerned largely with the mechanics of curriculum planning, development and innovation. There is no doubt that this is an important area of study and that there are many curricula which could profit enormously from the application of the understanding of the mechanics of curriculum planning which has been acquired through recent studies. There is much more to curriculum studies than this, however, and this further, and crucial, dimension is lost when we settle, or allow ourselves to be forced into settling, for a purely technicist approach. We have already seen that, if it is to help teachers and other curriculum planners with the most difficult theoretical task they face – that of justifying their curricular practices or proposals – it must go far beyond this rather limited scientific and technological level. As Bill Reid (1978:29) has suggested, curriculum problems 'are practical problems which are moral rather than technical in nature'. To deal with such problems, curriculum studies must embrace and tackle questions of what education is, or at least of what different approaches to schooling one might adopt. It must recognize that for some people the term 'education' means little more than instruction or the transmission of certain agreed bodies of knowledge; for others it carries connotations of the value of what is being transmitted; and yet again for some its central concern is the impact it makes, or is intended to make, on the development of the individual educands who are to be exposed to it.

To evaluate any curriculum plan or practice credibly, therefore, we need not only an understanding of the technicalities of curriculum planning and innovation but also the ability to discern the underlying values and assumptions of the curriculum specification. Indeed, it would not be difficult to argue that the latter may be far more important than the former. For to be subjected to some form of indoctrinatory process through lack of the ability to analyse critically and identify the value positions implicit in the forms of curriculum we are offered or exposed to is, in the long term, inimical to educational development in a way that some lack of understanding of the technicalities of curriculum innovation or planning or dissemination can never be. For, while the latter may diminish the quality of the educational experiences offered, the former must have the effect of rendering those experiences positively anti-educational.

The view of curriculum studies which underpins all that follows in this book will include, indeed emphasize, considerations of this deeper kind. For it is a major assumption that the narrower, mechanical, technicist version of curriculum studies, while important, does not in itself warrant a book of this scope or kind. In particular, it does not warrant a book whose prime concern is with the need for a critical approach to the study of the curriculum, since the mechanical view is by definition non-critical, value-neutral and raises no questions of whether the particular curriculum we might be planning is of educational value or not; its concern is merely with the mechanics of planning and 'delivery'.

Too much of what is called 'curriculum studies' these days is concerned with nothing more significant or more intellectually demanding than issues of methodology, usually within particular subject areas. The weakness, and the danger, of this is that, as Wittgenstein (1980:62) once said of traditional philosophy, it 'doesn't put the question marks *deep* enough'. Whatever one calls it, there is a need for a study of curricular theories and practices which goes far deeper than this; and it is with that kind of study that we shall be concerned here. Perhaps we should call it 'pedagogialogy', or some such, a term which might have the advantage C. S. Peirce once claimed for one of his linguistic creations, namely of being 'ugly enough to be safe from kidnappers'.

Curriculum studies, then, is seen throughout this book as a critical, analytical exploration of the curriculum as a totality, a theoretical/

conceptual and practical/empirical examination of all the many dimensions of the curriculum debate and of curriculum planning, a critical evaluation of curriculum theories and practices, and a form of inquiry which goes far beyond considerations of mere methodology and transcends both particular subject specialisms and particular age ranges.

Conceptual analysis

It follows, therefore, and this must be stressed, that a major concern is conceptual analysis, since its prime purpose must be to achieve conceptual clarity in thinking about the curriculum as a basis for ensuring practical coherence in the implementation of that thinking – again a proper matching of theory and practice. Its concern is to conceptualize the practice of education – at both the general and the particular levels. It requires, therefore, as was suggested earlier, the development of an understanding of a wide range of theories, views and empirical insights of the kind generated by the work of psychologists, sociologists and many others but, more than this, it demands the ability to sort through these ideas, theories and insights to identify and, if possible, resolve logical and conceptual mismatch and its resultant practical incoherence and confusion.

Many, perhaps most, of the concepts essential to any properly rigorous discussion of the curriculum or any attempt to implement curriculum proposals are highly problematic in nature, are complex in meaning and cannot, without detriment to the quality of both that discussion and its implementation, be treated as though they were simple, self-evident and non-controversial. This is another aspect of that attempt, which we commented on earlier, to treat educational planning and policy-making as forms of applied science. Concepts such as 'aims', 'objectives', 'processes', 'approaches', 'standards', 'ability', 'progression', 'continuity', 'coherence', 'evaluation', 'appraisal', 'accountability' and even 'subjects' or individually named subjects are far from being non-problematic in their meanings, just as they are equally far, as we saw above, from being ideologically neutral. Nor are they matters of empirical 'fact' or scientific 'truth'. One does not, or at least one should not, go out to 'discover' by empirical experiment aims, objectives, standards or any other of those things. This is another major intellectual flaw in many current policies and practices.

Further, the kind of deliberate obfuscation of these central educational concepts which characterizes recent official pronouncements on education and curriculum, such as that confusion of the concepts of education and teaching which we noted earlier, is intellectually dishonest as well as politically sinister. For one of its effects, and indeed intentions, is to sabotage and stifle the kind of open debate about the school curriculum which is essential to any genuinely democratic social context.

In any curriculum debate, therefore, a major concern must be with an analysis of what these concepts may mean, what, in the context of any particular debate or policy pronouncement, they are intended to mean, and, crucially, what, in that particular context, they actually do mean. In any curriculum planning conceptual clarity is a *sine qua non* of effective practice. In particular, it is crucial that the many concepts used in any statement of policy or practice be compatible with each other, and a major purpose in subjecting them to such conceptual analysis is to ensure that they are. A good example of this, and one we will find ourselves returning to constantly throughout this book, is the question of the compatibility of many of the concepts which are central to current policies with the notion of democracy.

Worthwhile and productive research into curricular matters, then, must embrace conceptual as well as, indeed perhaps more so than, empirical inquiry.

Engagement in curriculum studies of this kind, therefore, involves the development of skills with which to make this kind of challenging critical analysis and evaluation of curricular schemes, proposals and theories – whether these are one's own or are offered by others – to explore rigorously their underlying conceptual structures and to make similarly critical evaluations of educational practices – again both one's own and those of others – in terms not only of their effectiveness but also of their educational worth and their conceptual coherence. In short, it necessitates a raising of levels of perception and awareness in relation to all aspects of curricular theory and practice.

Finally, we must again note that many of the insights which had begun to emerge from this kind of critical questioning of the school curriculum have been lost as that questioning has been largely pre-empted at the practical level by the imposition of centralized political control, such as that which has characterized schooling in England and Wales since the 1988 Education Act. Teachers have now been told what they are to teach, and their trainers have been told how to train them, so that questions of the purpose or justification of this, or even of its logical or intellectual coherence, have effectively been removed from their sphere of influence. If, however, as a result of this, teachers and educationists generally cease to face these questions, even if at present they can approach them only in a largely theoretical way, then those questions will be faced by no one, and there are issues encapsulated in those questions which many would see as vital not only to the future of education but to the quality of the society in which future generations will live. The debate must go on, centralized control or not, and it must be conducted at a properly rigorous and critical level. It is that kind of debate which curriculum studies endeavours to fuel. And it is that kind of debate whose importance this book is seeking to reaffirm and to which it is attempting to contribute.

All that follows, therefore, should be seen by the reader as an attempt to provide him or her with the understanding and, particularly, the critical apparatus needed to engage in this kind of rigorous study of curricular practices, both as a sound underpinning for his or her own practice and as a firm basis for evaluating official policy and making appropriately professional contributions to what must be a continuing professional debate. The concern is to assist teachers and other serious students of education to acquire a critical apparatus which will enable them to reflect critically and rigorously on educational policies and practices, whether their own or those of others – especially when these are being imposed by force of law.

It is in this sense rather than in that of the purely mechanistic or technicist that the book seeks to improve the quality of educational provision at all levels.

Key isssues raised by this chapter

1) What is the most appropriate form of intellectual study of education and the school curriculum?
2) In what ways is this kind of study of importance – for teachers?
                                                              – for society?
3) How prevalent is this kind of study at the present time?

Suggested further reading

Carr, W. (1995) *For Education: Towards Critical Educational Enquiry*, Buckingham and Philadelphia: Open University Press.

2

Knowledge and the curriculum

Our exploration of the issues which are key to curriculum planning must begin from an analysis of the status of human knowledge for several reasons. First, it will be obvious that, however we conceive of education and curriculum, learning of some kind is central to it, so that what is to be learned must be a major planning consideration.

Second, it will become plain that what is crucial to curriculum planning is not merely **what** knowledge our curriculum should be concerned to transmit, but **how** that knowledge relates to other aspects of curriculum planning. We saw in Chapter 1 that there is a strong case for claiming that in curriculum planning and, indeed, in any debate about the curriculum, we must look beyond considerations of content alone and recognize that questions of the purposes or reasons for our decisions are logically prior to those about their substance. If we accept that curriculum planning must begin with statements about the purposes we hope to attain or the principles upon which our practice is to be based, all decisions about the content of our curriculum must be subsidiary to those prior choices. For, as Ralph Tyler said (1949:1), such decisions will be answers to the question, 'What educational experiences can be provided that are likely to attain these purposes?'

A third reason for starting with a discussion of knowledge arises from this. For it will already be apparent that there are different ways of conceptualizing the curriculum, and how we conceptualize it will depend on how we conceive human knowledge. One of the most significant, and also one of the most dangerous, fallacies with which the curriculum debate has been, and continues, to be beset, derives from the failure to recognize the problematic nature of human knowledge and the consequent assumption that it is possible to identify non-problematic elements which must form the core of the curriculum without further debate. Thus, decisions concerning the knowledge-content of the curriculum become the first, indeed the only, stage in curriculum planning. And the curriculum debate proceeds at the superficial level of shared assumptions about human knowledge – uncritical assumptions which do not acknowledge its problematic nature (Wittgenstein's (1980) question marks which do not go deep enough) – rather than at the deeper level where these assumptions themselves are recognized as a significant part of the debate.

Finally, this in turn draws our attention to a major result of recognizing the problematic nature of human knowledge and the consequent fact that there are different ways of conceiving it. For, once we recognize the problematic nature of human knowledge, we must also acknowledge that in making decisions about the content of the curriculum we are dealing in ideologies rather than in eternal truths. Thus the debate about knowledge reveals the degree to which all approaches to curriculum planning are ideological, and it alerts us to the political dangers which must be recognized and addressed.

Whatever view one takes of education, that view will be predicated on certain assumptions about the nature of knowledge and a particular set of values. All these elements need to be examined closely and, in particular, we need to ensure that, whatever our views are, they display a coherence and a consistency, that all these elements are compatible with and in harmony with one another.

Issues of knowledge-content, then, must remain central to the curriculum debate even if they must not be permitted to continue to dominate it. It is thus to an exploration of the problematic nature of human knowledge that we now turn.

The problematic nature of human knowledge

Absolutist theories

Two main kinds of theory have emerged during the development of Western European philosophy: those rationalist views that take as their starting point the supremacy of the intellect over other human faculties and stress that true knowledge is that which is achieved by the mind in some way independently of the information provided by the senses; and those empiricist views which have taken a contrary stance and maintained that knowledge of the world about us can be derived only from the evidence that the world offers us through the use of our senses.

This dispute further reflects two related beliefs which have characterized Western European philosophy from the beginning – the idea of the fallibility of the senses as sources of information and views that some have held of the infallibility of the intellect. Thus such philosophers as Plato, Descartes, Kant and Hegel have offered various versions of a rationalist epistemology which have shared the basic conviction that the evidence of our senses is misleading but that the rational mind can attain true knowledge independently of the senses by apprehending what lies beyond those sense impressions or in some way introducing a rational structure to our understanding of them.

Such theories, seeing knowledge as essentially independent of the observations of our senses, inevitably lead to a view of knowledge as reified, as in some sense (sometimes literally) God-given, 'out-there' and independent of the knower, having a status that is untouched by and owes nothing to the human condition of the beings who possess the knowledge they are concerned with. For them, knowledge is timeless, objective, in no sense related to the particular circumstances of individual eras, societies, cultures or human beings. True knowledge, on this view, is independent of all such ephemeral considerations. Furthermore, what is even more important for this debate, as we shall see later, is that these theories seek to embrace not only knowledge of a 'scientific' kind, that concerned with the 'factual' or empirical aspects of existence, but also, and more significantly, human values – aesthetic, moral and even social/political.

By their very nature too these theories elevate the universal above the particular, and thus the collective above the individual. Indeed, this can be seen as a major motive of Hegel in creating that elaborate rationalist system known as German Idealism which dominated the intellectual world of the nineteenth century and, in some quarters, much of the twentieth (Plant, 1997). And, through the development of Hegel's thinking by Karl Marx, the same kind of anti-individualism came to dominate the real politics of a very large proportion of the world's population, where the interests of the collective, the state, were regarded as superseding those of the individual in all circumstances.

Such a view of knowledge, then, has its attractions for the politicians, since it seems to offer a kind of universality and certainty which makes their lives easier – not least because it seeks to put an end to individual questioning and challenge. The political implications of this view of human knowledge are thus manifold and we must return to them later.

Less understandably, this view has had, and continues to have, its attractions for some theorists of education. It is this kind of epistemological belief, for example, which underlies the claims of some philosophers of education for the inalienable right of certain subjects, those whose intellectual content is high, to be included in the curriculum. For example, Richard Peters's 'transcendental' argument (1966) for the intrinsic value of certain kinds of human activity is in all major respects a reassertion of the rationalist arguments of Immanuel Kant. And similar arguments continue to be offered (Quinton, 1978; O'Hear, 1992). (Whether these are offered on philosophical or political grounds is a moot question, although it is important to note that the motivation is an important consideration, since it clearly makes a moral difference whether one is advocating such a view from philosophical conviction or political expediency.)

Objections to absolutism

Objections to this view of human knowledge have been mounted from a number of perspectives – philosophical, human and political. And these have recently coalesced in that movement currently known as postmodernism.

Empiricism

The philosophical objection began with the emergence of an alternative epistemology, that of empiricism which is perhaps best understood as a reaction against the mysticism of the essentially metaphysical nature of rationalism. Its fundamental tenet is well expressed in the claim of John Locke, the founder of the empiricist movement, that no knowledge comes into the mind except through the gates of the senses. The mind of the new-born child is seen as a *tabula rasa*, a clean sheet, 'void of all characters, without any ideas'. Such knowledge as it acquires, it acquires through experience. For the empiricist, there is no other source of knowledge, since he or she denies the validity of all *a priori* knowledge, that is, all knowledge which does not derive ultimately from experience.

A basic position such as this leads inevitably to a less confident view of knowledge and to a greater awareness of the tentative, indeed provisional, nature of human knowledge, since it is agreed by everyone that the rationalists are right at least in their claim that the evidence of our senses is unreliable. Thus a number of recent theories of knowledge and theories of education have begun from the conviction that human knowledge has to be treated in a far more tentative way than many who take a rationalist view would concede and that, in relation to curriculum planning, we are in no position to be dogmatic about its content. The whole pragmatist movement, as promoted by John Dewey, which has been highly influential in the recent development of educational practice, especially in the early years, has been founded on a view of knowledge as hypothetical and therefore subject to constant change, modification and evolution. Such a view requires us to be hesitant about asserting the value of any body of knowledge or its right to inclusion in the curriculum and encourages us to accept that knowledge is to be equated rather with experience, so that what it means for children to acquire knowledge is that they should have experiences which they can themselves use as the basis for the framing of hypotheses to explain and gain control over the environment in which they live. In other words, we cannot impose what is knowledge for us upon them; we must assist them to develop their own knowledge, their own hypotheses, which will be different from ours if the process of evolution is to go on.

This certainly results in a view of education as a much more personal activity than any rationalist could acknowledge. It may also suggest, however, that knowledge itself is personal and subjective. Thus some have stressed the phenomenological or existentialist claim that all knowledge is personal and subjective, that every individual's knowledge is the result of his or her own completely unique perceptions of his or her own world. This, however, is not a view that Dewey himself subscribed to. He believed that the proper model for all knowledge is that of scientific knowledge, where hypotheses are framed and modified according to publicly agreed criteria, so that while such knowledge has no permanent status it is objective in so far as it at least enjoys current acceptance by everyone. 'Meaning and truth are empirical affairs to be developed and tested by operational or experimental procedures' (Childs, 1956:143).

On this kind of view, then, human knowledge is seen as evolving but as subject to conformity with publicly accepted and agreed criteria. For Dewey, this further implies that its continuing evolution requires the kind of intellectual freedom which only a truly democratic political context can provide. Again, therefore, we glimpse some of the political ramifications of the knowledge question.

Existentialism

A second form of objection to the absolutism of rationalist philosophy appeared contemporaneously with Hegel's impressive statement of it. For his work induced an immediate revolt as some philosophers attempted to reassert the primacy of the individual over the collective, whether the latter has been conceived in terms of the state (as with Hegel) or social class (as with Marx) or humanity as a whole (as with Kant). The movement known as 'existentialism' embraces a wide range of, sometimes very different, theories. What they all have in common, however, is a concern to resist the submerging of the individual into some kind of whole. Every human being, it is claimed must be defined as a unique individual and not as a mere representative of some wider grouping. Furthermore, every human being must be encouraged to define him/herself in this way, and thus to accept full responsibility for his/her own 'essence', what he/she is and becomes. And this notion of individual responsibility is a key element in all versions of existentialist philosophy.

At root, therefore, this represents a revolt against the absolutes of rationalism, which, as we have seen, have the effect of dissolving the individual into some form of universal collective – again, the state, a social class or even humanity as a whole. And, as far as the curriculum is concerned, it again is warning us against the effects of imposing a universal curriculum on all pupils, particularly when that curriculum is regarded, or presented, as non-problematic, rather than offering scope for personal exploration and the development of individual values and perspectives.

Again too we see, lurking in the background, sinister political implications to which we must return.

The 'knowledge explosion' of the twentieth century

Before we move to a consideration of the key elements of that movement known as 'postmodernism' which is a major feature of the current intellectual scene and which it was suggested earlier can be seen as a culmination of the several strands of thinking we are attempting to identify, it is worth noting the significance for the knowledge debate of those major intellectual advances which the present century has seen.

There is no doubt that those advances have been primarily due to a jettisoning of the intellectual baggage of rationalism and the adoption of the kind of open, questioning approach to human knowledge and understanding which we have seen is characteristic of empiricist and/or pragmatist views. For it is largely because such views have led to a challenging of traditionally 'received wisdom' that humankind has been able to make those major breakthroughs which have led to the massive technological (and, consequentially, social) revolution we have experienced and indeed are continuing to experience.

A key feature of this development has been that shift which Karl Popper's analysis of human knowledge advocated, a shift from verification to falsification. Hitherto, in all areas, the concern has been to discover and identify 'truths'. It is this that underpins all absolutist systems. Popper's analysis suggested that human knowledge (and we must now call it that with great caution) develops not by discovering truths but by identifying falsehoods, by disproving rather than proving hypotheses. Thus theories are regarded as having validity until they are shown to be false or inadequate. And the corollary of this is that we must regard all such theories as potentially subject to falsification.

The significance of this, and its effects on the development of human knowledge in the twentieth century are expressed compellingly by Wellington (1981:21):

> Kant and his contemporaries strongly believed that the mathematics and physics of that time, and even the moral code, were true beyond all doubt. Kant thus assumed that the schemata employed in mathematical, physical and moral thinking were

unique and could not be otherwise. In 1981 we have non-Euclidean geometry, Einstein's relativistic view of the space-time continuum, Heisenberg's 'uncertainty principle' and the knowledge that Newtonian physics only applies to slow-moving objects . . . In the light of these alternative 'categorial schemata' or ways of understanding the world (Kant's *Anschauung*), who would be bold enough to ever attempt such a transcendental deduction today?

The answer to that final question is, of course, many people, especially among the ranks of politicians and their aides!

It is from here that postmodernism may be seen to begin. For one of its central tenets is a rejection of 'modernism', usually characterized by reference to Newtonian physics. Before we look at postmodernist theory in more detail, however, it will be helpful to consider an important movement against absolutism which began within education theory itself and which may be seen as one of the antecedents of postmodernism.

'New directions in the sociology of education'

An absolutist view of knowledge held almost unshakeable sway within education theory, and thus in the thinking of many teachers, throughout the 1960s and early 1970s largely as a result of the influence of Richard Peters and a posse of philosophers of education whose theory of the intrinsic value of certain bodies of knowledge we must consider in some detail in our exploration of curriculum ideologies in Chapter 3.

It was challenged from two sources. First, at the level of curriculum practice, the nature of the curriculum which it led to was challenged by teachers on grounds of its unsuitability for many pupils and the consequences of this in the alienation of these pupils and the inequalities which it inevitably generated. Thus the 1970s came to be characterized at the level of educational practice by attempts, such as those reflected in most of the projects spawned by the Schools Council, to devise forms of curriculum which would obviate this kind of alienating inequality. Inevitably these developments led practice away from traditional subjects, traditionally conceived, and towards a reconceptualization of many subjects and the introduction of new combinations of subjects in various versions of integrated studies.

It is important to note at this point that the motivation for all of this activity was a concern for equality of provision, a desire to provide pupils with experiences which would be genuinely educational and an awareness that the traditional form of subject-based curriculum, founded in absolutist conceptions of human knowledge, was inimical to these aims. For it is at this stage that we begin to see the political consequences and implications of the knowledge debate emerging.

Those consequences and implications began to be addressed explicitly as the dangers of absolutist theories of knowledge were strongly flagged within that movement known as 'new directions in the sociology of education' which appeared in the early 1970s, most famously through the publication of Michael Young's seminal work, *Knowledge and Control* (1971). This collection of papers introduced into the educational debate a perspective on knowledge which is distinctively sociological. For it suggested that human knowledge is not God-given but socially constructed, so that it is best understood not through any form of philosophoical analysis but through a study of the social and sociological conditions and context within which it is generated.

Its major claim, therefore, is that questions of the nature of human knowledge are sociological rather than philosophical and are concerned with the social relations through which knowledge develops rather than aspects or characteristics of the knowledge itself. Thus, Geoffrey Esland, in his contribution to this collection of papers, claims that it has been a mistake 'to leave epistemological issues to philosophy' (1971:70) and that the objectivist view of knowledge has led to the perpetuation of 'a view of man as a dehumanized, passive object' (1971:71). Man is seen 'not as a world-producer but as world-produced' so that 'one finds it difficult to disagree with the claim that this epistemology is fundamentally dehumanizing. It ignores the intentionality and expressivity of human action and the entire complex process of intersubjective negotiation of meanings. In short, it disguises as given a world which has to be continually interpreted' (1971:75). Thus the concern is that, as we saw earlier when discussing absolutist forms of epistemological theory, knowledge becomes reified and the knower is seen as a passive recipient of this kind of knowledge rather than as an active participant in its creation. A particular and important instance of this is the reification of school subjects which the work of Ivor Goodson (1981, 1983, 1985; Goodson and Ball, 1984) has highlighted. For that work has convincingly demonstrated that school subjects, far from being the rational entities which some philosophical theories such as that of Paul Hirst's 'forms of knowledge' (1965, 1974; Hirst and Peters, 1970) suggested most of them to be, are in fact the creations of interest groups whose prime concern has been with maintaining and extending their own status. The significance of this for views of the forms and functions of education are not difficult to see and we will return to them in our exploration of curriculum ideologies in Chapter 3.

Here, however, we can see that it is not only the reification of knowledge and the treatment of human beings as passive that is being flagged. Beyond this, we are now being alerted to the more serious consequences which follow when individuals are denied the right to negotiate meanings, to interpret and reinterpret their own experiences and thus, crucially, to develop their own systems of values. For, now, it is not merely that the collective takes over from the individual, denying individual freedom in the name of absolute truth. More than that, value systems, as manifested in cultural practices – religious beliefs and behaviour patterns generally – are created by groups and sub-groups in society: but, if this value pluralism, which is a feature of modern societies, is regarded as an aberration from true values, then the threat to individual and cultural freedom can now be seen as emanating from the control of society by the dominant sub-group within it through the distribution and the legitimation of knowledge. For, if one takes a view of knowledge as socially constructed, one must see the imposition of any one version of knowledge as a form of social control and as a threat to all of the major freedoms identified as essential constituents of the free and democratic society. Socially constructed knowledge is ideology and what is imposed through a politically controlled education system is the ideology of the dominant, controlling group.

Thus these new directions in the sociology of education immediately lead to those issues collectively denoted by the term 'the politics of knowledge'. Before we unpack that notion, however, we must briefly consider aspects of a further intellectual development which has brought us to the same kinds of conclusion – that movement which has been given the designation of 'postmodernism'.

Postmodernism

Postmodernism may be seen as a development of this theme but on a broader front. As an intellectual movement, it is highly controversial. It is strongly opposed and rejected by politicians and by those philosophers who also feel threatened by the loss of those spurious certainties of the traditional, absolutist view of human knowledge which seem to offer order and security to their lives and careers.

It is also a movement which is subject to many different interpretations from those who have advocated it, not least because it is a perspective which has been applied in many different intellectual contexts, from philosophy to art and architecture. And this makes the offering here of a brief overview of its main thrust a hazardous and perhaps foolhardy undertaking, since it is 'irritatingly elusive to define' (Featherstone, 1988:195). Nevertheless, such an overview must be attempted, because in general terms the movement offers a salutary antidote to the kind of confident pronouncements with which the planning and organization of the school curriculum has been beset both by politicians and by some theorists.

From the plethora of interpretations to which we have referred a common denominator can be seen to emerge. Postmodernism represents a rejection of all 'totalizing theories' (Boyne and Rattansi, 1990:12), an 'incredulity towards metanarratives' (Lyotard, 1984:xxiv), 'an interrogation of Western discourse's desire for certainty and absolutes' (Sholle, 1992:275). And from this perspective, 'we see our vision of the universe turning from the simple, stable one of Newtonian modernism to the complex, chaotic, finite one of postmodernism' (Doll, 1989:243).

It may be that this movement is better established in aesthetic theory than in epistemology or even sociology. Certainly, at the most superficial level, we cannot be in ignorance of the kinds of changes in artistic forms – in literature, in theatre, in music, in the plastic arts, in architecture – which the present century has seen. And it is also easy to see these as major steps away from traditional forms in all of these fields (although it is worth noting that for many of the advocates of postmodernism these developments have not gone far enough).

What is of most significance here, however, is the implications this movement has for our view of human knowledge and thus for our approach to the planning and organization of the school curriculum.

In relation, to knowledge, it seeks to take us some way further than those earlier theories we have noted. For, unlike them, in challenging absolutism, objectivism and positivism, it does not set out to offer us alternative theories or 'metanarratives', as we saw, for example, Dewey sought to do. It places everything in a cauldron of uncertainty and insists that that is where everything must stay. It thus adds great strength to the case for viewing what appears to count as knowledge, at any given time or in any given socio-political context, with continuing scepticism and without dogmatic confidence.

Its implications for the planning and organization of the school curriculum are consequently wide-ranging. For it undermines any theories anyone might mount for the God-given right of any body of 'knowledge', school subject or whatever to be included in a compulsory curriculum. Indeed, it alerts us to the dangers of all such theories. And, as we shall see, it suggests that we look elsewhere than knowledge-content for the foundation stone of our curriculum.

It further suggests the need to recognize that knowledge is ideology, and that all approaches to the school curriculum are ideological. This is an issue which will prove crucial to our discussion of curriculum ideologies in Chapter 3.

Central to the dangers it alerts us to are those political dangers which we have touched upon from time to time and which we must now face head-on. For the prime significance of postmodernism for students of curriculum is that it explicitly links theories of knowledge with political movements. A major target within social and political theory, for example, has been Marxism, which is precisely the kind of totalizing theory which is the *bête noire*, and which has dominated sociological enquiry for many years. This is a good example of the interpenetration of epistemology and political theory, as a political system is built upon a particular theory of knowledge, and ideology is conceived not merely as a point of view but as a form of deviance from the 'eternal truths' generated by that theory of knowledge.

Again, however, postmodernism would go further than this. For not only does it see all knowledge and all versions of the truth as ideological; it also makes an explicit link between knowledge and power, and sees power as being exercised through the distribution of knowledge and the manipulation of the discourses through which that knowledge, those 'totalizing theories' are expressed, 'the bureaucratic imposition of official values' (Turner, 1990:11). 'We live in a world in which there is no "knowledge", no "ultimate truths", in which all perception is subjective, so that we are the products of the discourse, the ideologies, we are exposed to' (Kelly, 1995:71).

In this way we see postmodern theory adding its weight to that conviction which has been growing throughout the second half of this century that knowledge and politics are inextricably interlinked and that serious political dangers, threats to individual freedom and to social democracy, ensue if we are not constantly aware of this and on the alert for instances of it. It is to an exploration of the politics of knowledge, then, that we must now turn.

The politics of knowledge

We have seen that the knowledge debate has shifted from being a philosophical concern focused on concepts of truth and questions about the source and validity of universal knowledge, by way of growing doubts about the adequacy of this conception of human knowledge – and its implications – to an awareness that a much more plausible characterization of human knowledge is that it is a social construct, and on to a number of concerns about the political implications of this latter view, and especially about the consequences of ignoring it. It is these political concerns we must now seek to unpack.

Totalitarianism – open and concealed

In doing so, the first point to be stressed is the inevitability with which the acceptance of an absolutist epistemology leads to an acceptance, even in many cases an advocacy of, totalitarian forms of government. For assumed certainty over human knowledge must include a comparable certainty in moral matters and thus in matters social and political. This, as we have seen, leaves no scope for individual freedom, since the individual must be required to accept the absolute imperative of universal knowledge, in Hegel's euphemism, he/she must be 'forced to be free'. For to exercise one's freedom to choose another course of action is *ipso facto* to be choosing what is wrong.

Thus Plato, who may be seen as the first major figure to advocate an absolutist epistemology and a comprehensive theory of education, reveals very clearly some of the features of both education and society which seem to be the inevitable consequences of this kind of epistemological stance. For Plato's 'ideal state' is not a democracy; it is a meritocracy, albeit with social status dependent on ability rather than on birth or social class. It is not a society of equals; it is hierarchically structured. Its education system is selective, designed to allocate individuals to their proper status within that hierarchy. And the focus of that education system is on the needs of the state rather than on those of the individual, whose freedom is to be curtailed in quite specific ways in the interests of social control and political harmony.

We can identify, then, from the beginning, a number of features which would seem to be the inevitable social and political, as well as educational, consequences of the adoption of an absolutist epistemology – in particular, social and educational inequalities, an acceptance of forms of elitism, the subservience of the individual to the collective, a consequent loss of individual freedom and no basis for the development of a form of governance which might be described as democratic in any coherent sense one might give to that term.

These features can be seen with even greater clarity in those German Idealist theories which, through the work of Kant, Hegel, Marx and others, dominated intellectual thought throughout the nineteenth century and into the twentieth and led to the emergence of what Hobhouse (1918) called 'the metaphysical theory of the state'.

Nor is this merely a matter of interesting philosophical debate. For the present century has seen the appearance, and the stark realities, of a range of totalitarian forms of government from the fascist governments of Franco's Spain, Mussolini's Italy and Hitler's Nazi Germany to the communist regimes of USSR, China and elsewhere. All of these regimes have evinced those characteristics of totalitariansim we have just identified – inequalities, especially in the form of racial, gender and religious intolerance, loss of freedom, the elevation of the interests of the state above those of the individual and the use of education to promote those interests.

What must be stressed here is that these political systems can be seen as direct consequences of the absolutist epistemological theories of the philosophers – of Plato, Hegel and Marx in particular. It is for this reason that Karl Popper (1945) identified those three figures as 'the enemies of the open society'; and Dewey claimed that most of German cultural and philosophical thought reached its natural fruition in Hitler. Nor is it surprising to learn that the subject of Mussolini's doctoral thesis was the philosophy of Hegel. As Sir Percy Nunn once wrote (1920:3),

> From the idealism of Hegel, more than from any other source, the Prussian mind derived its fanatical belief in the absolute value of the State, its deadly doctrine that the State can admit no moral authority greater than its own, and the corollary that the education system, from the primary school to the university, should be used as an instrument to engrain these notions into the soul of a whole people.

Finally, in case we are tempted to regard all of this as of mainly historical interest and as something which 'couldn't happen now', it is worth comparing this last quotation with one of more recent origin. 'Educators ought . . . to be more concerned with inculcating in the young a sense of awe and respect for the virtues of civilised life than with encouraging their pupils to regard these virtues as open to choice or simply a reification of defeasible preferences' (O'Hear in Haldane, 1992:53).

We must not lose sight of the fact that any political regime which embraces such a view of knowledge, which fails to recognize the problematic nature of human knowledge, even if it does so in ignorance rather than from deliberate intent, must in its policies, particularly those for education, veer towards a totalitarian – and thus away from a democratic – form of governance. It will in reality be nearer to the totalitarian than to the democratic end of the political spectrum. The current implications of this will emerge very clearly when, in Chapter 3, we discuss the range of educational ideologies which Denis Lawton has identified in the current scene.

It was a concern with ensuring the maintenance and development of democratic forms of social living which led John Dewey to reject Hegelian absolutism and to embrace a pragmatist view of knowledge, as we saw earlier. Dewey was of course concerned with the threat to democracy posed by totalitarianism, but to this he added a concern with the threat to the continued evolution of knowledge itself which totalitarian forms of government with their rigid value systems and dedication to the *status quo* also offer. For the evolution of knowledge, and indeed the continuing evolution of society require the kind of free and open social and political context which only democracy can provide. For him an important element in the definition of democracy is that it is a form of government open to continuous change. If, however, the adult generation imposes on the young its own values and its own knowledge, the process is one of indoctrination rather than education, and it is a process which inhibits rather than promotes the continued evolution of human knowledge and, indeed, of human society.

Here, then, we see another feature of totalitarianism, its resistance to change. And the threat here comes not from the state so much as from the generation currently in the ascendency. As we have just seen, however, it is an important threat. And it has led some commentators to suggest that it is a danger which cannot be avoided when society provides a universal system of education, since 'education is, first and foremost, a political act' (Harris, 1979:139). It has been claimed, for example, that American schooling, even when one accepts that it is 'a liberal institution conceived by liberal theorists and carried out by liberal practitioners' (Feinberg, 1975:v), nevertheless 'from Kindergarten through graduate school operates to reinforce certain basic aspects of the American political, economic and moral structure' (1975:vi). This is what Paulo Freire (1972) called 'the pedagogy of the oppressed', and it is what Ivan Illich (1971:9) described as 'the institutionalization of values' which he claims 'leads to . . . social polarization and psychological impotence', particularly in the areas of class, race and gender. And it is this that led him to advocate a deschooling of society as the only feasible solution, the only way to defend the young against this process, the only way to avoid this kind of limitation on freedom of thought and action, since 'universal education through schooling is not feasible . . . We must recognize that it [equal schooling] is, in principle, economically absurd, and that to attempt it is intellectually emasculating, socially polarizing and destructive of the credibility of the political system which promotes it' (1971:7). We must consider later whether there might be any less drastic solutions.

Ideological dominance

What the perspective of 'the politics of knowledge' adds to this sorry picture is the notion that this kind of indoctrinatory practice is more than an unhappy concomitant of state-provided education, and even more than the deliberate, but open, manipulation of education systems by politicians in pursuit of particular political goals or ideals. Within this perspective it is ideological dominance; it is the manipulation of education, and thus of society itself, by dominant power groups within it. It is not just a matter of the adult generation indoctrinating the young and thus inhibiting the evolution of knowledge and of society; it is a matter of one dominant group within society imposing its ideology on society as a whole and thus achieving political control at the expense of the freedom of others.

> Education in a class society is a political act having as its basis the protection of the interests of the ruling class. It is a mechanism . . . for securing the continuation of the existing social relationships, and for reinforcing the attitudes and beliefs that will help ensure that those social relationships will continue to be accepted. Education . . . is an ideological force of tremendous import . . . Education is the manipulation of consciousness . . . and it functions largely without serious opposition of any sort.
>
> (Harris, 1979:140–1)

It is the group within society which holds power, the dominant ideology, which controls the distribution of knowledge within a society and determines what kinds of knowledge will be made available. And the most effective mechanism for effecting this is the education system. And 'how a society selects, classifies, distributes, transmits and evaluates the educational knowledge it considers to be public, reflects both the distribution of power and the principles of social control' (Bernstein, 1971:47).

The legitimation of discourse

It is difficult of course in modern societies which pay lip-service to democracy for this kind of control to be exercised openly and coercively, although some of the mechanisms by which the National Curriculum for England and Wales was established and by which current political policies for education are maintained are quite openly coercive. The use of sanctions, particularly financial sanctions, is one example of such coercive measures; another is the powers and activities of Ofsted, threatening school closures, the firing of teachers and the public humiliation – the 'naming and shaming' – of schools. The sinister implications of such practices must not, however, be permitted to become too apparent to the general public. Hence more subtle devices must be found.

Pre-eminent among these is the legitimation of discourse. The notion that our thinking is controlled by forms of discourse is a major concern of postmodern thinking. For these forms of discourse are those totalizing theories which we saw that movement is concerned to challenge and debunk. And these totalizing theories are expressed in language and thus become forms of discourse which play a major part in determining how we think, how we view the world and respond to it. We are the creations of the knowledge and the discourse to which we are exposed. Yet, if, as postmodernism claims, these totalizing theories and thus the discourses in which they are expressed are not 'eternal truths' but ideologies, then our thinking is being controlled by ideological discourse which is both intellectually and politically highly suspect.

Thus discourse is seen as power and the legitimation of discourse as the exercise of that power. We are manipulated by those who possess that power through the control of discourse, 'the bureaucratic imposition of official values' (Turner, 1990:11). For the rules of discursive practices 'govern what can be said and what must remain unsaid ... [and] identify who can speak with authority and who must listen', so that, 'dominant discourses determine what counts as true, important, relevant and what gets spoken' (Cherryholmes, 1987:301).

At one level, this will take the form of imposing those totalizing theories we have discussed in a manner which encourages us to see them as eternal verities, to accept them uncritically and not even to contemplate the possibility of challenging them. Hence, other theories, different ideologies are debunked; in other words, alternative discourses are not accorded legitimation in the hope that they might thus die for lack of nourishment. A good example of this in the current scene in England and Wales is the excising of Education Theory from courses of teacher training, on the specious, but to the untutored mind reasonable, grounds that trainee teachers need practical experience rather than exposure to the theories of 'trendy academics'. We pointed out in Chapter 1 that it is a major function of Curriculum Studies to offer this kind of challenge to existing orthodoxy, and it will perhaps now be becoming clear why that is seen as important.

At another level, the legitimation of discourse can be seen in the subtle ways in which language is manipulated to ensure that the language we use carries the values we are intended to embrace. And again, as we argued in Chapter 1, it is an important function of Curriculum Studies to analyse critically the language in which official pronouncements are made and, perhaps more crucially, the ways in which the language we are encouraged to use when debating educational issues is being manipulated.

There are several major features of this use, or misuse, of language which we must briefly note (Blenkin *et al.*, 1992). First, there is the practice of blurring logical distinctions between assertions of different kinds. There is no acknowledgement, for example, of the importance of the distinction between conceptual assertions and those empirical claims for which, in any rational discourse, evidence is required. Bold claims are thus made in official documents and in public pronouncements by senior officials of Ofsted and QCA with no apparent awareness that these require substantiation. Indeed, we have recently reached the stage where such pronouncements are offered as valid refutations of contrary claims based on careful research and convincing empirical evidence. In short, we are encouraged to regard what officialdom says out of political expediency as carrying more weight than the evidence of painstaking research, as of course in a political rather than an educational climate it does. When the views of the Her Majesty's Chief Inspector are offered as if they carried more weight than the conclusions of extensive and careful research, and both the teaching profession and the press are expected to accept them as such, then it is clear that the context of the teacher's work is political rather than educational, and, at the level of society at large, totalitarian rather than democratic.

Second, and related to this, there is the deliberate failure to acknowledge the problematic nature of many, in fact most, of the concepts used in making these pronouncements. Thus terms like, 'standards', 'breadth', 'balance', 'continuity', 'progression' and many more are used as though there is no question about what they mean and as though their import will therefore be fully manifest to all who read or hear these pronouncements. We must note too that these terms are not merely used in discussion documents; in fact, no discussion is invited; they are used in documents which are intended to govern practice, as, for example, the activities of Ofsted inspectors.

Third, among the terms used we will find many which have clearly been selected because they have warm, happy and friendly connotations – even when they have been given quite new meanings through that lack of conceptual clarity we have just identified. Thus we hear of 'entitlement', of 'relevance', of 'coherence', and of 'development', as well as of those unanalysed concepts we noted above. Some of these terms have been hi-jacked from theories, such as progressivism or child-centredness, to which officialdom has been concerned to deny legitimation, even to rubbish (Kelly and Blenkin, 1993). The use of the terminology of such theories, however, serves to conceal the fact thay they have been so rubbished and that the concepts central to them have been emasculated. The use of emotive language is always persuasive. It can thus be misused in order to mislead or at least to deflect criticism.

Fourth, an extension of this use of emotive languages is the use, or again the misuse, of metaphor. Metaphors enrich our language and they can provide illumination and clarity to our thinking, as any teacher will know. They also have their dangers, however, especially when manipulated as part of the legitimation of official discourse. For, as Elliott Eisner (1982:6) has pointed out, they 'also have a cost. That cost resides in the ways in which they shape our conception of the problems we study'. They can thus be used as a rhetorical tool to shape those conceptions quite deliberately.

This is a particular problem when metaphors are allowed, or even encouraged, to become analogies, 'metaphoric models' (Ortony, 1979), and we are invited to develop arguments from such analogies. Once such a metaphoric model has become embedded in our discourse, it is difficult to resist the process of pursuing the analogy into false forms of reasoning. A prime example of this is the imposition of the commercial and industrial metaphor on the education system of England and Wales which recent years have seen. As Blenkin *et al.* (1992:141–2) have said,

> throughout the official literature on the National Curriculum, we are offered a commercial/industrial imagery which encourages us to see schools as factories. Teachers are invited to view their task as one of 'delivering' a 'product'; they are subjected to 'quality-control mechanisms'; they are encouraged to focus their efforts on 'increased productivity', usually at a more 'economic costing' (i.e. on the cheap); inspectors and advisers have in many places acquired new titles as 'quality control' specialists. Soon education will be run, like the Rev. Awdry's railway system by a 'Fat Controller' – if this has not happened already.

It takes only a moment's reflection to appreciate that, through such imagery, we have been encouraged to view curriculum as content (to be 'delivered') and as product (to be measured by outcomes). And education is now widely discussed, within the profession as well as outside it, in terms of 'delivery', 'product control', 'clients', 'managers', 'mechanisms', 'quality control' and so on. 'The language of educational purpose has undergone a sea-shift of transformation into business terminology and the going discourse of the corporate culture' (McMurtry, 1991:211).

And we must note also the corollary of this, that 'the language of the previous decade and of the post-war decades has been expunged from the record' (Lawn, 1990:388). We have been steered away from the erstwhile metaphors of growth, development, caring, tending, nurturing. The metaphors of child-centredness have been replaced by the harsher imagery of the factory floor. The notion of schools as places of nurture, as gardens, has been replaced by that of schools as those 'teaching shops' which the Plowden Report (CACE, 1967) repudiated. Thus the way in which we conceive the problems – and thus the solutions – of education have been dramatically changed by the subtle manipulation of the language and the imagery with which we have been encouraged to conceive and discuss them.

Finally, we must note how readily this kind of censorship has become a form of self-censorship – 'the most difficult of all kinds of censorship' (Hoggart, 1992:260). For this commercial/industrial metaphor, along with the values and attitudes implicit within it (competition, productivity, instrumentalism, value for money) and the loss of other values and attitudes perhaps more appropriate to education in a democratic society (caring, human development, intrinsic value) has been almost completely absorbed by the teaching profession, and has come to dominate not only the education debate but also educational policies and practices. And so 'it is difficult to avoid the conclusion that the educational process has been so persuasively subordinated to the aims and practices of business that its agents can no longer comprehend their vocation in any other terms' (McMurtry, 1991:211).

That is how control through the legitimation of discourse operates. It is a subtle and sinister process which threatens individual freedom and thus the future of democracy. The simple message is that if teachers, and indeed the population at large, do not develop, or, worse, are actively discouraged from developing, the ability to reflect critically on educational policies and practices (their own as well as those of others), then the education system will be led by the nose by those (including some in senior positions within that system) whose agenda is political rather than educational, geared to their own advancement rather than to genuine improvement in the quality of provision, and thus fundamentally totalitarian rather than democratic. Nothing illustrates better the dangers of the politics of knowledge to education and society.

Responses to the problem of the politics of knowledge

We have already noted that significant figures, such as Ivan Illich, have responded to the awareness of the problems posed by the politics of knowledge by suggesting that the only solution is to close the schools, to 'deschool' society. And some versions of postmodernism take an even more negative and deterministic view, seeing the control of the individual's thinking by the social and political context as inevitable,

whether it occurs through schooling or by other means. It is time to
seek for a more positive alternative.

Positive   interpretations   of   that   multi-faceted   intellectual
phenomenon known as postmodernism suggest that such a positive
alternative is to be found if we accept the problematic nature of human
knowledge and recognize the dangers of all totalizing theories but
respond to this by embracing the need for openness and constant
challenge.   Postmodern   thinking   is   only   now   beginning   to
interpenetrate educational thinking. It is important that it does so in a
form which offers positive directions for forms of educational planning
and practice which will take full cognizance of what that perspective is
telling, indeed warning, us about human knowledge.

First, we must stress that to claim that knowledge can never be
absolute is not to be condemned to a subjective form of relativism. It
reflects simplistic thinking of an extreme kind to assume that this is the
only possible alternative. 'The question mark that post-modernism puts
on the "truth" of all discourse means only that all knowledge is
contextual, not that all knowledge is false, nor that one cannot support
the validity of one claim over another in a specific circumstance'
(Sholle, 1992:276). Individuals construct their own worlds, but they do
so within a social context of shared meanings. There is a crucial
difference between private knowledge and public knowledge, and
education must be seen as a process whose central concern is to assist
the young to develop their knowledge within this kind of public
context. Education is a process of knowledge-making rather than
knowledge-getting, but this process has a public context. It is a matter
of developing what Elliot Eisner (1982) has called 'forms of
representation', but at the same time of recognizing, as he stresses, that
these are public modes, they are 'the devices that humans use to make
public conceptions which are privately held' and 'the vehicles through
which concepts . . . are given public status' (1982:47).

Second, a corollary of this is that, education must be open to, and
accepting of, difference, different world views and cultures. For to say
that knowledge, concepts and understandings are public is not to say
that they are universal.

Third, it is important to stress that, even if political power is
exercised through the distribution of knowledge, the legitimation of
discourse, 'the institutionalization of values' (Illich, 1971:9) and 'the
bureaucratic imposition of official values' (Turner, 1990:11), we are not
necessarily powerless in the face of this. On the contrary, to understand
these processes is to be on the way to being armed against them. As
Foucault (1979:100–1) has pointed out, 'discourse can be both an

instrument and an effect of power, but also a hindrance, a stumbling-block, a point of resistance and a starting point for an opposing strategy. Discourse transmits and produces power; it reinforces it, but also undermines and exposes it, renders it fragile and makes it possible to thwart it.'

The force of this is that the essence of education, if it is to be the education of free human beings in a free society, must be the development of powers of constant challenge, critique, dialogue, debate – what Freire (1976) called 'the practice of freedom'. Its central purpose must be the empowerment of the individual as a member of a free collective against those who would manipulate that collective against individual freedom. It must, as Freire (1972) also asserted, seek to provide pupils with the skills to see their problems in a reflexive perspective and thus enable them to gain some control over their own destinies and prevent them from becoming 'dopes' whose lives are determined for them by others. Education in a free and democratic society must be founded on an open and democratic view of knowledge.

This of course raises important questions about the ways in which curriculum can be perceived, and indeed conceptualized. We have been aware for some time that different models of curriculum exist, different ways in which we might set about our curriculum planning and provision. What should also be apparent as a result of this chapter is that these different models reflect different ideologies of education, and that these ideologies in their turn represent different theories of human knowledge and deeper ideological positions in relation to society itself.

The crucial interrelationships between ideological stances in relation to knowledge, society and the role of education within society must be borne in mind as we turn in Chapters 3 and 4 to a discussion of the major ideologies of curriculum. What this chapter has sought to demonstrate is that theories of human knowledge are central to them all.

Key issues raised by this chapter

1) What are the linkages between theories of knowledge and views of society?
2) What are the implications of these for curriculum planning, policy and practice?
3) What particular implications are there for education in a democratic society?

Suggested further reading

Doll, W. E. (1993) *A Post-Modern Perspective on Curriculum,* New York: Teachers College Press.

Kelly, A. V. (1986) *Knowledge and Curriculum Planning,* London: Harper and Row.

3

Curriculum as content and prod

We have noted on several occasions the analysis by Ralph Tyler (1949) of the key elements of curriculum planning – purposes, content, procedures and methodology. And we have suggested that a focus on any one of these, a selection of any as the prime consideration in curriculum planning, will lead us to a quite distinctive form for such planning. Chapter 2, through its discussion of the problem of human knowledge, also drew our attention to the fact that each of these forms will reflect and represent a different ideology not only of education but also of knowledge, of humanity and of society. This chapter and the next will seek to unpack the differing ideologies that each encapsulates. In particular, they will endeavour to elucidate what appear to be the three major ideologies which can be discerned – curriculum as content and education as transmission, curriculum as product and education as instrumental and curriculum as process and education as development.

Curriculum as content and education as transmission

We noted earlier that many people have not fully appreciated the force or the implications of Tyler's claim. For many, a curriculum is still a syllabus, and even among those who have discussed and even advocated a more sophisticated approach to planning there are those who continue, at least in the practical recommendations they make, to regard decisions of content as the starting point. Many of these people do operate with a concept of education framed in terms of the developing understanding of the child, the growth of critical awareness and other such elements which seem more closely related to the idea of education as development than to that of education as the mere transmission of knowledge. They still appear to assume, however, and sometimes endeavour to argue, that only certain kinds of knowledge will promote these forms of development or that exposure to certain kinds of knowledge will do so for all pupils.

And the politicians and those who produce the official documentation for them also continue to offer their curricular prescriptions in terms of the content to be transmitted, although they too wrap this up in a rhetoric of 'entitlement', 'progression', 'continuity', 'breadth', 'balance' and those other unanalysed and unexplained concepts which we noted in Chapters 1 and 2, again in a manner which suggests that they too assume that exposure to their chosen content will automatically, by some kind of magic or osmosis, ensure that these are the end results for all pupils.

There are thus two versions of this kind of planning which we must consider in rather greater detail. First, there is that version which derives from the adoption of the kind of absolutist epistemology we discussed in Chapter 2. And, second, there is the version favoured by the politicians, in which content is selected and dictated largely in terms of economic and social utility, whatever the accompanying rhetoric, and which can thus be seen as an amalgam of the content and product approaches to planning.

The philosophical case

The philosophical case for planning the curriculum in terms of its content is based on the kind of absolutist epistemology whose difficulties we explored in Chapter 2. We saw there that to view knowledge as being in some sense God-given, independent of the knower, as *sui generis*, is to approach the problem of the status of human knowledge by studying knowledge itself rather than the social context and the social relations within which it is produced. It is thus a view which leads to a loss of status, and indeed of freedom, for the individual, since objective, absolute knowledge is not to be argued or disagreed with, even in the murky area of values. And we also noted that this is not merely an academic issue, since societies which have been based on particular and unquestioned views of knowledge and values have all of them in reality been characterized by an absence of individual freedom, not only of thought but also of speech and action.

When this form of absolutist epistemology is applied to the planning of the curriculum, it assumes a planning model whose first question is 'What kinds of knowledge enjoy this kind of absolute status?', and education is then defined, in the famous words of Richard Peters (1965, 1966) as 'initiation into intrinsically worthwhile activities'.

There are two points to be identified here. First, if we are to see 'education' as a concept which is distinguishable from other kinds of teaching such as 'training', 'instruction', 'conditioning', 'indoctrination' and so on, one of the features which must distinguish it from these other teaching activities is that it must be focused on intrinsic value, it must be an activity we engage in for its own sake rather than as instrumental to some extrinsic purpose or purposes. This is an important distinction and one which has been largely lost in current policies and practices, as we shall see later.

The second point we must identify, however, is rather more controversial. For this approach to curriculum planning is asking us to accept, as its absolutist epistemology demands of it, that we see this intrinsic value as residing in some way in the knowledge itself rather than in the manner in which the learner approaches and views it. Unlike beauty, it resides not in the eye of the beholder but in some sense in that which is beheld. Thus, on this view, in a very real sense, we must plan our curriculum with little or no reference to its potential impact on the recipients of it. The justification for that curriculum is to be found in its content rather than in its effects.

A further point arises from this. For, as will have been seen from our discussion of the problem of knowledge in Chapter 2, what is important is not merely *what* knowledge we present *via* our curricula but also, and more so, *how* we present it. In a context of serious doubts about the status of all human knowledge, what is crucial is that we invite critical reflection and challenge of all that is so presented. The knowledge component of a democratic curriculum must be what Habermas (1972) has called 'emancipatory knowledge'. This has been described by Wilf Carr (1995:115) as deriving 'from a fundamental desire to be free from those constraints on human reason – constraints of authority, ignorance, custom, tradition and the like – which impede the freedom of individuals to determine their purposes and actions on the basis of their own rational reflections'. If knowledge is seen as emancipatory in this way (as it surely must in any genuine democratic context), then some God-given status of its own cannot be the justification for its selection for inclusion in the curriculum. There must be some other basis or bases for selection.

This approach to curriculum planning, then, has the merit of being concerned to ensure that all pupils have access to what is regarded as intrinsically worthwhile; its concept of entitlement is genuine rather than rhetorical. However, noble as its intentions may be, it falls well short of offering a satisfactory basis for curriculum planning for a democratic society, since it produces a form of curriculum which leads to the stratification of society, to elitism, to the disaffection and alienation of those who find themselves in the lower strata of such a society, especially when this is due to social class, ethnic origin or gender. Hence there has been a rejection not only of this approach to curriculum but also of the theory of knowledge on which it is based.

Education as cultural transmission

A common example of this content-based approach to curriculum planning is that which derives from a concern that the curriculum should be concerned to transmit the culture of society.

It must be recognized that schools exist in advanced or sophisticated societies as agencies for the handing on of the culture of the society, so that at least in part their purposes must be seen in terms of socialization or acculturation, attending to that induction of children into the ways of life of society which is achieved in more primitive societies by less formal methods. On this basis it has been argued that a good deal of what is to be taught in schools can be decided by reference to the 'common cultural heritage' (Lawton, 1973, 1975) of the society they are created to serve.

Even if one accepts the force of this claim in principle, in practice it creates more difficulties than it resolves. To begin with, difficulties arise because the term 'culture' has several different meanings (Kelly, 1986). In particular, confusions are created by the fact that the term is used, by anthropologists for example, to denote in a purely descriptive sense all aspects of the ways of life of a society, as when we speak of the cultural patterns of a primitive community. On the other hand, it is also used to denote what is regarded as being best in the art and literature of any particular society, what Matthew Arnold once described as 'the best that has been thought and said'. Thus a 'cultured individual' is not one who knows his or her way about the ways of life, the habits and beliefs of his or her society; he or she is an individual who has been brought to appreciate those works of his or her fellows that are regarded as being among the finer achievements of the culture.

When people talk, then, of basing the curriculum on the culture of the society, some of them are suggesting that we socialize the young, while others are encouraging us to frame the curriculum in terms of what is regarded as being best or most valuable among the intellectual and artistic achievements of the society.

A further difficulty arises for those who wish to base decisions about the content of the curriculum on considerations of the culture of the society when we attempt to state in specific terms what that culture is. For it is clear that in a modern advanced industrial society no one pattern of life, and no single body of 'high culture', that can be called the culture of that society can be identified. Most modern societies are pluralist in nature; that is, it is possible to discern in them many different, and sometimes incompatible, cultures or subcultures.

The question whether schools should endeavour to promote a common culture or help diverse groups to develop their own different cultures is a vexed one, not least in relation to those minority ethnic groups that are to be found in most societies (Jeffcoate, 1984; Kelly, 1986). What concerns us more directly here, however, is the implication that, even if we believe that the content of the curriculum should be based on the culture of the society, it will be impossible to assert with any real expectation of general acceptance what that culture is and therefore what the content of the curriculum should be. All that this line of argument will achieve is to remind us of the view of the curriculum as a battleground of competing ideologies and to bring us face to face with age-old issues concerning the appropriate educational provision for different social and ethnic groups. In fact, it is a line of argument which in the last analysis leads to a recognition of the need for diversity rather than uniformity of educational provision, and thus to an awareness of the inadequacies of any form of curriculum planning that lays too great a stress on the role of curriculum content.

This is one source of a further problem that arises if we attempt to establish as the content of our curriculum those things which we regard as being the essential valuable elements of the culture, a problem which we have seen is endemic to all forms of absolutist approaches. For recent practice has revealed very clearly that this can lead to the imposition on some pupils of a curriculum that is alien to them, which lacks relevance to their lives and to their experience outside the school and can ultimately bring about their alienation from and rejection of the education they are offered. This is probably the root cause of most of the problems that the educational system is facing today and it is certainly a real hazard if not an inevitable result of this kind of approach to curriculum planning. In a class-ridden society which is also multi-ethnic, it is not possible to break the cycle of poverty, unemployment, disaffection, alienation and social disorder by offering a middle-class, white Anglo-Saxon curriculum to all pupils. In fact, to do so is to aggravate and reinforce that cycle. So that the imposition of such a curriculum on all pupils is a clear indication that the breaking of that cycle is not high on the political agenda.

These last points lead us on to a much more general weakness of this line of argument. For it will be apparent that even if we see it as the task of our schools to initiate pupils into the culture of the society, it will not be possible to offer them the whole of that culture, however it is defined. A selection will have to be made and, since this is so, any notion of the culture of the society, no matter how acceptable in definition or content, will not in itself provide us with appropriate criteria of selection. We will need to look elsewhere for justification of the selection we do make, so that the arguments for a curriculum content based on the culture or cultures of society will not in themselves take us very far towards finding a solution to our problem. What they do offer, however, is a mechanism by which politicians can impose their own favoured versions of culture on a society, as is illustrated by recent pronouncements from senior politicians about such things as history and literature syllabuses, echoed as always by their spokespersons in the curriculum quangos.

This danger can be avoided only if it can be argued that what is valuable in the culture is valuable not merely because it is part of the culture but because it has some intrinsic merit which justifies its place not only on the curriculum but also in society itself. There are many people who would wish to argue that there are certain elements in the culture of any advanced society which go beyond the particularities of that society and reflect certain values which are timeless and, indeed, transcendental in every sense. It is on grounds such as these that many would want to press the case for the introduction of pupils to literature, music, art and ideas that are felt to be 'great' and to constitute a cultural heritage which is the heritage of humanity in general rather than of one particular nation. And it is difficult to mount a contrary argument and claim that such things should have no place on the curriculum.

However, this does bring us back to the whole issue of the nature of knowledge and the question whether any body of knowledge has or can have an intrinsic, objective, absolute value or status. The focus of the matter, therefore, continues to be the nature of human knowledge, and, if we have doubts about absolutist versions of knowledge, we must ask important questions about the forms of curricula that these must lead us to.

The problem is aggravated by the fact that most societies are far from static entities and this implies that one feature of their culture is that it is changing, evolving, developing. In particular, technological change must lead to changes in the norms, the values, the beliefs, the customs of a society; in other words, it must lead to a fluid culture. And moral change is more difficult in many ways to handle, since people shed or change their values more slowly, more reluctantly and, indeed, less consciously than they exchange their cars or their washing machines.

A recognition of the rapidity of social change and of the need for people to be equipped to cope with it and even to exercise some degree of control over it suggests that schools should in any case go beyond the notion of initiation of pupils into the culture of the society, beyond socialization and acculturation, to the idea of preparing pupils for the fact of social change itself, to adapt to and to initiate changes in the norms and values of the community. In short, it may be argued that the view of curriculum as cultural content is based on too narrow a concept of culture.

Thus more recent views have stressed that culture must be seen as the total environment within which the child develops and learns and which she/he must be helped to come to terms with, to operate effectively in and to gain some control over. Children learn, it is claimed, by making sense and constructing meaning through interaction with their environment, their culture. And so, the task of education is to help pupils towards this form of learning, 'to negotiate meaning in a manner congruent with the requirements of the culture' (Bruner and Haste, 1987:1). In this sense, culture is viewed as supporting cognitive growth by providing 'cultural amplifiers' through which children develop those 'modes of representation' (Eisner, 1982) we noted in Chapter 2, access to public structures through which the meaning of experiences can be not only internalized and understood, but also shared. On this kind of analysis, learning is interactive and the relationship between culture and the curriculum is two-way. This discussion, however, is taking us into a quite different curriculum ideology and we must delay further pursuit of it until Chapter 4.

What we must note here is the support such a view of culture gives to the argument that pupils must be offered much more than a selection of the culture of the society as it exists at the time when they happen to be in schools, even if this could be identified and defined clearly enough for adequate educational practice. It also constitutes, as we have seen, a strong argument for planning the curriculum by reference to the capacities we are endeavouring to promote in pupils rather than the bodies of knowledge we are concerned to pass on to them.

The idea of education as transmission or of curriculum as content, then, is simplistic and unsophisticated because it leaves out of the reckoning major dimensions of the curriculum debate. In particular, it does not encourage or help us to take any account of the children who are the recipients of this content and the objects of the process of transmission, or of the impact of that content and that process on them, and especially their right to emancipation and empowerment. Their task is to learn as effectively as they can what is offered to them. If the effect of the process on them is of any significance, this model offers us no means of exploring or evaluating that effect, beyond assessing the extent of their assimilation of what has been fed to them, any other consequences of such learning being beyond its scope. So far as this model is concerned, these are an irrelevance, since to ask this kind of question is to go well beyond what the model permits or acknowledges. Yet many would wish to argue that it is precisely that effect or these consequences which are at the heart of what we might mean by the term 'education', unless, as we have seen, we are to deny and reject any conceptual difference between education and instruction or even training. And for that reason it is claimed by many that this model is inadequate for proper *educational* planning; it does not go far enough; it asks one kind of question only and takes into account only one kind of consideration; in particular, it pays little attention to the purposes of education; it thus offers a distorted view of education and of curriculum and a seriously flawed and limited model for educational planning.

The approach to curriculum planning through content, then, raises problems even when it is proposed within the context of an epistemology which seeks to proclaim the intrinsic value of this content. When no such epistemological basis is claimed, when the selection of the content of our curriculum is not justified by reference to knowledge itself or to the culture of society, then further difficulties arise, since that selection will now be a result of considerations of an instrumental or utilitarian kind. And it is this kind of consideration which underpins the forms of content-based curricula which are hatched by politicians and their aides.

The political selection of curriculum content

Planning by nothing more sophisticated than statements of content is becoming increasingly prevalent in current curricular policies. It is the view of curriculum which clearly underpins most official statements which have emerged from the Department of Education and Science (DES) and the Department for Education and Employment (DfEE), and not only from the civil servants there, who might not be expected to show any depth of understanding of the complexities of educational planning, but also from Her Majesty's Inspectorate and that plethora of government quangos which recent years have spawned, whose ambitions to be regarded as the leading edge of professional planning and provision would seem to suggest that they should. Thus the series of publications under the general title *Curriculum Matters* (DES, 1984a, 1985a, b, c, d, 1986a, b, 1987b, c) which presaged the establishment of the National Curriculum for England and Wales, was planned, like most earlier statements emanating from the same source, in terms of separate curriculum subjects, and each concentrated very largely on outlining what its authors felt should be the essential content of those subjects. When they were not outlining content they were listing 'aims and objectives' and thus demonstrating a different, although related, lack of understanding and sophistication, as we shall see later.

It was not surprising, therefore, that this same, simple model was adopted by the politicians and their aides for the planning of the National Curriculum, whose core is 'the overall content, knowledge, skills and processes' (DES, 1987a:10) of every subject listed as an essential ingredient of the new national programme of instruction and testing. We will examine many aspects of this policy in later chapters, but we must note here that it is not only a good example but also a prominent and pressingly topical example of this view of education as transmission and of curriculum as content, but with the added dimension of a largely instrumental or utilitarian basis for the selection of the content to be transmitted. And the major weakness we should note is that at no stage does one find any justification, or even any attempt at justification, for either the subjects or their content, except in vague and unanalysed phrases such as 'which they need to learn' (1987a:4), 'relevant to today's needs' (1987a:10), or in overtly utilitarian considerations such as 'practical applications and continuing value to adult and working life' (1987a:4) and 'the challenge of employment in tomorrow's world' (1987a:2). We hear of 'bench-marks', of 'attainment targets', of 'programmes of study' and of 'standards', all defined in terms of subject-content and offered as though they are non-problematic, and, although we get an impression that attempts are being made to 'cash in' on the kinds of philosophical argument we considered earlier, these arguments are nowhere adduced nor are the utilitarian arguments made explicit.

However, it is clear from the most superficial analysis that, behind the rhetoric, the fundamental thrust of these policies is instrumental (Kelly, 1990, 1994). And the survey of events leading up to the implementation of these policies which will be offered in Chapter 7 will lead us inexorably to the same conclusion. Indeed, the change of name from Department for Education and Science to Department for Education and Employment (or is it the Department of Education for Employment?) indicates a shift of ideology towards an instrumental view of schooling and the school curriculum. The education system is now geared to economic productivity and the curriculum planned to promote forms of learning which are regarded as useful, in terms both of future employment for individuals and the continued economic growth of society. Neither of these considerations of course can be responsibly ignored. In current policies, however, they are being bought at the expense of any notion that schools should also offer education in that full sense of learning for its own sake and for the development of the individual. Indeed, as we have seen, any conceptual distinction between education and training, instruction or teaching is ignored, and, indeed, specifically rejected.

However, the merits of this approach are not the concern here. What we must identify are its implications and consequences. And those implications and consequences must be precisely the same as those we saw emerging inexorably from the content-based approaches we considered earlier, although this time there is not the saving grace of attempted objectivity in views of knowledge or culture, nor, as we have just noted, any associated concept of education for its own sake. For, if we have been right to claim that content-based approaches to curriculum must lead to elitism, inequalities, disaffection and alienation, then this must be, perhaps especially, the case when the choice of content is made not by reference to the knowledge itself nor by reference to the children who are the objects of the curriculum but in relation almost solely to the economic needs of society and the interests of social control.

Furthermore, it is clear that these consequences are accepted, if only tacitly, by the authors and the proponents of those policies. The view of society, the social ideology, to which they are committed is fundamentally elitist. For, in spite of all the rhetoric of entitlement, it is clear from policies, practices and proposals, that there are strong and influential pressure groups whose weight is behind policies which would reduce entitlement for large sections of the child population.

Hence we can see quite clearly the surfacing of those ideologies (we might in this context call them sub-ideologies, since they are sub-variants of the general ideological position we are exploring) which Denis Lawton (1989, 1992, 1994) has drawn our attention to. For, in opposition to the faction he names 'the comprehensive planners', those who press for the provision by the state of 'a good general education for all' (Lawton, 1989:52), he identifies three contrary ideologies which would deny such provision.

First, there are those he calls the 'privatisers'. These are those who, on the philosophical grounds of their objections to 'collectivism', interference by the state in individual privacy (what is now known as 'the nanny society'), and the much more practical grounds of costs, 'would advocate the dismantling of the whole state education service or gradually privatising the system' (1989:49). A notable step in this direction was the introduction of vouchers for nursery education, a policy which has now been discontinued. This group would leave all to market forces, as, for example, by permitting, and indeed encouraging, the 'opting out' of schools from the state system.

The second group he calls the 'minimalists'. These hold to a tradition which derives from nineteenth century 'Tory paternalism' (1989:50) and which now reflects 'a set of values supporting the provision of a state education system provided that value for money can be demonstrated, and also that education can be shown to be "useful" particularly in the sense of servicing the labour market with well-trained and disciplined school-leavers who have been convinced of the value of such virtues as punctuality and hard work' (1989:50). Thus they 'support a state education service which concentrates on the basics' with parents having the right 'of buying additional extras or opting out altogether' (1989:50).

Lawton sees 'Mr Baker's City Technology Colleges' as an example of this ideology in practice.

The third group are the 'pluralists'. This group favours the establishment of a good state system of education, but views such a system in meritocratic terms, 'favouring the metaphor of 'the ladder of opportunity' rather than that of 'the broad highway'' (1989:51). It may well be argued that in most countries, and especially in England and Wales, it is this group which is currently in the ascendant.

These then are all sub-variants of, and natural consequences of, the instrumentalist ideology we are describing. Their curricula will emphasize content, but they do not embrace an epistemology which requires them to select this content for its own sake. Rather, they lead to a viewing of all knowledge and all forms of learning as justified only on utilitarian grounds, so that the basis for the selection of curriculum content is a consideration of nothing more than its instrumental value.

It is for this reason that official policy statements and pronouncements, in addition to being framed in terms of subjects and knowledge-content, are also laden with references to the 'aims and objectives' of these subjects and this content. They can thus be seen as attempts to conflate the traditional model of curriculum as content with that model which emerged with the aims and objectives movement, with particular force in the second half of the twentieth century.

Before we consider the implications of such a conflation, however, we must turn to a detailed consideration of that movement and the ideology it represents.

Curriculum as product and education as instrumental

The aims and objectives movement

The growth of the movement
A concern with curriculum objectives was one of the most striking features of the move towards deliberate curriculum planning to which we referred in Chapter 1. Statements of objectives were, for example, the starting points for many curriculum projects developed under the aegis of the Schools Council, and we have witnessed a growing pressure on teachers to pay due regard to them in their planning.

The impetus for this came initially early in this century from those who were impressed by the progress of science and technology and believed that the same kind of progress might become possible in the field of education if a properly scientific approach were to be adopted there also. As is so often the case, the origins of this movement can be traced to the United States; in the United Kingdom it appeared somewhat later.

The tone of this movement was set by one of its earliest proponents, Franklin Bobbitt, who expressed great concern at the vague, imprecise purposes he felt characterized the work of most teachers, announced that 'an age of science is demanding exactness and particularity' (Bobbitt, 1918:ch.6; Davies, 1976:47) and suggested that teachers be required to write out their objectives in clear, non-technical language that both pupils and their parents might understand.

The cry was taken up by others. In 1924, for example, Werrett Charters attempted a 'job analysis' of teaching and offered a method of course construction based on this kind of approach. His suggestion was that we first determine what he called the 'ideals' of education, then identify the 'activities' that these involve and finally analyse both of these to the level of 'working units of the size of human ability' (Charters, 1924; Davies, 1976:50), those small steps that need to be mastered one by one. In this way the curriculum could be reduced to a series of working units and its whole structure set out on a chart or graph.

Thus, early pioneers of the movement, like Bobbitt and Charters, gave it from the beginning a scientific, behavioural, job-analysis flavour, their general purpose being to introduce into educational practice the kind of precise, scientific methods that had begun to yield dividends in other spheres of human activity and especially in industry.

The spread of interest in testing that was a feature of educational development in the 1930s can be seen as another aspect of this same movement. For the link between the prespecification of objectives and the testing of performance has long been a close one, and that it continues to be so is apparent from the emphasis on attainment targets, allied to assessment procedures, within the National Curriculum in England and Wales.

This link was made quite explicit in the work of the next major exponent of the objectives approach, Ralph Tyler. For Tyler's original aim was to design scientific tests of educational attainment and his solution to this problem was to suggest that this could be done most readily and easily if a clear statement had been made of the kind of attainment that was being aimed at. If course objectives had been formulated and those objectives defined in terms of intended student behaviour, that behaviour could then be evaluated in the light of those intentions (Tyler, 1932; Davies, 1976).

This provided the foundation upon which Tyler was later to base what has come to be regarded as the classic statement of the objectives approach to curriculum design. In a book in which he expressed alarm at the level of generality he claimed to have detected in teachers' responses to questions about their work, he set out the four questions which he said must be faced and answered by curriculum planners. Those four questions, as we saw in Chapter 1, are concerned with the purposes, the content, the organization and the evaluation of the curriculum (Tyler, 1949).

The next milestone was reached in 1956 with the publication by Benjamin Bloom and his associates of their *Taxonomy of Educational Objectives Handbook 1: Cognitive Domain*. For this introduced a new dimension into this form of curriculum planning with its division of objectives into three categories or 'domains' – the cognitive, the affective and the psychomotor – and at the same time it offered the most detailed and ambitious classification of objectives in the cognitive domain that had yet been attempted. This was matched by the publication in 1964, under the editorship of D. R. Kratwohl, of a second handbook that offered a similar classification within the affective domain.

It was some time before the work of either Tyler or Bloom began to have any real impact but by the mid-1960s their influence was beginning to be felt not only in the United States but in the United Kingdom too.

And so the prespecification of clear course objectives was a major feature of most of the curriculum projects that emerged during that period of widespread innovation that followed the establishment of the Schools Council in the United Kingdom in 1964, and this was a key factor in the growth of interest in this approach to curriculum planning that came in the 1960s. The allocation of public money (although never a large sum) to curriculum development on this scale brought with it the requirement that a proper account be given of how that money was being spent. For this reason, as well as for considerations of a purely educational kind, evaluation was a central concern of most new projects from the outset, and in those early years a proper evaluation was interpreted as requiring a clear statement of goals, aims, purposes, objectives.

It was through the work of the Schools Council, therefore, after a long and interesting history, that the concept of curriculum planning by objectives finally entered the consciousness of the practising teacher. And so, when in the late 1970s, as a result of several factors of a largely political kind which we will explore more fully in Chapter 7, pressures began to be felt by teachers to plan their work more carefully and precisely, it was to this model that they were inclined and, indeed, encouraged to turn (Blenkin, 1980).

This approach to curriculum planning, however, requires more careful analysis than most teachers were able to give it, and it is to that kind of examination that we must proceed.

Some problems presented by this model – a passive view of humanity

One fundamental criticism which has been levelled at this approach to curriculum planning is that its attempt to reduce education to a scientific activity, analogous to the processes of industry, commits it to a view of humans and of human nature that many people find unacceptable and even unpalatable. To adopt this kind of industrial model for education is to assume that it is legitimate to mould human beings, to modify their behaviour, according to certain clear-cut intentions without making any allowance for their own individual wishes, desires or interests. Like the materials upon which the industrial worker operates, children's minds are to be fashioned by teachers according to some preconceived blueprint. It thus represents a serious threat to individual freedom.

And, indeed, the major proponents of this view leave us in no doubt that they see objectives as behavioural and consequently regard schooling as a form of behaviour modification. Tyler, for example, tells us that 'the most useful form for stating objectives is to express them in terms which identify both the kind of behaviour to be developed in the students and the context or area of life in which this behaviour is to operate' (1949:46–7). Bloom calls them 'intended learning outcomes' and says that they are to be defined in terms of the behaviour the pupil is intended to display through his or her thoughts, actions or feelings. Mager (1962:13) says, 'A statement of an objective is useful to the extent that it specifies what the learner must be able to *do* or *perform* when he is demonstrating his mastery of the objective.' And Popham (1969:35) tells us that 'a satisfactory instructional objective must describe an observable *behaviour* of the learner or a *product* which is a consequence of learner behaviour'. The observable behaviour might take the form of something like 'skill in making impromptu speeches or performing gymnastic feats' (1969:35). Products might be an essay or 'an omelet from the home economics class' (1969:35). This being so, 'a properly stated behavioural objective must describe *without ambiguity* the nature of learner behaviour or product to be measured' (1969:37). [All emphases original.]

The important thing to recognize, therefore, is that the notion of behaviour modification is essential to this model of curriculum planning. Again, we may note that there may well be areas, such as that of vocational training, where this is entirely appropriate. Whether it is appropriate to *educational* planning, however, is highly questionable, as we shall see. What we must note here is that to adopt this as the model for all educational planning is to be committed to the idea of education as the modification of pupil behaviour, whether one defines what one means by 'objectives' in behavioural terms or not, or, indeed, even if one does not bother to offer a definition at all.

The focus of this approach to educational planning, then, is essentially on the modification of pupil behaviour, and the success of such a curriculum is to be gauged by an assessment of the behaviour changes the curriculum appears to have brought about in relation to those it was its stated intention to bring about. Fundamental to the view, therefore, is a psychological theory of a behaviourist kind, and it is with behaviourist psychology that the movement has been associated from the start. In fact, most of its theoretical proponents have been psychologists rather than educationists or teachers.

This passive model of humans is endemic to the theory and it is thus not acceptable to those who take the view that the individual is to be regarded as a free and active agent, responsible for his or her own destiny and who, as a direct consequence of this, believe it to be morally wrong to deny him or her that responsibility and freedom by attempting to mould his or her behaviour to suit the ends of someone else. Such a process, they argue, is indoctrination rather than education and thus to be deplored. This, as we have seen before, is a problem which is endemic to all forms of instrumentalism in educational planning. This model, then, must be recognized as fundamentally at odds with the notion of education for emancipation or empowerment.

This becomes particularly evident when we consider the use of this approach in those areas of the curriculum which most obviously involve content of a kind which is highly controversial. For to approach these areas with a clear prespecification of intended learning outcomes in behavioural terms is to abandon education altogether for what must be seen as a much more sinister process. In the teaching and learning of music and the fine arts the prime concern is to elicit an individual response from the pupil; it is clearly not appropriate to decide in advance what that response should be (Eisner, 1969). 'How can you put on the blackboard the mysterious internal goal of each creative person?' (Pirsig, 1974). In literature too the whole purpose of introducing pupils to great literary works is lost if it is done from the perspective of intended learning outcomes (Stenhouse, 1970). Again that purpose is to invite the pupil to respond in his or her own way to what he or she is introduced to. To approach a reading of *Hamlet*, for example, in any other way is either to reduce it to an instrumental role, designed to promote an understanding of words, poetic forms, even philosophy, or to attempt to impose one's own moral and aesthetic values, one's own subjective interpretation of the play and response to it on one's pupils. If appreciation of literature or any of the arts means anything at all and has any place in education, it cannot be approached by way of clearly prespecified objectives.

This is one of the major reasons why the Schools Council's Humanities Curriculum Project, which may be identified as the first major rebellion against the use of this model, deliberately eschewed any kind of statement of objectives. Being concerned to introduce older pupils in secondary schools to some of the controversial issues that face modern society, such as relations between the sexes, living in cities, war and so on, and being of the opinion that these are issues upon which a number of different value stances can be taken with equal validity, it recognized that the involvement of pupils in these issues could not be undertaken justifiably with clear objectives as to what the outcome of their learning and discussions should be, but only according to certain procedural principles designed to allow them to reach their own informed opinions on them. To do anything else would be to indoctrinate rather than to educate, to deny them their right to think for themselves and to reach their own conclusions as emancipated human beings.

This has also led some people to reject the behavioural objectives approach to the planning of the curriculum for children with special needs (Goddard, 1983). It is perhaps in this field that the model has been adopted most readily and extensively and in its starkest form. Indeed, in this kind of context the notion of 'behaviour modification' seems to have been adopted with few qualms, and there has been little objection to the view that in the case of children with special needs or learning difficulties it is not only acceptable but even necessary to concentrate all one's attention on modifying their behaviour and improving their performance of certain kinds of behavioural task. Thus Wilfrid Brennan (1979:97) tells us that 'clarity of terminal and intermediate objectives in the curriculum is seen as essential if the teacher is to use the total learning situation in order to continuously "shape" [note the metaphor] the development of the pupil', and we are also told (Leeming *et al.*, 1979:68) in relation to the education of children with special needs that 'the only way we can hope to change children and know we have succeeded, is to change their behaviour. This is the basis for the use of an objectives approach to the curriculum.'

However, if this approach leads to forms of indoctrination, if it treats human beings as passive recipients of experiences intended to bring about behavioural changes felt to be desirable by others, if it denies individual freedom, and if it negates the notion of learning for learning's sake, then it is at least as unsatisfactory as the sole approach to the teaching of children with special educational needs as it is in the case of other pupils. And it is right that Alan Goddard and others should be insisting that there be more to the education of such children than that, that 'what we often want to teach is not behaviour, neither can it be reduced to behaviour' (Goddard,

1983:272 – referring to Swann, 1981). Indeed, it is difficult to see the point of the Warnock Report's (DES, 1980c) recommendation for the integration of pupils with special needs wherever possible into ordinary schools and classrooms on any other grounds – unless of course behaviour modification is to be the aim for all pupils.

A view of learning as a linear process

A second feature of the aims and objectives model which has been seen as posing serious problems is its view of the learning process as linear. Aims are usually seen as very general statements of goals and purposes. Such aims by themselves, however, have often been regarded as too general and lacking in specificity to provide clear guidelines for planners or teachers, so that curriculum planning has been seen as a process of deriving more precise statements of goals from these general aims; these more precise statements of goals are normally termed objectives. Indeed, some writers have even suggested that we should recognize three or more levels of specificity (Kratwohl, 1965): general statements of goals that will guide the planning of the curriculum as a whole, behavioural objectives derived from these which will guide the planning of individual units or courses, and a third level of objectives appropriate in some cases to guide the planning of specific lessons; to use Wheeler's terms, 'ultimate', 'mediate' and 'proximate' goals, the last providing specific classroom objectives (Wheeler, 1967).

This, as we saw earlier, is the kind of structure that was envisaged by the early pioneers of the movement, and the important point to note is that this approach to curriculum planning assumes that education must be planned in a step-by-step linear manner. It is in fact an attempt to translate into classroom terms that linear step-by-step process which is not only claimed to be characteristic of industrial processes but which behavioural psychologists have discovered to be the most effective way of conditioning animals – dogs, cats, rats, pigeons and so on.

It is important to stress that it is only through this kind of linear and hierarchical scheme that one can make any real sense of the distinction between aims and objectives, in short, that it is an essential feature of the aims and objectives model of curriculum planning. The term 'objective' might of course be used to mean merely any 'goal' or 'purpose'. There is nothing fundamentally wrong or mistaken in such a usage. However, the attempt to distinguish 'aims' and 'objectives' implies that these terms denote different kinds or levels of educational goal or purpose, so that to make this distinction reflects either a clear acceptance of a hierarchy of goals, and thus of the objectives model and all it entails, or a disturbing failure to achieve conceptual clarity over what one's planning model really is. For, if there is a distinction between the two concepts, it can consist only in their hierarchical relationship with each other.

Thus, for example, the taxonomy which Bloom and his associates (1956) offer us requires us to prespecify our objectives at varying levels of specificity in order to outline in great detail the kinds of behaviour which are the objectives of our curriculum. We are offered a hierarchy of goals, of 'intended learning outcomes' defined in terms of the kind of behaviour the pupil is intended or expected to display through his or her thoughts, actions or feelings if we are to be able to claim that our objective has been achieved.

It is easy to see why this approach has proved, and continues to prove, so attractive to some curriculum planners. Indeed, as we will see shortly, the National Curriculum for England and Wales is firmly entrenched in this model, offering in fact a classic example of the combination of the content and aims-and-objectives bases, its statements of the essential content of each of its subjects being set out in the form of attainment targets (ATs) and levels of attainment in a step-by-step linear hierarchy. On a similar model, the curriculum for schools in Hong Kong was originally termed Targets and Target-Related Assessment (TTRA) and is now known as the Target Oriented Curriculum (TOC).

However, the hierarchical form of the relationships between objectives that is characteristic of taxonomies such as that of Bloom (1956) does not reflect the realities of the learning process. The linear model that it assumes, which attempts to break down all learning into a step-by-step procedure, is not suitable for most of the learning that goes on in schools. We do not acquire knowledge and then, at some later stage, attain understanding; the two must go hand in hand. Real learning is developmental rather than linear. The acquisition of knowledge or the transmission of knowledge-content may be linear processes; the development of understanding certainly is not; it is a far more subtle process and much more likely to be brought about by some form of what Jerome Bruner has termed a 'spiral curriculum', where one returns to concepts at ever higher levels of complexity and understanding, than by a 'Thirty-Nine Steps', linear and hierarchical set of offerings. Any view of the learning process that does not recognize this must be regarded as too simplistic to serve as a basis for any but the most unsophisticated of teaching activities.

A good example of this is the suggestion often made by the advocates of this approach, and which is implied by all the assertions we hear about the need for the teaching of 'the basic skills', that we ought to set about teaching these skills before we attempt more sophisticated forms of teaching and learning; in short, that our approach to teaching and learning should be not only linear but also hierarchical.

The teaching of basic skills, however, even those of a psychomotor kind, cannot be separated out from other kinds of goals without risking the loss of that essential ingredient of education that we must also be concerned with. It is possible to teach basic skills in an instructional manner – the basic skills of reading, for example, of using a saw or a wood-chisel, of drawing straight lines or circles and many others – and in this area the use of the behavioural model has appeared to be successful. However, if we do not at the same time have clearly in mind the educational dimensions of the activities we are engaged in, then, while our efforts might well result in highly skilled performance at the behavioural level, they are likely to result in our achieving little beyond that and may even be counterproductive to any further attainment and, indeed, to education itself. For, as the Bullock Report (DES, 1975) pointed out, it is possible to help pupils to a high level of reading performance and at the same time to kill or to inhibit any love or appreciation they may have developed for the written word. Indeed, as the Report also pointed out, even that high level of skilled performance itself will be short-lived. There are more 'non-readers' about than those who merely cannot decipher the symbols of the written word. Written language too is 'far too complex a system for any simple description in terms of a build up of sub-skills to account for it', so that 'if we try to offer a logically pre-programmed sequence of knowledge we simply interfere with the sense-making opportunities which real reading and writing offer to the learner' and 'any attempt to make learning literacy easy by offering only parts of the whole experience is almost certain to violate the meaningfulness of normal written language' (Money, 1988:142). And, in mathematics too, it has been suggested (Metz, 1988:187) that 'an emphasis . . . on applying rules in a step-by-step manner ignores not only the need to make general sense of a situation first, but also the importance of reflecting on any solution obtained after the rules have been applied'. Education is far too complex a process to be broken down in this kind of way.

This is a major danger of attempts to measure standards of attainment in schools in terms simply of performance or behaviour. It is thus a danger not only of the objectives model of curriculum planning but also of those popular, public and political demands for improved standards in the 'basic skills' which have this kind of simplistic model of learning at their tap-root.

An inadequate concept of education

It is for this reason that the model has also been attacked as being based not only on inadequate and unacceptable models of humanity and of human learning but also on an equally unsatisfactory concept of education. The aims-and-objectives approach to curriculum planning, like all scientific approaches to the study and planning of human activity, endeavours to be value-neutral. Those who have advocated it have been concerned only to present teachers and curriculum planners with a scheme or a blueprint for them to use as they think fit; it is not their concern to tell them how to use it. They regard education as a matter of changing behaviour but they do not accept responsibility for questions about what kinds of behaviour education should be concerned to promote or what kinds of behavioural change it should be attempting to bring about. They maintain their scientific stance, therefore, and leave it to the persons using their scheme to make the decisions about how it should be used.

Thus this approach deliberately side-steps the most difficult and intractable problem that faces curriculum planners – that of deciding what kinds of activity shall be deemed to be educational. And in itself it can offer no help or guidance with this aspect of educational decision-making. It sets out to provide a methodology for curriculum planning and nothing more. This must be regarded as a very serious disadvantage in this model as a basis for *educational* planning, and it may explain why most of those who have promoted the model (as opposed to those who have merely accepted and attempted to use it uncritically) have been inclined to use the word 'instruction' for what they are concerned to plan rather than the much more pregnant term 'education'. As a model for planning schemes of instruction, it may well have much to recommend it; as a model for educational planning, it is seriously flawed.

However, although the proponents of this planning model have claimed that it is value-neutral, in fact there is implicit within it a very clear ideology of education. For its failure, or refusal, to distinguish education from teaching or learning itself constitutes an ideological position. Those who have attempted to disentangle the concept of education from other related concepts such as training, instruction or indoctrination have done so by drawing attention to certain features of education that are not necessary parts of these other processes and, indeed, are sometimes explicitly excluded from them (Peters, 1965, 1966). One of these features is that of individual autonomy without a concern for which, it is argued, no process of teaching can be called education. Such a view of education clearly entails that we adopt an active model of humans and precludes an approach to educational planning that begins from a clear idea of the kinds of behaviour modification that teachers are to try to bring about in their pupils. In this context, it is interesting to note again how many of the books and articles written to promote an approach to educational planning through the prespecification of objectives contain the word 'instruction' in their titles or use that word to describe the kinds of teaching they have in mind. It is also interesting to consider the examples that they give, since most of them are of a relatively simple, instructional kind.

Instrumentalism

A second feature which it has been claimed is essential to education in the full sense is that the curriculum activities proposed should be undertaken for their own sakes. In a properly educational process the teacher must view the content of his or her teaching as being of value in itself and his or her intention must be to persuade his or her pupils so to view it. For if its justification lies in what it leads to, if, in short, the process is an instrumental one with ends or purposes outside itself, then, as we have seen, we would more naturally refer to it as 'training' or 'instruction'.

If one of the things that characterizes education as opposed to other activities that involve teaching and learning, such as training or instruction, is that education is essentially concerned with activities undertaken for their own sakes, such a notion of education is clearly at odds with the idea of activities planned according to extrinsic behavioural objectives, goals extrinsic to the activity itself. John Dewey first drew our attention to this feature of education when he asserted that education can have no ends beyond itself, since it is its own end. This view was subsequently developed more fully by Richard Peters (1965, 1966, 1973a) who claimed, for example, that 'to be educated is not to have arrived at a destination; it is to travel with a different view. What is required is not feverish preparation for something that lies ahead, but to work with precision, passion and taste at worthwhile things that lie at hand' (1965:110).

On this kind of analysis not only does the notion of prespecified behavioural objectives run counter to the very concept of education but the broad aims of education must also be seen from a different perspective, not as what education *is for* but as what *it is*, so that to assert that education is concerned with the development of personal autonomy, understanding, a cognitive perspective, a recognition of the value of certain kinds of activity and so on is not to state extrinsic goals for education but to identify features that should characterize any process that is to be described as educational, a point we will pick up again in the next chapter.

Any approach to educational planning that ignores this, that sets out deliberately to be value-neutral, as we have seen the behavioural objectives approach does, must be inadequate as a basis for the planning of activities which are educational in the full sense. Such an approach might be quite satisfactory for the planning of schemes of training or instruction. But for those activities that most teachers would wish to argue constitute the education they offer their pupils, the things they would claim were for their 'personal development' rather than for their vocational advancement, those things whose presence on the curriculum would be justified in educational or intrinsic terms, the model is quite inadequate. In fine, while the concept of an *instructional* objective is not difficult to grasp, that of an *educational* objective would appear to have no substance at all and to be, in fact, a contradiction in terms.

There is a further, important implication in this, and one that reveals an underlying ideology of society. For this form of schooling must lead to the emergence of a society which has never learned, except perhaps by accident, to value things for their own sake, a society in which utility is the sole concern, a society in which all are absorbed only by the means of existence and never by a consideration of its ends. This approach to educational planning, then, has wide-sweeping implications not only for education itself but for the nature, and indeed the future of society and for attitudes to human life and existence (MacIntyre, 1964). It represents what Enoch Powell (1985) once described as 'a modern barbarism'. Confucius once said, 'If you have twopence to spend, you should spend a penny on bread and a penny on a flower, the bread to make life possible, the flower to make it worthwhile'. The objectives model can offer no help or guidance with the second element of that advice. Its adoption as the planning base must therefore imply that its users have no interest in this aspect of human existence or, more likely, that they have not recognized the full implications of the model they have adopted. It must be emphasized, then, that the model must lead to an instrumental view of schooling and that it cannot accommodate, and thus offers no basis for, planning any other form of educational provision.

An instrumental approach to the curriculum, then, precludes a number of characteristics deemed to be essential to education, and must therefore be seen as incapable of supporting, indeed as inimical to, educational provision in the full sense. Further, this ideology is one which implies a rejection of other concepts and dimensions of teaching and schooling which some would claim would make them more worthy of being described as 'education'; it requires us to settle for something considerably less than many would wish to see and/or get from an *education* system. One quite crucial effect of the adoption of this model, then, is that the use of this model places at risk all of those educational activities for which it cannot adequately cater. It thus leads to a loss of those essential dimensions of the educational process which, as we have seen, cannot be planned from the perspective of this linear, hierachical and behavioural model.

Loss of freedom

The final criticism which has been levelled at this planning model and which we must note here is the charge which Charity James (1968) made that this approach restricts the freedom of teachers as well as pupils. For both will be inclined to see the objectives as fixed or given, just as secondary teachers have always tended to see examination syllabuses as immutable, so that not only will they concentrate on what must be rather simple instructional goals, they will also lose the opportunity to play an active role in the educational process, a process which, it is claimed, is fully educational only if both teachers and pupils are active within it. The curriculum on this view is seen as the dynamic interaction of teacher and pupil and this cannot be promoted by a scientific, 'industrial' model requiring careful preplanning of outcomes. If education is seen as a continuous, ongoing, open-ended activity, and if the teacher's role is central to its effectiveness, as we claimed in Chapter 1, the idea of constant modification and reassessment must be endemic to it, so that any approach to planning an educational activity that starts with a clear specification of objectives will be based on a misunderstanding of what an educational activity really is. Every act of education takes place in its own individual context (Sockett, 1976a) and thus cannot be predetermined. Education is an art as well as a science and far too complex and sophisticated an activity to be elucidated in terms of this kind of simple model.

Again, therefore, we see the close connections between the model adopted for curriculum planning and the ideological stance of the planner. And again, we must note the significance of this in the context of current political realities. For the adoption of the aims-and-objectives model by politicians is a clear indication of an ideological position which cannot, or does not wish to, accommodate the notion of freedom for teachers or pupils. We can now see, however, that this means that they have also failed to recognize, or at least to acknowledge, what this implies for the quality of educational provision. As a consequence their policies lack any clear concept of education; indeed, we have seen that this is deliberate and that they are choosing to regard state maintained schooling as merely a matter of teaching and instruction.

However, this view of education as an ongoing, open-ended process, subject to constant reassessment and modification as a result of pupil-teacher interaction is supported by the practical experiences of many teachers. Teachers and student teachers, even in the face of concerted pressures upon them to prespecify the objectives of their lessons, have in practice rejected this approach, and it is precisely those teachers who are concerned to offer something that goes beyond mere training or instruction who have found this model impossible to use. The realities of the teacher's task are too complex to be met by an approach like that of the industrial planner. This was reinforced by the experience of many of those curriculum projects that attempted to use this kind of model. For even when sets of objectives were presented to them in clear terms, many teachers found it impossible not to modify them continually in the light of the experiences that they and their pupils had from the moment the work began. As John Dewey once pointed out, objectives have a tendency to change as you approach them. It is thus not bloody-mindedness on the part of teachers that causes them to cannibalize what they are offered; it is a realization that, if they do not make this kind of constant adjustment, the goals of their teaching will remain at a simple level and that which is truly educational will be at risk. It is here that the most serious threats are posed to the quality of *educational* provision by the simplistic, objectives-based prescriptions of the National Curriculum and its supporting documentation.

One major reason, then, why some people have recently wished to argue against the prespecification of objectives is the conviction that education is a more sophisticated activity and curriculum planning as a result a more complex process than this simple theoretical model suggests. This is a point we have noted several times already. And, to foreshadow what we shall discuss in greater detail in the next chapter, what teachers need is a set of principles which will guide them in making the minute-by-minute decisions which this complex process requires.

Any model we adopt for curriculum planning must allow for a degree of personal and professional autonomy for the teacher. If we do not allow for this, we create constraints on the activity of teachers and their scope for exercising their professional judgement on the spot, and, far from ensuring that quality which the documentation proclaims, this will act to the detriment of the quality of their provision when that is defined in any but the most simplistic terms. This is clearly a very real danger with the aims-and-objectives model.

All of these criticisms suggest that the aims-and-objectives model is appropriate only for the planning of relatively low level forms of teaching and aspects of the school curriculum. And attempts to develop it to a more sophisticated level, by, for example, suggesting we regard our objectives as 'provisional' (Blyth, 1974) or as 'mutable' (Kelly, 1973), or that we accept 'unintended learning outcomes, (Hogben, 1972), or that we seek to devise non-behavioural objectives (Eisner, 1969; Hirst, 1975), bring their own difficulties, not least in failing to provide adequate criteria and principles for practice. And so, this would appear to suggest that rather than seeking to modify it in some way in order to extend its use to the planning of the more complex and sophisticated aspects of educational provision, we might be better employed looking for a completely different model. It is to this that we shall turn in Chapter 4.

The combined model – 'mastery learning'

It is quite common to see the content-based approach to curriculum planning in practice – curriculum content selected without any real consideration of its aims and then 'delivered'. It is less common to see the aims-and-objectives model at work, at least in any genuine form, to see planners deciding on their aims and then selecting the content felt most likely to achieve these. The tradition of the view of curriculum primarily in terms of its content is too strong.

What is common, however, is to find a combination of the two, what the proponents of the aims and objectives model have called 'mastery learning' (Bloom, 1971). On this model, the content which is selected, on whatever grounds, for 'delivery' is viewed as the aim, and the objectives are the 'bite-sized pieces', attainment targets or whatever, into which the content is broken down for ease of 'delivery'. This approach has been characterized by Basil Bernstein (1996) as a 'performance' mode of pedagogic practice.

Thus we have a fundamental commitment to the content model and an adoption of the aims-and-objectives scheme as a methodology for achieving the most effective 'delivery' and assimilation of the selected content. This is the model employed, whether by design or accident, in the National Curriculum for England and Wales.

No doubt the advocates of this combined model feel that they are getting the best of both worlds. In fact, what they are getting is the worst of both, all of the inadequacies which we have identified as features of both models – in particular, the inequalities, potential disaffection and alienation of the content model, and the behaviourism, the instrumentalism and the loss of any genuine concept of education of the objectives model.

For the recommendation that content be broken down into 'bite-sized pieces' clearly indicates through its choice of metaphor that the 'education' process is seen as the force-feeding of content to pupils and its ingestion by them – whether this is also a process of digestion or not. And the use of the 'delivery' metaphor indicates that the process is seen as one of handing something over; it leads to a view of curriculum as an entity, a body of knowledge to be transmitted. 'Deliver' is a transitive verb; it must have an object; and, in this context, that object can only be a curriculum viewed as substantive rather than adjectival, as prescriptive rather than descriptive, as static rather than dynamic.

This is of course again an attempt to turn teaching into a scientific process. And it is perhaps worth noting here that, if completely successful, in an age of high technology, it will do away with the need for human teachers altogether; teaching machines will ultimately do the job far more efficiently – and more cheaply. It will also of course do away with *education* in the sense of 'what survives when what has been learnt has been forgotten' (Skinner, 1964:484).

For such a curriculum is clearly based on a view of teaching as the transmission of knowledge in a form which does not and cannot adequately cater for those wider dimensions of education which we have identified – autonomy, personal and social development, aesthetic awareness, literary appreciation, the valuing of experiences and activities for their own sake and so on. All of these can only be promoted by the provision of appropriate experiences, since they all involve changes in the way that people view the world and not merely the acquisition of more and more inert knowledge. They involve the development of understanding rather than mere knowledge, and the development of understanding cannot be broken down into 'bite-sized pieces'; it is a far more complex matter than that. Education is much more than a form of mastery learning.

The underpinning curriculum model of current policies, then, is an amalgam of the content and the aims-and-objectives approaches. There is, however, no evidence of an awareness of the problematic aspects of either of these models. None of the documentation acknowledges that there are different models or approaches which might have been adopted; thus none attempts to offer any kind of justification for the model chosen. One can only assume that this is because their authors are not aware of, or are not permitted to acknowledge, either the fact that one might approach curriculum planning in any other way or the many inadequacies of the approach they have chosen or been forced into. As a result, they all reveal a disturbing confusion between a concern for the subject content of their prescriptions, the wish to organize it in a linear and hierarchical fashion by the clear prespecification of objectives and a lingering desire for the kind of educational justification which might come from viewing their subjects as 'areas of experience' with something to offer to children's development above and beyond the transmission of the knowledge-content itself.

All this reveals a failure to appreciate the deep conceptual issues which underlie the differences between these approaches. This comes out perhaps most clearly in that failure to distinguish conceptually between aims and objectives, to which reference has already been made on more than one occasion.

It does seem too that the conceptual confusion arises from a desire to embrace the rhetoric of more attractive approaches to educational planning and the vocabulary of the increasingly fashionable process model, which we shall explore in Chapter 4, while at the same time advocating the more politically acceptable and 'hard-headed' view of education as instrumental and as primarily directed towards economic success. Or perhaps it reflects a conflict between the vestiges of a concern with education in the full sense and the realities of political expediency. Or again it may result from an unwillingness to acknowledge all the inevitable implications of the instrumental, economic, political view. Whatever the reason, it leads to a highly confused and unsatisfactory set of prescriptions for educational practice.

What we have seen in this chapter is that both the approach to curriculum planning through content and that through the prespecification of aims-and-objectives have serious drawbacks in relation to the planning of *educational* provision. Whether we first select the content of our curriculum and use the aims-and-objectives schema as a methodology for planning the teaching of it, or establish our aims and objectives and select that content that we believe will achieve these most effectively, both models create more difficulties than they solve.

The objectives movement has rightly drawn our attention to the importance of being clear about the purposes of the curriculum, and that is a lesson we must not lose sight of, since there is nothing wrong with the advice of those such as Ralph Tyler who have told us we must begin our planning with a clear view of its aims and purposes. And the advocates of planning through content have raised important questions about the selection of the content of the curriculum, in particular by stressing the claims to inclusion of those aspects of culture which might be deemed to constitute that which is valuable in the heritage of human experience and understanding.

Neither, however, can help with the selection of what should be included, unless we are prepared to accept the absolutist epistemology of some of the proponents of the content model in its pure form. We need basic principles of a kind which will enable us to make these choices, and neither of these models can provide these.

Further, both of them can be seen to make tacit assumptions concerning not only education but also the nature of human beings and of the societies they form, assumptions which constitute ideological positions of a kind which must be challenged and questioned. In particular these are ideologies which in themselves are difficult to reconcile with any reasonable concept of democracy, so that, not surprisingly, they lead to practices which are clearly impossible so to reconcile.

What is needed for *educational* planning is a model which accepts the need for clear purposes and for the initiation of the young into that which is deemed to be worthwhile, but which at the same time seeks to do this while respecting the freedom of the individual and promoting social equality and empowerment. In short, we need a model which will provide us with fundamental principles to underpin our planning and one whose ideological base is genuinely democratic.

Those who have been exploring and advocating a curriculum planning model focused on education as development and curriculum as process have been doing so because they believe such an approach can meet these needs. It is to a detailed consideration of this model that we turn in Chapter 4.

Key issues raised by this chapter

1) Is the selection of content an adequate basis for an educational curriculum?
2) How might 'valuable' content be identified?
3) On what bases should content be selected?
4) How effective is the use of aims and objectives for the planning of classroom practice?
5) How might one reconcile the instrumental functions of the schooling system with its wider educational purposes?

Suggested further reading

Grundy, S. (1987) *Curriculum: Product or Praxis?*, London: Falmer.
Kelly, A. V. (1994) *The National Curriculum: A Critical Review*, London: Paul Chapman.

4

Curriculum as process and development

We explored in the previous chapter the model of curriculum which would have us begin our educational planning from a selection of the knowledge-content to be transmitted, that which would start from a declaration of aims and objectives and that which combines these two approaches. We found that all had something of value to offer, the idea, for example, that education should involve learning for its own sake and an introduction to what is deemed to be of value in our human heritage, the notion that it cannot be planned without reference to the national economy or the career prospects of the individual and the claim that in our curriculum planning we should be clear about what we are seeking to achieve.

However, we also noted that all of them displayed many inconsistencies and inadequacies, side-effects, such as the generation or maintenance of inequalities and a failure to allow for many important aspects of educational development, which suggested that there is a need to search for a more comprehensive model. A particular weakness we noted was the fact that neither offers any real help with that decision which must precede all others in educational planning, namely the choice of content and/or aims. The content model offers, or takes as read, a number of arguments based on a view of the nature of both knowledge and culture which we suggested was far from convincing; the objectives model does not even attempt that but side-steps the issue by claiming to be value-neutral.

We also saw, however, that, far from being value-neutral, all of these approaches to curriculum planning reflect particular ideological stances in respect of education, society, human knowledge and, indeed, humanity itself. We noted that these ideological stances are not always overtly stated or admitted, but often have to be teased out by a careful analysis of the policies and practices which they lead to. As a result, the value positions which underpin them are never made explicit – except of course in the terms of the spurious rhetoric of approved official pronouncements.

In this chapter we will examine an approach to curriculum which endeavours to face up to the value issue as the prime concern in educational planning, which suggests that our educational purposes should be framed in terms of the processes which we regard education as able, and concerned, to promote, which advises us to select the knowledge-content of our curriculum not by reference to some supposed intrinsic value which it is claimed it has or by a reference to its assumed effectiveness in securing certain extrinsic aims or objectives, but in relation to its likely contribution to the development of the pupil, and which recommends that we see these purposes not as goals to be achieved at some later stage in the process but as procedural principles which should guide our practice throughout. All these features of this model we will consider in greater detail in what follows.

We must first note, however, that in seeking to face the value question squarely, it is a model which cannot in itself be value-free, or rather which cannot ignore questions of value or assume that these are unproblematic. There is no suggestion here that we can engage in educational planning without attending to the matter of choices, and especially to the justification of those choices, or that we can make those choices in a pseudo-scientific manner or by reference to some philosophical or epistemological theory which will offer God-given and objective answers to questions of value and of choice. Nor is there even an appeal to some kind of consensus view, whether spurious or verified, such as that which forms the only justification offered for current educational policies in England and Wales. Rather it acknowledges that choice in any sphere will be made from one ideological position or another, so that it recognizes the necessity of setting out one's basic ideological position from the outset.

Thus it is an approach which accepts its own status as an ideology and does not allow its value system to remain implicit in its policies and practices and thus to go unchallenged, and even unrecognized. Its ideological stance is made quite explicit and is stated as the first principles of the form of curriculum it advocates. For the approach begins from a view of society as democratic, of human beings as individuals entitled within such a society to freedom and equality and of education as to be designed and planned in such a way as to prepare and empower such individuals for active and productive life within a democratic social context.

In other words, its essence is a positive awareness of the ideological nature of all educational (and, indeed, all social) prescriptions, and a concern to explicate clearly its own ideology as the only basis it can see for planning education and the school curriculum in a form which acknowledges and caters for that central element of values we have noted so often already. Whereas most of the other models we have considered are models of curriculum *planning*, this model also offers a clear concept of curriculum, and, indeed, of education.

Finally, we must note that what provides a cutting edge to this particular ideology is that it is firmly rooted in a concept of social democracy. Whereas the other models we have considered appear to leave much to be desired in terms of the basic principles of democratic living – freedom and equality in particular – this approach seeks to base itself on those very principles and to justify itself in terms of its specific aim to promote them. While not seeking to offer a philosophical justification for itself, then, and certainly not an economic, instrumental justification, it does make a logical claim. For its strongest argument is that it offers a form of curriculum which is consonant with the concept of democracy in a way that, as we have seen, other ideologies are not. It seeks to offer a form of curriculum which is essential for any society claiming to be genuinely democratic.

The growth of this view

The view which we are about to consider begins from the premise that the starting point for educational planning is not a consideration of the nature of knowledge and/or the culture to be transmitted or a statement of the ends to be achieved, whether these be economic or behavioural, but from a concern with the nature of the child and with his or her development as a human being. Its purposes are plain, although it has often been accused of lacking clear aims. It sees education as the process by which human animals are assisted to become human beings (Kelly, 1998).

The idea that, in seeking answers to our questions about what should be taught, we look to an examination of the nature of the child is not new; it is certainly not a product of the twentieth century. The revolt against the traditional view of education as concerned with the purveying of certain kinds of abstract knowledge and the development of rationality was begun by Rousseau in the eighteenth century and carried forward by other, perhaps more influential, educators, such as Froebel and Montessori, in the last century. The main thrust of that revolt was against the idea that we should plan our educational practices by a consideration of knowledge or of society. Its recommendation was that we begin to look instead to the children who are the objects of those practices and plan according to what we can discover about them. It is for this reason that this general movement has been termed 'child-centred'.

What is recent is the rigorous examination of what this entails, since for many years, while admittedly encouraging a more humane approach to education and requiring a more careful consideration of the child's feelings and his or her reactions to educational practices, it was highly suspect theoretically, leading more to the generation of a romantic reverence for childhood than to any rigorous analysis of what education fundamentally is or should be. It is one thing to claim that education should be planned according to what we know about the nature of children; it is quite another to spell out precisely how our knowledge of children should be reflected in our educational planning. Thus some of the early theories seemed to suggest that no planning should be done at all, since they advised us to leave the child alone to develop naturally, to grow like a plant in a garden, free from the corrupting or confining influences of adults.

This lack of a properly rigorous and substantiated theoretical base for this approach to education and curriculum was also reflected in the Plowden Report (CACE, 1967); and it is probably the main reason why subsequent studies revealed that its practice, at least in our junior schools, was not as widespread as the rhetoric might lead us to believe (Bennett, 1976; Bennett *et al.*, 1984; DES, 1978; Galton *et al.*, 1980).

However, a sound theoretical base does exist, and this has been strengthened in recent times from two main sources. First, the pragmatist philosophy of John Dewey, which he himself applied and related quite directly to education and the curriculum, has been recognized as reinforcing this general view of educational theory and practice (Blenkin and Kelly, 1981, 1987, 1988a; Kelly, 1986), and especially the notion that education should be seen in terms of the continuous experience of the individual, a process which 'has no ends beyond itself' and one which promotes not only the development of the individual educand but also the evolution of knowledge and thus of human society.

Second, the work which has been done in the study of children's development, especially in the cognitive sphere, by people such as Jean Piaget, Lev Vygotsky and Jerome Bruner, and which has been taken on in more recent times by the work of Margaret Donaldson (Donaldson, 1978, 1992; Donaldson *et al.*, 1983), Elliot Eisner (1982, 1996) and others, as well as by Bruner's latest work, has done much to reveal to us not only how children learn but, more importantly, how their minds develop, and has thus led to the emergence not merely of a new theory of learning but, much more crucially, of a new concept of learning, one which sees it in terms of the development of understanding rather than the acquisition of knowledge.

These developments have led to three consequences of great relevance to us here. Firstly, they have led many people to that rejection of the knowledge base for curriculum planning which we noted in Chapter 3. Secondly, they have led to the emergence of the view that educational planning must be based on clear statements of its underlying principles or of the processes it seeks to promote rather than of the goals it is concerned to attain (Stenhouse, 1975). And, thirdly, and most recently, they have led to the idea that those principles are to be sought in the nature of the development of the child, that education should be seen not just as any process or series of processes but as a process of development, and that, consequently, the fundamental values of education are to be found in the nature of human development and its potentialities (Blenkin, 1988; Blenkin and Kelly, 1981, 1987, 1988a, 1996).

The first of these, the rejection of the knowledge base, we examined at some length when exploring in Chapter 3 the inadequacies many have found in the notion of curriculum as content. We need now, however, to consider the two other developments more carefully, since they constitute major elements in the case for planning the curriculum in terms of the development of the child.

Curriculum as process – aims and principles

Paul Hirst's claim (1969) that all rational activities are characterized by having clear goals or objectives has perhaps been accepted by many educationists too uncritically. For, while this may be a major characteristic of rational activity, it is certainly not peculiar to human activity, since it is quite apparent that much of the behaviour of animals is goal-directed. It is also true that much animal behaviour is characterized by the ability to generalize, since, as Mark Twain wrote, a cat who sits on a hot stove-lid will not sit on a hot stove-lid again. It is a reflection on the quality, rather than the existence, of the ability to generalize that he is able to go on to claim that such a cat will not sit on a cold stove-lid either.

What is uniquely characteristic of human behaviour and does offer a valid and important contrast with animal behaviour is that it is based on adherence to principles; it is fundamentally moral. It might be argued, therefore, that it is this feature of human behaviour which offers the most appropriate basis for planning the education of human beings, so that some educationists have advised that we turn from the search for objectives of any kind and devote our attention instead to achieving agreement on the broad principles that are to inform the activity or course we are planning and in the light of which all on-the-spot decisions and modifications will be made.

Lawrence Stenhouse, for example, has suggested that 'in mounting curriculum research and development, we shall in general . . . do better to deal in hypotheses concerning effects than in objectives' (Stenhouse, 1970:80). Such an approach, he is claiming, will encourage us to be much more tentative, less dogmatic and more aware of the possibility of failure and the need for corrective adjustments than statements of objectives which may lead us to feel we know where we are going without fear of contradiction. This approach provides us also with criteria for evaluating those 'unintended learning outcomes' which other models cannot handle. He thus suggested that we should begin by defining the 'value positions embodied in the curriculum specification or specifications' (1970:82). Again, to do this will provide us with a clear view of the principles upon which the original planning was founded, which can act as a basis either for changes in our procedures or for modification of these value positions themselves in the light of subsequent experience.

It was on this kind of base, as we saw in Chapter 3, that the Schools Council's Humanities Curriculum Project (HCP), which Lawrence Stenhouse directed, was established, making no attempt to specify learning outcomes but stating quite clearly the principles to be adhered to in the classroom. In fact this has been the practice of most curriculum projects. For where objectives have been stated, these have seldom been really short term, but usually have had a kind of 'middle-ground' appearance and have been stated in general procedural terms. In other words, they have often been neither very broad educational aims nor immediate intended outcomes but rather statements of the general principles that the project team felt should underlie the work of a particular curriculum initiative.

The issue, then, is not whether the curriculum should have aims *or* objectives; it is whether it should have aims *and* objectives. In general, planners describe what they are doing as framing objectives but then proceed to make these of such a general kind that they are not objectives in the instructional and behavioural sense of the term at all, but rather expressive objectives or principles of the kind we have been discussing. The conceptual confusion arises from their attempts to divide these stated goals into 'aims' and 'objectives', since, as we saw in Chapter 2, if there is a conceptual distinction between the two terms, this can derive only from the fact that each refers to purposes of a different order and level of specificity, in other words that it implies a hierarchical and linear relationship between these different kinds of purpose. The essence of the objectives model, as we saw, is that it advocates the making of this kind of conceptual distinction and thus the establishment of this kind of linear hierarchy in which *aims* are used as the base from which more specific *objectives* are derived.

The essence of the process approach is that what is derived from what are stated as overall aims is not a series of short-term goals or objectives but rather a detailing of the principles which are inherent in those aims and which are to inform and guide subsequent practice – a breaking down of an aim such as 'the development of literary awareness' not into an elaborate series of sub-goals or objectives, 'bite-sized pieces', beginning with what are deemed to be 'the basic skills', but into a clear listing of what literary awareness means, what its essential elements are, what its constituent processes are, so that we can plan the work and the activities of pupils throughout in the light of the principles these give rise to.

Thus the model allows us to have our goals, purposes, intentions, aims as educators but frees us from the necessity of seeing these as extrinsic to the educational process and from the restrictions of having only one, step-by-step, predetermined route to their achievement. It allows us to have our content, but frees us from the need to select this by reference to anything other than the principles inherent in our aims or purposes. It thus enables us to focus attention on developing the understanding of the pupil rather than on the transmission of predetermined content or the achievement of prestated behavioural changes. And it provides us with a firm and clearly articulated base from which to make all the decisions that curriculum planning and educational practice require of us.

Aims and processes cannot be separated; the aims are reflected in the processes and the processes are embodied in the aims. As Dewey said almost a century ago in his 'educational creed', 'the process and the goal of education are one and the same thing'. It is, as we noted in Chapter 3, a matter of what education *is* rather than of what it is *for*.

We must note, therefore, a crucial difference, which is more than a semantic one, between a principle and an aim. For an aim can be seen as extrinsic to the activities which constitute the attempt to attain it, while a principle is integral to those activities. An aim can be viewed as something which will be attained at a later stage in the process, while a principle must be seen to be present at every stage. Thus a teacher of young children who regards literary appreciation as an aim of education, if persuaded to adopt an objectives model and thus to see this aim as extrinsic, will be encouraged to adopt a linear, 'Thirty-Nine Steps' approach, to view his or her task as 'preparatory' and to undertake the teaching of reading as if it were merely a step on the road to that extrinsic goal, and so may adopt methods of teaching, perhaps unduly emphasizing the 'basic skills', which may even turn out to be counterproductive to its attainment, as we saw in Chapter 3. On the other hand, one who sees it as a principle will be concerned to ensure that it should inform even the earliest steps of linguistic development. For the same reason, ideas such as those of autonomy, freedom of thought, critical awareness and all those other qualities we might include in a definition of what it means to be educated, are of as much concern to teachers in nursery schools as to those in universities, and they must be recognized as intrinsic to the educational process at every stage. In short, the adoption of a principle ensures that the end justifies only those means which are compatible with it.

It is because aims have been seen as extrinsic by most of those concerned with major attempts at changing the curriculum in recent years that they have been tempted into proceeding to deduce from these aims more specific teaching objectives. It is because they have done this that teachers have felt the need to modify and change those objectives, as well as to accept the educational validity of some of the learning outcomes which were unintended. Where teachers have done this, however, they have usually done it in response to and in accordance with principles which they have felt to be embodied in the broader aims. It would avoid much confusion at all levels of both theory and practice if this were acknowledged, the status of such principles as the essential starting point of educational planning recognized and the principles themselves clearly articulated. Another way of putting this was once suggested to me by a friend and colleague, HMI Roger Shirtliffe, who suggested the acceptance of the maxim of the artilleryman, that if the aim is good enough the objectives are destroyed.

In summary, let us note that education must of course have aims. Much depends, however, not only on what those aims are but also on how they are conceived, whether as extrinsic or intrinsic to the educational process itself. Even more crucial is how these aims are translated into practical planning, whether they are seen as the source of working principles of a procedural kind or of a hierarchy of short-term sub-objectives. It is also vital to note that these two approaches are quite different from, and indeed incompatible with, each other. To offer educational and curricular prescriptions which do not clarify which of these two approaches they are recommending, or which, worse, like much of the documentation emerging from officialdom, offer a mishmash of the two, is to do the opposite of 'contributing to the search for greater clarity and definition' in relation to the curriculum debate and, more seriously, to deny teachers the advantages of clear advice and a conceptually sound base for the realities of their practice.

Teaching is of itself a complex activity, so that teachers shou̇
excused the added complexities of having to cope with incohere
of curriculum guidelines.

This model, then, does not suggest that in educational planning we should take no account of outcomes or products, and it is certainly not advocating that we should not have clear aims. It does propose, however, that in both the planning and the execution of an educational curriculum the major emphasis should be on its underlying principles and on the processes of development it is setting out to promote, so that, if it can be said to be concerned with products or outcomes, these will be defined in terms of intellectual development and cognitive functioning rather than in terms of quantities of knowledge absorbed or changes of behavioural performance.

This takes us to that other point which we noted earlier when tracing the growth of this approach to educational planning – the idea that not only should our planning begin from statements of the procedural principles which are to underlie our practice but, further, that these principles should be derived from the view that the prime concern of the educational process is with human development, and, further, that such development is to be conceived within a democratic social context.

Education as development

It is worth noting first that education cannot be planned without some reference to development, that 'formal education cannot take place without the adoption of some stance towards development' (Blyth, 1984:7). Formal education cannot be conceived in any way other than as some kind of guided development. The key issue is thus the nature of that guidance. We have noted before that even content-based approaches to education have some notion of development at their base. Certainly, objectives-based approaches to curriculum are concerned to bring about certain changes in pupils' behaviour and performance, in short to develop them in certain ways. One of the strengths claimed for the developmental view of education and the process model of curriculum from which it is derived is that they both accept this as the essence of education and thus as the only logical starting point for educational planning.

However, one of our major criticisms of the objectives model of curriculum planning was that it assumes a passive model of the individual and feels it right and proper to regard education as concerned to mould the behaviour of children according to certain predetermined goals or blueprints. This must be the case with any approach to education whose prime concern is with extrinsic goals, unless, of course, those goals are set – as they seldom are in schools – by the person being educated.

The central feature of the developmental planning model is that it begins from the opposite view of human nature, of human development and of human potentiality. It sees the individual as an active being, who is entitled to control over his or her destiny, and consequently sees education as a process by which the degree of such control available to each individual can be maximized. Its central concern is with individual empowerment. It is what Bernstein (1996) has called a 'competence', as opposed to a 'performance', mode of pedagogic practice.

All the fundamental, underlying principles of the developmental model derive from this basic position, which, as was pointed out earlier, is offered not as a scientifically demonstrable theory but as the ideological position which its advocates adopt and which they recognize the right of others to reject, provided that they appreciate to the full what it is they are rejecting.

To begin with, if one takes this kind of view of the individual, a central feature of one's educational theory and practice must be with the development of the child's growing ability to act autonomously, so that the promotion of autonomy becomes a major principle of one's educational practice. It should be noted that this is not now being offered merely as a feature of the concept of education, although it can of course be seen as one of those several elements which distinguish education *per se* from other acts of teaching. The case for autonomy here is also that it is a logical consequence of the value position from which we started, the idea of the individual as an active being responsible for his or her destiny. For one cannot coherently take that view of the individual and then argue that education must be some form of moulding or indoctrinatory process.

Several further points follow from this commitment to autonomy. To exercise autonomy, people need a range of consequent capabilities. Autonomy is not merely a negative concept signifying a freedom from constraints; it is also a positive notion implying the development of those capacities which will, or can, enable one to make the personal choices, decisions, judgements that autonomous living implies, and will give one as much genuine control over one's destiny as is possible. Thus, to become as fully autonomous as possible as a human being, one needs to develop the greatest possible depth and breadth of understanding, one needs the capability to look critically at the world, and one needs to develop the ability to make up one's own mind about the many aspects of that world. And so, for example, however the content of our curriculum is selected, the crucial thing is that it must be presented in a

manner which promotes critical consciousness and invites cr
reflection, personal response, even rejection. As we saw when discus
the problematic nature of human knowledge in Chapter 2, what is
central is not *what* our curriculum offers but *how* it is offered. These, then,
become further procedural principles to underpin our educational
planning; and, again, these are not qualities whose educational
justification is to be found solely in an analysis of the concept of
education; they are necessary and logical consequences of the
underpinning view of the individual and of society.

It is for this reason that John Dewey stressed the importance of
experience as the only route to anything one could describe as education
– 'not knowledge but self-realization is the goal' (Dewey, 1902); that the
Hadow Report (Board of Education, 1931:para.75) claimed that 'the
curriculum is to be thought of in terms of activity and experience rather
than of knowledge to be acquired and facts stored'; and that present-day
advocates of this approach, with the advantage of recent work in the
field of developmental psychology, speak of 'active learning' as opposed
to the mere learning of 'facts'. Thus education is seen as a process of
growth, as the developing experience of the individual, and a further
procedural principle emerges by reference to which we may plan our
curriculum and, perhaps more importantly, evaluate its effectiveness –
the degree to which it supports this kind of continuous experiential and
active learning.

It must follow next that this must be an individual matter. It is a
nonsense to assume that this kind of active learning can be promoted in
all pupils by exactly the same kind of educational diet, as provided, for
example, by the National Curriculum or even by the programme of
'intrinsically worthwhile activities' advocated by the philosophers of
education. That kind of content-based curriculum, as we have seen, leads
for many pupils to failure, inequality and ultimate disaffection and
alienation.

This is why the advocates of this view have constantly stressed the
necessity of taking into full account the needs and the interests of
individual pupils (Wilson, 1971), of building the educational experience of
each child on what that child brings to school with him or her. This is also a
way of ensuring that the curriculum does not become the vehicle for the
imposition on the child of knowledge and values which are alien to him or
her (Keddie, 1971).

To all these general principles can now be added refinements of a
much more detailed kind. The work of Jean Piaget (1969) drew our
attention to certain important qualitative differences between the
thinking of the child and that of the mature adult. This view has been

refined extensively by others, such as Vygotsky and Bruner, especially in relation to its 'stage theory', since it has more recently been argued that what Piaget described as stages of cognitive development and suggested all must pass through in an invariant sequence if they are to reach full intellectual maturity, are rather to be seen as modes of thought or representation, all of which persist into adulthood.

The important point to be emphasized here, however, is that, whether they are stages through which we must pass or modes of thought we must learn to work within, if we are to pass through them or acquire a facility within them, we will need the right kind of educational provision. Intellectual maturity does not just happen in the way that, at least to a very large extent, physical maturity does. There are many physically mature adults, including some who are drawing their pensions, who have never reached Piaget's final stage, that of 'formal operations', when ideas can be handled conceptually rather than only in concrete form, or have never acquired a facility with what Jerome Bruner called the 'symbolic' mode of representation. Such people remain forever cognitively and intellectually stunted, and thus deprived of much of the richness life can offer to those who are helped to this level of mature cognitive functioning. They are also, perhaps more crucially, extremely limited in relation to the kind of autonomy we suggested earlier is essential to a fully human form of existence.

Thus we begin to see further, more detailed, principles emerging as the basis for our educational planning and practice, principles deriving from a concern for what has been called 'the growth of competence' (Connolly and Bruner, 1974).

Once started on this train of deduction, we can go on to derive many more principles which will reflect in greater detail that basic value position from which we started. We can see, for example, how the rather simplistic notion of cultural transmission can be, indeed must be, translated into the rather more complex and sophisticated idea of access to a critical understanding of aspects of the culture in which one lives and is growing up, as well as to the important notion which Bruner also offers us of 'cultural amplifiers'. We can see how the similarly simplistic notion of instruction in various bodies of knowledge-content can and must become the more subtle notion of the selection of knowledge-content in terms of the promotion of that growth of competence, initiation into the many modes of representation we have seen Eisner (1982, 1996) has identified and, indeed, the achievement of greater control over the circumstances of one's life.

And so we might go on. Nothing we deduce, however, will take us in any way beyond what is implicit in our basic notion of the individual as an active, autonomous being. And we must remind ourselves of the point made in the last section, that we can bring about this kind of development only if we see all these principles as ever present in the educational process and not as end-states to be achieved at some later date.

One final point needs to be made. The autonomy from which we begin is essentially a moral autonomy, since the making of autonomous decisions and judgements must imply the making of autonomous moral choices. Thus this model is not only able to cater for the moral dimension of education, indeed the whole affective dimension, in a way that others cannot (Kelly, 1986, 1998), it specifically requires of us that we face up to the idea that education is moral development, that it is thus also social development, in fact, that it must embrace the whole spectrum of affective development, and that it cannot be viewed solely in terms of cognitive or intellectual growth. Recent work in developmental psychology has highlighted the crucial importance of the social context for cognitive development itself. And Elliot Eisner has claimed with some conviction that, if development is the concern, the cognitive forms of development cannot be isolated from the affective, since 'there can be no cognitive activity which is not also affective' (Eisner, 1982:28). There are many dimensions to human experience and, as Eisner (1985:240) also suggests, 'the very existence of such varieties should be clue enough that they perform important functions in helping us grasp concepts of the culture in which we live'. Any form of education which ignores these affective aspects of experience, as Eisner claims schooling in Western cultures does and, as we suggested in Chapter 3, the curriculum models and ideologies we considered there do, is limited and diminished. The developmental model of curriculum regards this affective dimension as a central feature of that form of human development which it is being claimed education should be concerned to promote. It seeks to support development on all fronts and in all modes of representation.

Thus the developmental model of curriculum planning goes beyond the process model in that it not only advises us to base our planning on clearly stated procedural principles rather than on statements of content or of aims and objectives but, further, it suggests that we should look to a particular view of humanity, of society and thus of human development, including crucially social development, as the source of those principles. Further still it would claim that this is the only view of education one can take if one sees the individual in this light, so that to reject this view of education is to reject also the view of the autonomous individual, and of the democratic society, upon which it is based. Unlike the objectives model, it thus offers us, as we saw at the outset, an overtly stated ideological position from which to make our subsequent educational judgements and decisions and, unlike the content model, it encourages us to see that value position as itself problematic rather than assuming or claiming some pseudo-scientific or epistemologically objective status for it.

In this way it promotes not only a particular model for educational planning but also, and perhaps more crucially, the idea that there must be continued debate about and consequent development of that model. The very notion of change, development, evolution is built into it and must therefore discourage the kind of dogmatic prescriptions we have seen emerging from other sources based on other models.

The social dimension of development

An awareness of the importance of the social dimension of human development takes us on to discussion of the part played in the genesis of this curriculum ideology by a commitment to democracy and to democratic emancipation and empowerment.

Democracy is not merely a political concept; it is also a moral concept. It not only offers criteria for the management of society; it also provides a basis for the generation of moral principles governing our conduct towards each other within that society (Kelly, 1995). And those principles extend to the activities of government and all other major agencies.

Within a democratic society, morality is not a free-for-all. It is subject to clear rules. Those rules, however, are not derived from governmental edict, nor from religious beliefs or pronouncements, but from the concept of democracy itself. And they include essentially respect for the freedom of every individual within society, equality of treatment for all and adequate scope for participation in the government of society, whether this takes the form of direct involvement in that government or opportunities to evaluate the actions, the decisions and the policies of those who are so involved.

Several things follow from this which are of consequence for curriculum planning in such a society and especially for the notion of education as development.

First, education must make adequate provision for moral development – not as a matter of choice, preference or ideology, but as an inevitable consequence of the democratic context for which the educational planning and provision is being undertaken. In a democratic society, the young must be initiated into democratic morality (Kelly, 1995, 1998).

Second, that planning and that provision must in themselves conform to the moral criteria which the concept of democracy generates. The curriculum in such a society, then, must be planned in such a way as to promote equality of provision and entitlement for all. And it must do this not by offering a package of subjects and programmes of study on a take-it-or-leave-it basis, and thus creating, as we have seen, more opportunities for failure, disaffection and alienation than for freedom, equality and participation. It must do so by seriously and genuinely seeking to provide all young people with an educational diet which will secure them entry to and involvement in the democratic social context of which they are a part.

Consequently, this means, thirdly, that the education provided must be focused on ensuring the emancipation and empowerment of every individual, on developing a real sense of involvement and control of the social context of one's life. Basil Bernstein (1996:6) speaks of the democratic necessity of ensuring three interrelated pedagogic rights in educational institutions: (1) the right to individual enhancement; (2) the right to be included, socially, intellectually, culturally and personally; (3) the right to participate in procedures 'whereby order is constructed, maintained and changed'.

The concept of education as development seeks to provide a means by which this can be accomplished. It advocates the adoption of a model for curriculum planning which will seek to promote 'the right of each individual to a form of education which will advance his/her development as an individual, which will offer enrichment and, indeed, social and political empowerment' (Edwards and Kelly, 1998b:xii).

In any other sense, the claim to be providing an entitlement curriculum is mere rhetoric. Entitlement is to be gauged by reference to what is received rather than to what is offered or provided. Genuine democratic entitlement is not merely entitlement to a range of school subjects; it is entitlement to a process of development in which all of one's potential and capacities will be cultivated and amplified to the fullest possible degree. And this is why the developmental model has throughout been so closely linked to developmental psychology, since the understanding of human development – cognitive, social, emotional and aesthetic – which studies in developmental psychology have promoted is essential if we are to achieve the goal of such cultivation and amplification.

What the developmental model offers us, then, is a solution to the problem of values in education. It has no doubts about the value position upon which it is founded. Furthermore, that position is not merely ideological, not plucked from a range of possible choices. It is put forward as the only position on curriculum provision which can coherently be adopted in a democratic society, the only position which is compatible with the values of democracy itself. Its advocates would claim, therefore, that it can only be rejected by those who, like the adherents of those ideologies we noted in Chapter 3 Denis Lawton has identified, are prepared to deny democracy itself.

Neverthless, it is a view of education which has attracted more criticisms than most, and it is to a consideration of some of the more serious of these that we now must turn.

Some criticisms of the developmental model

Criticisms of this approach to education have come from two main sources – the politicians and the philosophers of education.

Political objections

There are three main reasons why this approach is unpopular with politicians. First, it is expensive, although we should note that all the major government reports – those of the Crowther, Newsom and Plowden Committees – have pointed out that to provide a proper form of universal education would be an expensive undertaking, and all have commended this as money well spent. Second, the effectiveness of this form of curriculum depends crucially on professional decisions made on the spot by teachers, since it acknowledges the point we made in Chapter 1 concerning the centrality of the teacher's role to the quality of educational provision. Hence, if there is to be a national curriculum, on this model it will need to be one which consists of broad guidelines rather than tight prescriptions. And thirdly, the corollary of this last point is that such a curriculum cannot be tightly controlled through central direction. Nor does it permit of the assessment of pupils or the evaluation of schools by simplistic devices and the production of spurious, if superficially convincing, statistical data.

None of these constitutes a theoretical critique, and none such has been forthcoming. Hence this line of objection has taken the form of putting this model down, rubbishing it, especially by describing it as outmoded or 'old hat'. No serious intellectual critique has been offered, so that there is nothing of substance to which one might respond.

Philosophical objections

Such intellectual critique as has been offered has emanated from those philosophers of education who have advocated that content base for curriculum planning which we discussed in Chapter 3. And one line of criticism they have offered we can deal with very quickly. For they have suggested that the methods adopted for the implementation of a developmentally appropriate curriculum – enquiry, discovery and active forms of learning generally – are inefficient devices for ensuring that children learn all that they have to learn (Dearden, 1968, 1976).

Two weaknesses in this line of criticism become immediately apparent. First, this kind of criticism errs in regarding this approach as a form of methodology, when, as we have seen, it represents a quite different way of conceptualizing curriculum, not merely of 'delivering' it. And, second, it is mounted from a particular epistemological and ideological viewpoint, that objectivist position which we discussed in Chapters 2 and 3, and thus fails to recognize that the developmental approach to curriculum is founded, as we have seen, on an epistemology and an ideology of a completely different and incompatible kind, one that has no concept of 'all they have to learn'.

Needs, interests and growth

Particular attention has also been focused on concepts such as 'needs', 'interests' and growth which are central to this view of education and curriculum, as well as on the concept of development itself. Such criticism has in the main focused on the claim that these are all value-laden terms. The concept of 'need', for example, we are told, offers us no help with the value issue of deciding what criteria we should or can appeal to in evaluating needs. Some further basis is required, it is claimed, to enable us to do this. And similar claims are made concerning the notion of basing the curriculum on children's interests.

We have seen, however, that the main point of the developmental view has been to face that value issue, and the notion that education is, or should be, about individual development is designed to make very plain the criteria we should appeal to in evaluating children's needs and interests. For it advises us that the main needs we are to be concerned with are the child's developmental needs, the provision of whatever experiences seem most likely to promote his or her educational development in accordance with those principles we attempted to unpack earlier. It suggests that the needs we should take most account of are those whose satisfaction is most likely to lead to continued growth and development. And the central criterion of choice among children's interests is the degree to which their pursuit is likely to enable us to promote their continued development along the lines we set out earlier.

The notion of 'growth' too has been said to raise similar difficulties. For again, if growth is not to be haphazard, we need some criteria by which to decide how, when and where to direct and guide it.

Dewey's answer to this problem is an interesting one. He is aware that growth must be directed and he is also aware that this implies the existence of some kind of goal. On the other hand, his view of knowledge, as we saw in Chapter 2, will not allow him to produce any theory that implies that teachers, parents, adults generally or even society as a whole have the answers to this question of goals, since, as we have seen, for him knowledge must be allowed to develop and evolve and this cannot happen if the knowledge of one generation is imposed on the next, no matter how gently this is done. His answer is to assert that the only criterion we can use in attempting to evaluate one kind of activity, one body of content, one set of experiences in relation to others is an assessment of the extent to which each is likely to be productive of continued experience and development. Thus he speaks of an 'experiential continuum' (Dewey, 1938) which is for him the essence of education as a continuous lifelong process and which offers us the principle by which we can reach decisions concerning the content of each child's curriculum and the nature of our intervention in his or her learning, that principle being always to choose or promote that activity or those experiences likely to be most productive of further experience. 'The educative process is a continuous process of growth, having as its aim at every stage an added capacity of growth' (Dewey, 1916:54). And, furthermore, 'the criterion of the value of school education is the extent in which it creates a desire for continued growth and supplies means for making the desire effective in fact' (1916:53). Thus he offers us the notion of development, rather than those of needs, interests or growth, as the ultimate criterion of educational choice.

Again, therefore, it might be claimed that the notion of education as development meets many of the criticisms raised by offering us the basic values upon which a more positive theory might be built. For its view is that guided growth means growth directed towards the attainment of those competencies we discussed earlier, towards the maximization of potential, towards the achievement of the highest possible levels of functioning – cognitive, affective, psychomotor and, above all, human and moral.

There is a good deal that is of value in this concept of the teacher as one who keeps constantly open the options available to each pupil and tries to ensure continuous development and progress, forever widening horizons and steering pupils away from any experience that will have the effect of closing them down. The idea is an attractive one and as a principle to underlie all of our educational practice it would appear to be of great importance.

However, if the notion of development is being offered as the solution to many of the difficulties which people have seen in this view of education and model of curriculum planning, there are those who have claimed that the concept of development itself needs to be analysed and explored rather more closely. Hence, the concept of development has been singled out for particular scrutiny.

The concept of development

Development, it is said, is another value-laden, normative concept, which can mean many things to many people, or even all things to all people. And there are two major aspects of this criticism which we need to pursue in greater detail.

The first is that discussions of development, particularly those which have been critical of the concept as a basis for educational planning, have tended to see it as a process leading to some kind of end-state. Thus there has been discussion of the concept of development as an aim of education (Kohlberg and Mayer, 1972), some at least of the problems of which disappear if, as was suggested earlier, we view it not in terms of extrinsic goals but of intrinsic guiding, or procedural, principles. The mistake is, as Dewey (1916:50) puts it, that 'growth is regarded as *having* an end, instead of *being* an end', or, as we have expressed it on several occasions, that the focus is on what education is *for* rather than on what it *is*. Central to this concept of education as development, then, is Dewey's notion that education is a continuous lifelong process which has no ends beyond itself but is its own end, so that it must be stressed again that to speak of education as development is to view it as a process and to focus attention on the intrinsic features of that process rather than on clearly defined extrinsic aims or goals.

We must note further that for some this concept of an end-state to human development has been interpreted in the form of some notion of the ideal or perfect human being. This is perhaps most obvious in Plato's discussions of education and of society, but it is no less significant, even if it is less overt, in modern versions of philosophical rationalism (Kelly, 1986, 1995). If we have some concept of human perfection, as rationalism clearly has, we must see education as a process by which people can be led towards this state. It is perhaps worth noting too that, on this view, childhood is regarded as some kind of imperfect and inferior form of existence, from the inadequacies of which children are to be liberated, as from the 'original sin' of Christian theology.

The view of education which is being explicated here, however, begins from a rejection of this notion of human perfection, regarding it in fact as a quite meaningless concept, since it is a view which rejects that rationalist epistemology which is essential to such a concept. Again, therefore, it must eschew the notion of an end-state to the process of development, since its basic epistemological stance renders such a notion illogical. On the other hand, as we have also seen, it is an approach which is predicated on a view of the child's thinking as being qualitatively different from that of the adult, so that it must see the educational process as concerned to liberate children from the limitations imposed by these early and primitive levels of cognitive functioning. To say that, however, is not to say that it is a process directed towards some definable end-state; it is merely to say that its concern is with the enhancement of capability, the extension of the individual's powers, the growth of competence and, in general, control over his or her environment and, indeed, destiny.

This takes us naturally to the second major aspect of this criticism. For this concept of the end-state of development has led some critics back into the value issue. Thus, Paul Hirst and Richard Peters ask:

> What, too, at the human level, corresponds to the mature oak-tree or elephant which represents the end-state of plant or animal development? Does not human life offer a great variety of possibilities of development? And do not these depend partly on cultural pressures and partly on individual choice – factors which do not apply at the plant or animal level? And *is* not our conception of such an end-state irredeemably valuative in nature?
>
> (Hirst and Peters, 1970:45)

On their view, only certain kinds of development are appropriately fostered by education, namely the development of those God-given forms of rationality of which they also speak. Thus, for them, education is not just any kind of development; it is the development of the rational mind along all of the several dimensions of rationality they claim to have identified. And their criticism of the concept of education as development stems from the fact that in itself it appears not to go as far as they would want it to go in identifying the particular kinds of development it is concerned with.

It will be plain, however, from what has already been said in this chapter, that the notion of education as development it has been concerned to analyse and explicate is one which recognizes only too clearly the need to be quite specific about the forms of development it is concerned with, and thus the value positions implicit in its stance. A major difference, however, and one which reveals the heart of the problem, is that while Hirst and Peters, and indeed the whole band of rationalist philosophers of education, have sought to answer these questions through their analysis of the nature of knowledge, an analysis whose weaknesses we identified in Chapter 2, those who are currently offering this as a theory of education and as a model for curriculum planning are doing so on the basis of explorations of the nature of children's thinking, of aspects of their cognitive development and an analysis of the nature of human cognition, and in relation to certain imperatives deriving from the essential characteristics of democratic social living.

Development is thus not the vague concept its critics have claimed; nor, as we have seen, are its advocates unaware of the need to specify very clearly their value stance, the forms of development they are concerned to promote. These can be specified with increasing clarity as a result of the recent work of developmental psychologists (Bruner and Haste, 1987; Donaldson, 1978, 1992; Donaldson *et al.*, 1983; Tizard and Hughes, 1984; Wells, 1981a and b) and of those curriculum theorists who have been attempting to translate this work into curricular terms (Blenkin, 1988; Blenkin and Kelly, 1987, 1988a, 1996; Eisner, 1982, 1985, 1996). They can be clearly seen to include development through all the stages of cognitive functioning or command of all the modes of representation which this work has identified; they embrace development of the ability to operate on all dimensions of human functioning – moral, social and affective as well as cognitive; they include a facility for thinking within whatever forms of understanding we might identify – mathematical, scientific, historical and so on – provided that we appreciate that the significant differences are those in the thinking processes themselves not in the knowledge-content towards which they might be directed; and they can be seen to add up to a deliberate process of maximizing the individual's powers and widening his or her horizons in the interests of the greatest possible enrichment of experience and control over one's destiny, placing, as the Hadow Report, *Infant and Nursery Schools* (Board of Education, 1933), suggested, 'less weight on the imparting of an ordered body of knowledge and more on the development of the child's innate powers'. And all of this is predicated on the principles of the democratic context for which such a curriculum is being offered.

This concept of development, then, while it can be, and in some discussions clearly has been, vague and thus unhelpful in educational planning, need not be so. Recent work in fact is enabling us to be increasingly clear and specific about what it does entail. And the fact that it is a concept which is manifestly value-laden is offered by its advocates as a positive strength, rather than a weakness, since it acknowledges the value-laden nature of the educational process itself and seeks neither to avoid the implications of that, as the objectives model does, nor to resolve it by an appeal to some highly problematic notion of the God-given status of certain kinds of knowledge, like the content model. It is thus seen by its advocates as offering a more satisfactory, and certainly more honest, basis for curriculum planning, since it requires that we analyse and make quite explicit what our educational ideology is rather than pretend that we do not have one.

The process/developmental model of curriculum planning, therefore, has the merit of seeking to take account of all the many dimensions of education and curriculum – purposes, principles, values, content. It thus may be seen to have certain advantages over the other models which, as we have seen, emphasize one or another of these features but cannot effectively embrace them all.

It also has the merit of offering a theoretical model which might be recognized as reflecting more accurately, and thus supporting more constructively, the realities of educational practice. For teaching, especially that which purports to be educational, cannot often be undertaken by reference merely to its subject-matter. And only seldom, and then at very low levels, is it a linear, step-by-step process. It requires the making of day-to-day and even minute-by-minute decisions; it is a complex process of dynamic interaction between teacher and taught. It thus needs a planning model which will ensure that those interactions reflect the complexities of the sophisticated goals from which it starts. This the translation of those goals into procedural principles offers to teachers in a way that the attempt to reduce them to ever more simplified objectives can never do.

It has been said that this approach to education is idealistic and, indeed, unrealistic. It is, however, no more idealistic than those notions of education as initiation into intrinsically worthwhile activities which we have noted on several occasions. And if it requires of teachers higher levels of professional performance, so be it. Those higher levels were being reached by many student teachers on B.Ed. courses before these were discontinued in the interests of National Curriculum subject-based forms of training. And there are many teachers who, before the advent of the National Curriculum, Desirable Learning Outcomes, and enforcement by the thought-police of Ofsted, were doing a most effective job in implementing this kind of curriculum, perhaps especially in some of our nursery and first schools. And if we are right in suggesting that it reflects more closely the actualities of most teachers' practice, to adopt it fully requires little more than that they reflect more deeply on that practice and the theoretical considerations which underpin it (Blenkin and Kelly, 1997). In fact, a further merit of this model is that it demands what Lawrence Stenhouse (1975:123) called 'an evaluative response', suggests 'a further possibility which I shall call here *the research model*' (1975:13) and takes us towards his notion of 'the teacher as researcher' which we shall look at in more detail when we consider strategies for curriculum change and development in the next chapter. Education is a complex undertaking. It is all too often viewed in simplistic terms by those outside the school. If teachers themselves shy away from its complexities, then all is certainly lost.

Curriculum planning models

Now that we have considered the main features of the three models of curriculum planning we have identified, it might be worthwhile to attempt briefly to pull some general points together.

First of all, let us note that we have here three different approaches to the question of the purposes of education, three different ideologies – one which sees these in terms of the acquisition of knowledge, whether seen as intrinsically valuable or as economically useful, a second which has no kind of view of what the aims of education are or should be but offers us a mechanism for achieving those we have decided to pursue and thus sees it as essentially an instrumental process, and a third which puts to us the notion of education as the promotion of human development. The last two offer us also a methodology, the aims and objectives model advising us to break down our aims (once we have decided on them) into a series of sub-aims or objectives, the process model suggesting that we would be better advised to translate our aims into procedural principles by reference to which we can undertake both our preplanning and our practice. Broadly, the distinction is between what we have seen Basil Bernstein (1996) describe as the 'performance' and the 'competence' models of pedagogic practice.

Further, the reasons behind these differing concepts of education, as we have seen, are to be found in the commitment to quite different ideologies of knowledge, of social living and of humanity.

Each offers us too a distinctive view of the role of content in the curriculum and quite different criteria for the selection of curriculum content. The first sees the role of content as central and finds the criteria of selection in the content itself – either its presumed intrinsic value or its usefulness. The objectives model places its aims and objectives first and offers these as the criteria for selecting content, suggesting that we select that content which seems to be most likely to help us to achieve our aims. The process model requires us to select that content which will promote the processes or the forms of development which are its concern and to make such selection in the light of the procedural principles derived from these.

The next point we should note is that, since these models are based on quite different views of the purposes of schooling, quite different concepts of education, knowledge, society and, indeed, humanity, and, as a consequence, quite different notions of the role of subject-content in the curriculum and the basis for selecting this, as well as offering quite different schemes for educational practice, it is important that anyone undertaking curriculum planning should be absolutely clear about the fundamental conceptual and, most importantly, ideological differences between them.

We have already noted the failure of the HMI/DES *Curriculum Matters* series of publications to recognize the important differences between the concepts of 'aims', 'objectives', 'principles' and 'processes' or at least their failure to achieve clarity in their own use of these terms. It is worth noting also here the tendency of those documents to see those differences they do recognize as being merely methodological. Thus the authors of *Curriculum Matters 2* (DES, 1985a) (the only non-subject-specific contribution to the series, and so the one to which one might look for some understanding of general curriculum issues) view approaches to the primary curriculum not as reflecting a different concept of education and its purposes, that concept, for example, which is encapsulated in the Plowden Report (CACE, 1967), but merely as a different method of achieving the goals of transmitting predetermined knowledge-content, telling us that 'parts of the programme for the younger children may be organised through carefully planned activities, such as domestic role play and the use of constructional toys, within which desired knowledge and understanding can be developed' (op.cit.:8). It would seem clear from this that a major reason why this series attempted no justification or explication of whatever its model of curriculum is and why it also revealed such conceptual muddle was that its authors did not (or were not permitted to) recognize the existence of different concepts of education but only of different methodologies.

This complete lack of conceptual clarity and the failure to recognize the fundamental distinctions we have seen to be crucial to productive curriculum planning come out most clearly in the following passage in which notions of aims, objectives, content, intrinsic value, development and others are hopelessly interwoven:

The criteria for selecting content should be in the aims and objectives which the school sets for itself. That which is taught should be worth knowing, comprehensible, capable of sustaining pupils' interest and useful to them at their particular stage of development and in the future. It should be chosen because it is a necessary ingredient of the areas of learning and experience or because it has an important contribution to make to the development of the concepts, skills and attitudes proposed.

(DES, 1985c:37)

It is salutary to reflect that it was this kind of muddled thinking which provided the basis for the framing of the National Curriculum, and to note that the tradition is being maintained in subsequent and current emanations from officialdom.

It must be stressed, then, that adequate curriculum planning requires a full recognition of the deep conceptual differences between these approaches to education and curriculum and of the fundamentally different forms of practice they lead to and demand.

It follows from this that curriculum planners must not only recognize the need to make informed choices between these alternative approaches, they must also have clear reasons for the choices they make and they should be prepared to make these reasons plain. It is quite unacceptable for anyone to plan a curriculum or a piece of work, at any level but especially at the national level, without first setting out quite clearly, both for himself or herself and for others, the curriculum model adopted and the reasons for its adoption. For, as we have seen, this choice is not only of a methodology, it involves also a commitment to an ideology of knowledge, of education, of society and of humanity. It is thus inexcusable for curriculum statements and prescriptions, again like those in the *Curriculum Matters* series and those which have subsequently emerged from NCC, SCAA and QCA, which are offered as guidance to the whole educational system, to refuse or to fail to do this. All curricular recipes must be based on a clear concept of education and a clear model of curriculum planning, and they must make plain their reasons for adopting these. Otherwise, they are at best unhelpful and at worst dishonest.

The emergence of several, clearly defined approaches to education and curriculum planning, then, has offered teachers and all other would-be curriculum planners a range of choices. It has also imposed on them the consequent requirement that they consider these choices very carefully in their planning and that they have good reasons for their decisions. There is, or should be, no longer any excuse for that muddle or lack of clarity which has characterized curriculum planning and thus diminished educational practice for far too long.

It was claimed that the developmental model reflects more appropriately the actualities of the teacher's task and role in relation to the education of pupils. For it seeks to allow for the interactive nature of the educational relationship in a way that the other models cannot – not least by providing the teacher with a clear set of principles as a basis for the making of day-to-day, minute-by-minute professional judgements, rather than offering a rigid syllabus of content to be 'delivered' or a fixed hierarchy of objectives to be achieved. This is a point which takes us naturally into an exploration of the strategies of curriculum planning and change which is the subject of the next chapter.

Key issues raised by this chapter

1) What are the essential features of education for a democratic society?
2) Why is it important to distinguish conceptual and methodological issues in curriculum planning?
3) What might an analysis of the implicit assumptions of official documents tell us about their underlying ideology? (A detailed analysis of any one official document in the light of what has been said in Chapters 3 and 4 may be an interesting and illuminating approach to this issue.)

Suggested further reading

Cornbleth, C. (1990) *Curriculum in Context*, London: Falmer.
Edwards, G. and Kelly, A. V. (eds.) (1998) *Experience and Education: Towards an Alternative National Curriculum*, London: Chapman.

5

Curriculum development, change and control

We have noted in the earlier chapters of this book that if curriculum development is to be promoted and if curriculum change is to be effected, a good deal of attention must be given to the choice of a suitable theoretical model for curriculum planning and, in particular, to some important questions about the kind of emphasis which can or should be placed on the selection of curriculum content and the use of curriculum objectives. In later chapters we will note the account which must also be taken of a vast range of constraints and influences which together provide the context within which curriculum change and development must occur. This chapter will address itself to questions concerning the possible strategies which might be employed for changing the curriculum, the techniques which have been shown to be effective in attempts to bring about curriculum change or to promote curriculum development.

Again we must begin by noting that the most significant change which has occurred since the publication of the third edition of this book in 1989, especially in England and Wales, is the politicization of the curriculum. The effect of this in relation to curriculum change has been twofold. First, quite sweeping changes have been made by centralized diktat. And, second, all other forms of change and development have been arrested, since deviation from the prescribed form is not permitted, and this, as was predicted in earlier editions, has had the effect of bringing the natural evolution of curriculum to a halt. Some changes may be allowed to occur within subject-content or methodology, but nothing more sophisticated than that is now possible. Curriculum development is now no more than tinkering with content, attainment targets, profile components, levels and so on; the overall structure is set in stone. As a result, the understandings we were developing about the complexities of educational planning and provision have not been extended significantly, nor, as we shall yet again see, have they been incorporated in the curriculum which has now been imposed.

Those understandings, however, continue to be important and interesting to any serious student of curriculum. And, indeed, the strategies which have been employed by those who have taken responsibility for implementing these new policies are interesting in their own right, especially when compared and contrasted with those which had emerged from earlier experience of curriculum change in less overtly political contexts. Both, then, will form the substance of this chapter.

First of all we will look at what can be learned from the work of major national agencies established to promote and support curriculum development. Secondly, we will explore some of the problems of disseminating curriculum innovations, by looking at some of the models of dissemination which have been either postulated or employed and by considering their relative effectiveness. Thirdly, since this kind of exploration must lead to a questioning of the role of any centralized agency in curriculum development, since in fact the main lesson to be learnt from a study of dissemination techniques is that local initiatives have always been more effective than national projects in bringing about genuine change, we will examine the theory and the practice of school-based curriculum development and the associated concepts of 'action research' and 'the teacher as researcher'. And, fourth, against the backcloth of the understandings which we will see emerged from those developments, we will consider the devices which have been employed for effecting the massive changes in schools in England and Wales required by the 1988 Education Act and its associated policies and practices.

National agencies for curriculum development

The most illuminating, and indeed appropriate, way to set about an exploration of the effectiveness of national agencies in supporting curriculum change and development is to trace the work of the Schools Council in England and Wales. For this was the largest non-statutory and politically independent body established with the set task of promoting curriculum change. And it will be interesting not only to identify the important lessons which can be learnt from its work but also to compare and contrast that work with the procedures which have been adopted for the implementation of centrally dictated change by the several political quangos which have been created to enforce that change on schools and teachers.

It was suggested in Chapter 1 that the 'unplanned drift' (Hoyle, 1969a), resulting from the product of external pressures, which characterized such change as the curriculum once sustained, at least at the level of secondary education, was replaced by attempts at deliberate planning and curriculum construction only in the late 1950s and early 1960s. This was largely as a result of a concern felt throughout the Western world that it might be falling behind in the race for technological advancement.

In the United Kingdom that period saw the beginning of a number of attempts to change the curriculum, supported in some cases by the injection of money for research and development from such bodies as the Nuffield Foundation, until all these threads were drawn together by the establishment in October 1964 of the Schools Council for the Curriculum and Examinations, whose brief was 'to undertake research and development work on the curriculum, and to advise the Secretary of State on matters of examination policy' (Lawton, 1980:68). It was to be funded jointly by the Department of Education and Science and the local education authorities. It is worth noting also, that its constitution implicitly endorsed the idea of teacher control of the curriculum in that teacher members formed a majority on virtually all of its committees.

There are perhaps two major kinds of general lesson to be learned from the work of the Schools Council – first, those relating to its role as a politically independent, professional body for curriculum development, and, second, those deriving from its failure to bring about change on any significant scale. Both throw light on the issue of the role such an independent body can play in promoting the continuing development of the curriculum.

A politically independent professional agency

It is worth remembering that at the time when the Schools Council was first established there was little in the United Kingdom which could be called professional curriculum theory (Blenkin *et al.*, 1992). The major intellectual influences on curriculum came from those contributory disciplines whose inadequacies we noted in Chapter 1 – philosophy, psychology and sociology. Curriculum theory, as we defined it there, was virtually non-existent. That by the time the first edition of this book was published in 1977 there was a wealth of theoretical understandings which that book attempted to summarize was largely due to the Council's work.

For the many research and development projects it sponsored opened up all of the issues of curriculum theory which we are still exploring here – curriculum models and ideologies, curriculum evaluation, pupil assessment, the role of the teacher and, perhaps above all, strategies for the dissemination and promotion of innovation and change.

In the course of doing this, it also generated a great legacy of materials, handbooks and other artefacts which, as Lawrence Stenhouse (1983:354) said, embody 'ideas of great power . . . and are the best outside source of ideas about pedagogy and knowledge for teachers who will approach them as critical professionals who perceive ideas not as threats to their own professional autonomy, but as supports for it'. He goes on to add a point which is particularly relevant to our discussion here, that, although these ideas were generated at a time of optimism, they still have importance at a time of gloom and recession.

These ideas, insights and understandings, it might be said, came largely from the mistakes which were made by many of the Council's earlier projects – the too ready adoption of the aims and objectives model, for example, especially because it seemed to be required for purposes of evaluation, and the simplistic strategies which were initially adopted for the dissemination of its planned innovations. However, without the freedom to make these mistakes, these lessons would not have been learnt. And so there is some force to the argument that the main significance of the Schools Council's work lay not in the changes it brought about in the school curriculum (its own Impact and Take-Up Project (Schools Council, 1978, 1980) revealed how slight these were), but in the fuel it provided for the developing curriculum debate and the insights and understandings it helped us to achieve.

The virtual cessation of that debate and the loss of those insights and understandings which are key features of the era since the Council was disestablished and replaced by a number of politically driven quangos is perhaps the most eloquent testimony to the value of its work in this respect. And it is also perhaps the best evidence of the importance of a politically independent agency for curriculum development in a genuinely democratic society.

Lessons from the Schools Council's work

The first lesson to be learned relates to the duality of the role given to the Council – its responsibility for both curriculum development and the public examination system – which was a major factor in determining its policies and its actions. For its task was to maintain a balance between two potentially conflicting elements of the education system (Becher and Maclure, 1978). There is no doubt that these two must be planned in phase, not least because, as we shall see when we consider in Chapter 7 some of the external constraints on curriculum planning and development, the public examination system is probably the most influential of these; and, indeed, as we shall see when we consider the implementation of current policies and practices in England and Wales, control of assessment procedures is the most effective element in control of the curriculum. Hence the Council's inability to bring about significant changes in the examining system severely limited its effectiveness in promoting curriculum change. Its advice on examinations was never taken seriously by the Department of Education and Science, as is demonstrated by its attempts to introduce a common system of examinations at sixteen-plus (Schools Council, 1971a, 1975b), a change which was given official sanction only after the demise of the Schools Council when it was implemented through the General Certificate of Secondary Education in 1988.

If a national agency is to influence the development of the school curriculum to any significant degree, then, it must be able to effect changes on a broad front and, in particular, to address the issues raised by the many constraints on curriculum change and development, especially the public examination system.

This dual role also determined the major flavour of its work at least during the first ten years of its life. For, like the examinations system, its work was largely subject-based and this made it difficult for it to respond to changes of focus within the curriculum. It also led it to adopt a differentiated approach to curriculum planning. Because the constraints of the examination system were less significant in relation to those pupils regarded as 'less able' or those whose examination targets were within the newly established Certificate of Secondary Education (CSE), where examination requirements, and even subject content, were more readily malleable, it could be claimed that it was at its most influential in recommending changes in the curriculum for the 'less able' pupil in the secondary school. Indeed, a major part of its brief was to advise on a suitable curriculum for the early leaver, the school leaving age having been raised to 16+, with effect from 1972, on the advice of the Newsom Committee (CACE, 1963). It must also be recognized, however, that its influence here often took the form of advising schools to offer such pupils a different curriculum, consisting largely of low-status knowledge and little else (Kelly, 1980a). This is a point we will return to when we discuss the issue of curriculum entitlement in Chapter 8.

A third aspect of the work of the Schools Council from which many lessons have been learnt was the encouragement it offered to most of its early projects to adopt an objectives-based planning model. Again it must be conceded that this was understandable in the context of the general climate existing at the time when it was established. Whatever the reasons, however, it is clear that from the beginning the Council was not only concerned that, in order to demonstrate its proper use of public funds, the work of all its projects should be evaluated, but inclined also to the view that this could best be done, perhaps could only be done, if they began by making clear statements of their objectives. There were, of course, notable exceptions to this general trend, among which, as we saw in Chapter 3, was the Humanities Curriculum Project (Schools Council, 1970), but these exceptions merely prove the rule and there is no doubt that as a whole the Schools Council added its weight to that growing trend towards regarding this as the only proper basis for curriculum planning, a trend which we both noted and vigorously questioned in earlier chapters. The link between the prespecification of objectives and the evaluation of the curriculum we will explore more fully in Chapter 6; we must merely note here that the Schools Council can be criticized for lending its general support, at least in its early years, to the view that this link is non-problematic, although this must be offset by a recognition that it was some of its own later projects which led to the opening up of this issue.

Lastly, we must note that further lessons were learnt from the methods of dissemination adopted by many of the Schools Council's projects. Again, we will look at the problems of the dissemination of curriculum innovation later in this chapter. We must comment here, however, that on the evidence of its own Impact and Take-Up Project (Schools Council, 1978, 1980) the work of the Council was less effective than one would have hoped and that this was to a large extent attributable to the forms of dissemination it adopted, particularly in its early years, or to its failure to pay adequate attention to the problem of dissemination.

The force of most of these difficulties and criticisms was recognized by those responsible for the work of the Council, so that its later years saw new trends arising from the emerging inadequacies of the old. We have already seen in Chapter 3 that there was a development away from the starkest forms of objectives-based planning, for example, as more soph- isticated forms of evaluation were developed. The emergent problems of dissemination, too, led to a greater concentration on the idea of support- ing local, school-based initiatives.

However, it is quite clear not only that the early patterns and structure adopted by the Schools Council influenced curriculum development generally but also that they acted as a continuing constraint on its own work and thus inhibited these later developments (Blenkin, 1980). It is equally clear that they provided ammunition for those who argued that a teacher-controlled Schools Council had failed to make a significant im- pact on the curriculum of the schools. It was claimed above that the success of the Schools Council is to be judged not by its direct influence on curriculum change but by the contribution its work made to pro- moting debate about the curriculum, to developing insights and under- standings and to extending awareness of the complexities of curriculum planning and to creating an interest and concern for curriculum issues among teachers. But the influence of the Council's work on general development in both the theory and the practice of curriculum change, while it may be very extensive, is difficult, if not impossible, to quantify, while its failure to achieve direct changes through its own projects was manifest from the evidence of its own Impact and Take-Up Project (Schools Council, 1978, 1980). Its attempts to learn from the inadequacies of its earlier practices, then, were thwarted not only by those practices themselves but also by the strength they added to the case of its opponents.

These criticisms of the achievements of the Schools Council under a system of teacher control then led to its reconstitution. For the move to reduce the teachers' control of the curriculum, which we will explore in Chapter 7, gained strength from the criticisms by outsiders of its work (Lawton, 1980), as well as from the economic stringency which led to a reduced availability of money for curriculum development. Thus the main thrust of the reconstitution of the Council was towards reducing the influence of teachers in the formation of its policies and increasing that of many other bodies with an interest in education. In short, in unison with the general trends of the time, it was designed to open educational policy to public debate, and thus to bring it under the control of the administrators.

It was but a short step from this to complete disestablishment. Problems of the kind we have listed and the criticisms they led to were the major stated reasons why the funding of the Council was withdrawn in 1984. There is no doubt, however, that there were also significant underlying political reasons for this action, as we shall see when we explore the political context of curriculum change and development more fully in Chapter 7. This was clearly a step towards the establishment of the new National Curriculum and, in that context, perhaps the greatest significance of this action is that it had the effect of removing the only major source of politically independent research in education and the only politically free professional agency for curriculum change and development.

Its role in curriculum development was in theory to be taken over by the School Curriculum Development Council (SCDC), but this was clearly a politically controlled body and merely paved the way for the establishment of those several political quangos which have subsequently been established to oversee the implementation and maintenance of those policies and practices which were decreed by the 1988 Education Act and subsequent policy changes.

The strategies adopted for this implementation are interesting in themselves as devices for effecting curriculum change, and we must consider them presently. Before we do so, however, we need to explore in some detail the three most significant understandings relating to curriculum change and development which emerged from the Schools Council's work – the issue of the dissemination of innovation, that of school-based development and the concept of action research.

The dissemination of innovation and change

It was suggested earlier that a major reason for the failure of the Schools Council to influence curriculum change more directly and more widely was to be found in the dissemination strategies that were adopted. The dissemination of innovation is another problem that was created by that shift we have noted on several occasions from unplanned drift to deliberate planning, from random evolution to positive engineering. The essence of the change is that dissemination replaces diffusion (although the terms are not always used with meanings as clearly distinct as this). 'Once the curriculum reform movement got into "third gear" the term "diffusion", suggesting a natural social process of proliferation, gave way to the term "dissemination", indicating planned pathways to the transmission of new educational ideas and practices from their point of production to all locations of potential implementation' (MacDonald and Walker, 1976:26).

The intentions behind this process were several. It was hoped that it would lead to improvements in the channels of curriculum change; there was optimism that it would accelerate the speed of curriculum change; it was expected that the quality of the curriculum would be improved; and greater cost-effectiveness was also envisaged (MacDonald and Walker, 1976).

The problems which rapidly became apparent arose from two major and interrelated sources. First, the effectiveness of this process was seen to be affected to a high degree by those many constraints which limit all forms of curriculum development. At an early stage in its existence, the Schools Council identified several of these as being particularly significant in the constraining effects they were clearly having on innovation – 'finances, staff attitude, the mobility of pupils, parental pressures, and examinations' (Schools Council, 1971b:15).

Models of dissemination

The second set of problems for programmes of dissemination arose from the models of dissemination which were used, and some discussion of the models which have been identified must be undertaken as a prerequisite to examining the problems themselves.

Two major attempts have been made to identify different models of dissemination – those by Schon (1971) and Havelock (1971). These have been taken as offering the bases of an understanding of the problems of disseminating educational innovation, but it must be noted and emphasized straight away that their analyses are based on evidence culled from spheres other than education, a process whose dangers and inadequacies we have had cause to comment on in several other contexts.

Schon identified three models of dissemination, which he called the Centre-Periphery model, the Proliferation of Centres model and the Shifting Centres model. It is not unreasonable to see the second and third of these as elaborations of the first and thus all three of them as different versions or methods of what is fundamentally a centre-periphery approach.

The essence of the simple Centre-Periphery approach is that it assumes that the process of dissemination must be centrally controlled and managed, that the innovation is planned and prepared in detail prior to its dissemination and that the process of that dissemination is one-way – from the centre out to the consumers on the periphery. The effectiveness of this approach depends on several factors, which include not only the strength of the central resources but also the number of points on the periphery that are to be reached and the length of the 'spokes', the distance of these points from the centre.

The Proliferation of Centres model attempts to overcome these factors, or at least to reduce their significance, by creating secondary centres to extend the reach and thus the efficiency of the primary centre. The intention is that the work of the central development team is supported and extended by local development groups. In turn, these local groups are supported by the central team through the provision not only of advice but also sometimes of courses of training.

Schon's third model, the Shifting Centres model, was posited to explain the spread, witnessed in recent years, of ideas such as those of civil rights, black power, disarmament and student activism, in other words changes of values and attitudes of a more subtle and less deliberate kind. These developments are characterized by the absence of any clearly established centre and of any stable, centrally established message. Indeed, this is a model which appears to be more successful at explaining how unplanned diffusion occurs than at offering a strategy for planned dissemination. Schon believes it has potential value for curriculum change but this must be questionable, since it is a model which appears to offer no basis for the development of any specific message (Stenhouse, 1975).

Havelock's analysis of dissemination strategies can be seen as an attempt to take us beyond the notion that these must always assume a one-way, centre-to-periphery process. His Research, Development and Diffusion (R, D & D) model has many affinities with Schon's basic Centre-Periphery approach. For it assumes a developer who identifies the problem and a receiver who is essentially a passive recipient of the innovation developed to resolve that problem. It is a 'target system' and is regarded as the model to be adopted when large-scale curriculum change is the aim.

His Social Interaction (SI) model, however, places great stress on the social interaction between members of the adopting group. Again it is a form of the centre-periphery model; again it is a 'target system'; and again the needs of the consumer are determined by the central planner. But it recognizes that the key to the adoption and implementation of the innovation is the social climate of the receiving body and that success or failure will hinge on the channels of communication there. It thus represents, like Schon's Proliferation of Centres model, the beginnings of a shift of focus from the centre to the periphery.

It is with Havelock's third model, the Problem-Solving (PS) model, that this shift is completed. For the essence of this model is that the problem is identified by the consumer and the process of innovation is thus initiated also by him or her. The individual on the periphery is thus himself or herself active and involved from the beginning and the process is essentially one in which he or she recruits outside help. The relationship between the consumer and the external support agent is one of mutual collaboration rather than that of the receiver and the sender of a message; and the whole process is personalized to the point where it has to be recognized that this is not a model of mass dissemination, since the solution that is devised for the problem need not be seen as solving the problems of other consumers. In short, it might be fairly claimed that this is not a model of dissemination at all but rather a model for school-based curriculum development.

The inadequacies of the centre-periphery approach

It will be appreciated that there is a good deal of overlap between these schemes and models. It is not an over-simplification, however, if we suggest that the major division is between those which adopt a centre-periphery approach of central development and planned dissemination and those which encourage initiatives from the consumer and have led to the development of the notion of school-based curriculum development. The latter is a relatively new concept, which, as we saw, the Schools Council came to late in its life; the former was the strategy adopted by the early projects of the Schools Council and, as we suggested earlier, this was a major factor in its failure to influence curriculum development as directly as it was once hoped it might.

For there are some problems which it might be argued are endemic to this approach and which make it quite inadequate as a device for bringing about effective curriculum change. In particular, there is a wide gap between the ideas of a project held by its central planners and the realities of its implementation, if that is even the word, in the classroom by the teachers. The existence of this gap between policy and practice was viewed by Lawrence Stenhouse (1975) as the central problem of curriculum development and, indeed, of the advancement of education itself. Even when a project team sets out deliberately to support teachers in their own developments rather than to provide a teacher-proof blueprint (Shipman, 1972), as was the case, for example, with the Humanities Curriculum Project, the Keele Integrated Studies Project and the Goldsmiths' College Interdisciplinary Enquiry Project, the same difficulties have been experienced. It has proved impossible to get across to teachers the concept of the project, the theoretical considerations underlying it, in such a way as to ensure that these were reflected in its practice. And so a gap emerges between the ideals and the realities, a gap that in some cases is so wide as to negate the innovation entirely, at least in terms of the conception of it by its planners.

The main danger then becomes a possible loss of credibility for the project, a rejection of the principles behind it, if an ill-informed or maladroit or even malignant implementation of it, derived from lack of adequate understanding, has led to disastrous practical consequences. That something has not worked leads too readily to the assumption that it cannot work, rather than to a consideration of the possibility that one has got it wrong.

Such a situation is clearly unsatisfactory since it means at one level that the sums of money spent on central curriculum development have not produced anything like adequate returns and at a further level that they can be positively counterproductive, in so far as failures of this kind can lead to an entrenching of traditional positions.

This kind of reaction, however, is easy to understand, once one acknowledges that schools are living organisms and must be helped to grow and develop from within rather than having 'foreign bodies' attached to them from without, like barnacles attaching themselves to a ship's bottom. This kind of attempt at transplantation must lead in almost every case to 'tissue rejection' (Hoyle, 1969b), and that has been the experience of all such attempts at the dissemination of innovation.

Various hypotheses have been put forward to explain the inadequacies of the centre-periphery model of dissemination. One piece of research has indicated that even where a lot of positive effort has gone into promoting the dissemination of a project to the schools, barriers to its implementation exist in both the failure of teachers to perceive with clarity their new role and also the absence of conditions appropriate to their being able to acquire such a perception (Gross *et al.*, 1971). 'Our analysis of the case study data led us to conclude that this condition could be primarily attributed to five circumstances: (1) the teachers' lack of clarity about the innovation; (2) their lack of the kinds of skills and knowledge needed to conform to the new role model; (3) the unavailability of required instructional materials; (4) the incompatibility of organizational arrangements with the innovation; and (5) lack of staff motivation' (1971:122). The first four of these conditions, they claim, existed from the outset; the last emerged later. Nor would this seem surprising.

It has also been suggested that another major factor in the ineffectiveness of this approach to curriculum change is its failure to take proper account of social interaction theory (House, 1974). Broadly speaking, the argument is that centre-periphery approaches to dissemination in education are using the wrong model of social interaction or 'personal contact'. They are attempts at imposing a highly depersonalized model and thus they reduce the level of personal contact, leaving the teacher as a largely passive recipient of the innovation. This not only restricts the flow of the innovation but invites teachers to modify and adapt it to conform to the norms of their own group.

Another perspective on this difficulty sees these attempts to impose new ideas and approaches to curriculum on teachers as examples of the use of 'power-coercive' strategies (Bennis *et al.*, 1969), attempts to bring about change or innovation by enforcement. This kind of approach is contrasted with 'empirical-rational' strategies, which attempt to promote change or innovation through demonstrations of their validity and desirability, and 'normative-reeducative' strategies, which approach the task of innovation through devices for changing the attitudes, the values and the interrelationships of the teachers and for providing them with the new skills needed to implement the change. Again, therefore, we can see that a major concern is with the quality of the social interaction within the school and with the teachers' response. We can also recognize that the contrast is between imposition, whether from an outside agency or from within the school through, for example, a powerful and strong-willed headteacher, and the involvement of the teachers themselves both in identifying the need for change and in developing responses seen by them to be appropriate to that need. It will be interesting to remember this analysis when we review the methods by which recent changes have been imposed on schools as a result of central government directives.

Finally, it is worth noting briefly the implications of this debate for notions of teacher professionalism or the professional concept of the teacher. It would not be appropriate here to engage in detailed analysis of the concept of professionalism. It is important, however, to note, not least because of the enhanced significance this has in the context of the National Curriculum in England and Wales, that to adopt power-coercive strategies, to attempt to develop 'teacher-proof' schemes, to endeavour to bring about change from outside the school, is to view the teacher as a technician rather than as a professional, as an operative rather than as a decision-maker, as someone whose role is merely to implement the judgements of others and not to act on his or her own. We must note, therefore, that the difficulties of this approach to curriculum planning and innovation derive not merely from the fact that it seems to have proved ineffective in practice but also because it has serious implications for the professional standing and responsibility of teachers. Again it represents a technicist rather than an ethical approach to curriculum development.

These, then, have been some of the criticisms of those early attempts at curriculum innovation and change which did not plan their dissemination but rather hoped that their ideas, once propagated, would spread with the wind, and of those which, while deliberately planning the dissemination of their ideas and materials, did so in a somewhat authoritarian manner, offering what they hoped would be 'teacher-proof' schemes and packages, and expecting teachers either to accept the imposition of these upon them or to recognize unaided their supposedly self-evident attractions.

Some consequent modifications

In response to these criticisms, therefore, many devices have been used to improve the processes of dissemination both by deliberately planning it and by doing this in a manner designed to take greater account of the difficulties of ensuring proper acceptance. Most of these may be seen as indications of a move towards Schon's proliferation of centres. House (1974) recommends the creation of more incentives for local entrepreneurs, the leaders of Schon's secondary centres; he also wishes to increase the number of those participating in the exercise; and his major aim is 'to reduce political, social and organisational barriers to contact with the outside world' (MacDonald and Walker,

1976:20). In pursuit of much the same goals, the Schools Council attempted to establish local development groups, to involve teachers' centres, to gain the support of local education authorities, to promote the in-service education of teachers, to mount regional conferences and even, in some cases, to involve members of the project teams in the work of the schools, as change agents working in secondary centres (Schools Council, 1967, 1971b, 1974b). Many of these devices were also adopted by the Assessment of Performance Unit in the final stages of its work, when it sought to support teachers in effecting changes in their curricula (Kelly, 1987).

In spite of all such developments and the use of all these detailed strategies for planned dissemination, major difficulties have continued to exist. Some of these were identified by those concerned with the dissemination of the Humanities Curriculum Project. In particular, failure to achieve adequate dissemination was attributed to difficulties in communication between the project team and the schools (MacDonald and Rudduck, 1971). It would be a mistake, however, to interpret that statement at too simple a level, for a number of features of this failure of communication have also been identified. One is the tendency of teachers 'to invest the development team with the kind of authority which can atrophy independence of judgement in individual school settings' (1971:149). The converse of this was also observed, namely the anxiety of some teachers not to lose their own style by accepting too readily the specifications of method included in the project. Both these factors would seem to point to the need for a full and proper involvement of the teachers with the development of a project. Both of them too draw attention to the significance of House's insistence on a proper regard being paid to the different forms of social interaction.

This emphasizes the importance of the manner in which innovations are introduced. It will be clear that if an innovation is to have a chance of 'taking' in a school, it will be necessary for more to be done than the mere provision of resources and in-service support for teachers. Teachers will need to become committed to it, an ideological change will need to be promoted, if they are to be expected willingly to adapt their methods and approaches to meet the demands of the new work. This offers a far more subtle problem. It is here that the manner in which the proposed change is made becomes important. For if it is imposed by the headteacher, for example, or by powerful pressure from outside, the dictation involved will be counterproductive and will promote opposition and hostility in teachers rather than support. Not only will teachers in such circumstances not work to promote the change planned; they will often quite deliberately and actively sabotage the efforts of others. It is plain that power-coercive strategies do not bring about real or effective change.

To bring about effective curriculum change, then, we must take full account of the micro-politics of the school (Ball, 1987). Indeed, the attitudes of staff were one of the major constraints on curriculum change that the early work of the Schools Council drew attention to. It asserted that 'innovation cannot succeed unless the majority of staff are, at worst, neutral; but it was clearly important to have a majority positively inclined to curricular change' (Schools Council, 1971b:15). That report went on to say that 'one solution suggested was that innovation should begin by attempting to solve existing dissatisfactions' (1971b:15). This suggestion clearly points to the desirability of shifting the focus from the centre to the periphery, of adopting a model more akin to Havelock's Problem-Solving model, and of employing empirical-rational and/or normative-reeducational rather than power-coercive strategies. In fact, it would appear to indicate that artificial dissemination by donor is not as good as the real thing.

Support for this view is to be found elsewhere too. For it has further been suggested that this problem goes beyond a mere failure of communication or of the strategies employed to introduce the innovation and is in fact the result of the different views and definitions of a curriculum project that we have already suggested are taken by different bodies of people involved in it (Shipman, 1972, 1973). The question must then be asked whose definition is to be seen as valid. For this reason, it has been suggested that 'the process of curriculum dissemination, in so far as it assumes a stable message, does not occur. The process to which the term 'dissemination' is conventionally applied would be more accurately described by the term 'curriculum negotiation' (MacDonald and Walker, 1976:43). In other words, having recognized that a gap exists between the ideals of the planners and the realities of the work of the teacher in the classroom, we should be concerned to close it by attempting not only to bring the latter nearer to the former but also by seeking to bring each closer to the other. To see the need to do this is to recognize that curriculum development is essentially a matter of local development, that it requires a form of 'household' innovation.

This, then, constitutes a further argument in favour of school-based curriculum development. For it is clear that, if the social climate of the school is to be supportive of innovation, if, to change the metaphor, the organizational health of the school is to be such as to ensure that there will not be any kind of 'tissue rejection' (Hoyle, 1969b), it is necessary for the initiatives to come from within, for the process to be one of growth and development rather than of transplantation. In short, the main reason for the failure of attempts to change curricula from outside was that the dissemination model itself was wrong, so that attention came to be directed towards the development of alternative models, in particular the idea of school-based curriculum development.

School-based curriculum development

It was the relative failure of external attempts at the dissemination of innovation, then, that led to the emergence of the idea of school-based curriculum development. There is, therefore, a real sense in which this must be seen not as a form of dissemination so much as an alternative to it. We have just noted that the failure of descending models of dissemination is in part due to the need for the social and organizational climate of the school to be such as to create the conditions for any planned innovation to 'take' in the school, and that this realization, by shifting the focus of attention from the innovation to the school, from the seed to the soil in which it is to be planted, suggests that the process must be considered first from the other end and the initiative sought in the school rather than outside it.

Several major principles are reflected in this notion of school-based curriculum development. First, it acknowledges that a large measure of freedom for both teacher and learner is a necessary condition for curricular provision which is fully educational (Skilbeck, 1976). Second, it views the school as a human social institution which must be responsive to its own environment (Skilbeck, 1976), and which must, therefore, be permitted to develop in its own way to fit that environment. Lastly, it regards it as vital to this development that the individual teacher, or at least the staff of any individual school, should accept a research and development role in respect of the curriculum (Stenhouse, 1975), modifying, adapting and developing it to suit the needs of individual pupils and a particular environment.

Fundamentally, therefore, it is an acceptance of that developmental view of education which we attempted to unpack in Chapter 4 which has provided the basis for the positive arguments which have been offered in support of this shift of emphasis. Malcolm Skilbeck, for example, argues that school-based curriculum development 'provides more scope for the continuous adaptation of curriculum to individual pupil needs than do other forms of curriculum development' (Skilbeck, 1976:93–4). Other systems are

> by their nature ill-fitted to respond to individual differences in either pupils or teachers. Yet these differences . . . are of crucial importance in learning . . . At the very least, schools need greatly increased scope and incentive for adapting, modifying, extending and otherwise reordering externally developed curricula than is

now commonly the case. Curriculum development related to individual differences must be a continuous process and it is only the school or school networks that can provide scope for this.

(Skilbeck, 1976:94)

For these reasons, then, there came to be a growing conviction that the only satisfactory form of curriculum development is likely to be school-based, so that in the years preceding the advent of centralized control of the school curriculum, we saw a proliferation of sub-variants of this generic concept – School-Focused Curriculum Development and School-Centred Innovation (SCI), for example – of supportive agencies, such as Guidelines for Review and Internal Development of Schools (GRIDS), and of consequent schemes for evaluation at this level, such as School Self-Evaluation (SEE) and School-Based Review (SBR).

Key features of these developments

We must now remind ourselves of some of the key features of these developments, not merely from nostalgia but, more importantly, because they contribute to a clearer appreciation of the changes which recent years have seen.

Change agents

We must begin by noting that, to meet some of the problems this approach creates, some schools made senior appointments of teachers with special responsibility for co-ordinating and guiding curriculum – curriculum co-ordinators or curriculum development officers, change-agents within the school. If the conditions are to be created for the continuous development and evolution of the curriculum, this is a practice which has much to recommend it. It is a step towards achieving that kind of co-ordinated development across the curriculum which we said in Chapter 1 was often lacking, especially in secondary schools where the tradition has been for development to go on within individual subjects in isolation from one another. It also ensures that there is one person in the school who can be expected to attempt to organize support from outside agencies for any group of teachers engaged in any particular innovative activity. Such a person can also act as a focus for curriculum study groups in the school, an essential innovation if teachers are to be made fully aware of what is entailed in school-based curriculum development.

Outside support agencies

Secondly, the importance of outside support agencies became increasingly apparent. We have already noted how the Schools Council in its later phases directed most of its attention to supporting school-based developments, and it is clear that schools need this kind of external support and advice. Perhaps more important, however, was the support provided by local education authorities. Curriculum support teams were created in several areas and the impact of these was often crucial to school improvement and the school-based development of curricula. Furthermore, at this time local authorities employed an array of advisers rather than inspectors, and their role was also to support the schools within their responsibility rather than to police their activities through inspections. This kind of support has now been largely lost with the reduction in the powers of local authorities which current policies have brought.

This kind of link with external agencies is important for at least two reasons. One is that without it what occurs may well be change but will not necessarily be development or lead to improvement in the quality of education experienced by a school's pupils. There has been a tendency, in response to those difficulties of prompting innovations from outside which we noted earlier, to assume that school-based curriculum development must be worthwhile merely because it is school-based. There is, however, no guarantee of this. Engagement with outside agencies may contribute to ensuring that it is worthwhile.

There is also the related danger that, if teachers' attention becomes too closely focused on their own institutions, and their possibly narrow concerns, they may fail to address curriculum issues at an appropriate level or depth. In particular, there may be a tendency to see these issues largely in managerial or organizational or even bureaucratic terms, again to adopt a technicist rather than an ethical stance towards them, a tendency which has been reinforced by recent governmental policies emphasizing these dimensions of schooling. However, we have seen in earlier chapters the important conceptual issues which curriculum planning and development raise, so that we can appreciate how important it is that teachers are able to address these issues in the course of their school-based curriculum development. Again, therefore, contact with supportive and illuminative outside agencies is crucial.

The centrality of the teacher
The third, and perhaps most crucial feature of school-based curriculum development to emerge was the centrality of the individual teacher to the process. If we have been right to identify the teacher in the classroom as the person whose role is quite fundamental and crucial to the effectiveness of educational provision, then the teacher must be the hub of all this activity. The most important need which arose, then, was that

for adequate support for him or her. It is clear that what we have been describing involves a major change in the teacher's role and it entails major changes in the organization and even the staffing of schools if he or she is to have the time and the ability to respond to this.

It also became increasingly clear how important it is for initial courses of training to prepare teachers to take this central role in curriculum development, and that it is even more important that they be given adequate opportunities for continuing in-service education to enable them to obtain any new skills that the innovations require and a developing insight into the wider issues of education, a deep understanding of which is vital for any kind of adequate planning, research or development.

This is why major curriculum changes such as the introduction of mixed-ability groupings in secondary schools worked most smoothly and effectively when, as in the West Riding of Yorkshire under Sir Alec Clegg's guidance, suitable in-service courses were made available on demand and tailored not to the advisory staff's ideas of what is needed but to what the teachers themselves asked for (Kelly, 1975). It is for the same reason that, where national projects have developed training courses for teachers wishing to make use of the project materials, teachers who have had this training achieve more success than those who have not (Elliott and Adelman, 1973).

In short, there can be no curriculum development without teacher development and, if, as we have claimed, the teacher's role is crucial to the quality of the pupil's education, it becomes most important that they be given all possible support of this kind. What is needed is help and advice, from the stage of initial training onwards, in the process of becoming 'reflective practitioners', professionals able to evaluate their own work with a view to continuously improving it.

Hence we must now explore what we have identified as the third major development which emerged from the work of the Schools Council – the development of the notion of school-based curriculum development into that of action research and 'the teacher as researcher' (Stenhouse, 1975).

Action research and 'the teacher as researcher'

Action research has been defined as 'the systematic study of attempts to improve educational practice by groups of participants by means of their own practical actions and by means of their own reflection upon the effects of these actions' (Ebbutt, 1983), and as 'the study of a social situation with a view to improving the quality of action within it' (Elliott,

1981:1). The important aspect of this notion is that it represents a claim that the only productive form of educational research is that which involves the people who are actually working on an educational problem or problems and is conducted *pari passu* with the development of solutions to that problem or problems. It is a view which has developed out of a growing sense of dissatisfaction with the pointlessness of much research which has been conducted outside the field of practice and has thus produced generalized findings which it is left to the practitioner to 'apply'. This latter kind of research has often not only failed to be supportive of teachers in the development of their practice, it has sometimes even been counterproductive to that purpose (Kelly, 1981). Its inadequacies, then, are precisely those of centre-periphery models of dissemination. The notion of action research is offered as an alternative form of research and one which it is claimed should provide teachers with a proper kind of support. As Elliot Eisner has said (1985:264), 'what . . . we need if educational research is truly to inform educational practice is the construction of our own unique conceptual apparatus and research methods'.

The first aspect of this approach to research is that it requires the teachers themselves to be actively engaged in the activity. They must be constantly evaluating their work, critically analysing it with a view to its development and improvement. It is this feature which brings in Lawrence Stenhouse's associated notion of 'the teacher as researcher' (Stenhouse, 1975). 'The ideal', said Stenhouse, 'is that the curricular specification should feed a teacher's personal research and development programme through which he is progressively increasing his understanding of his own work and hence bettering his teaching' (1975:143). 'It is not enough', he adds later, 'that teachers' work should be studied: they need to study it themselves' (1975:143).

Several further issues arise as a result of adopting that basic position. It is clearly vital, if teachers are to develop and if the quality of their work is to improve, that they engage in this kind of continuous evaluation of their work. Indeed, it might be argued that this is a *sine qua non* of teaching, certainly of good teaching, and that it is something that all teachers naturally do. It must be said, however, that not all teachers do it well. School-based curriculum development, as was suggested earlier, is not necessarily good just because it is school-based; and similarly teachers' own evaluations of their work are not necessarily sound and productive merely because they are their own evaluations. Teachers can be, and should be, assisted to develop the skills and techniques needed for proper and effective self-evaluation, as we shall see in Chapter 6. And there will always remain that psychological difficulty which makes objective self-evaluation difficult in any sphere.

Thus questions now arise about whether there is a role for an external figure or figures in action research and, if there is, what that role is and who this external figure or figures might be.

These were among the questions addressed by the Ford Teaching Project (FTP). One of the main purposes of the Ford Teaching Project was 'to help teachers by fostering an action-research orientation towards classroom problems' (Elliott and Adelman, 1973:10). This was offered as an alternative to the model of action research in which researchers from outside come into the classroom and work with the teacher. It was felt that this kind of relationship erodes the teacher's autonomy and that if this is to be protected he or she must be enabled to take responsibility for his or her own action research as part of his or her responsibility for his or her own curriculum development (Elliott and Adelman, 1973). This the Ford Teaching Project attempted to encourage.

However, a second-order focus of the FTP's research was the question of the role of the outside 'expert'. At the same time as helping teachers to develop the ability to engage in their own 'research-based teaching', the team wanted also to explore how best this kind of teaching might be assisted and supported from outside.

The logic of the FTP's own approach would seem to be that, once teachers have acquired a research-based teaching orientation as part of their basic weaponry, the need for outside support will disappear, so that perhaps the role of the curriculum developer or other external 'expert' is to be seen as provisional only, his or her services being needed only until such times as teachers themselves have acquired the necessary skills.

Two questions, however, must be asked before we too readily accept such a view. In the first place, we must ask how far the average teacher is likely to be able to develop the abilities this will require of him or her. Apart from the problem of adding yet another chore to an already heavy task, we shall see in Chapter 6 that it was not easy for the FTP team to develop in teachers the detachment and the security of confidence necessary to be able to make reasonably objective appraisals of their work, although the team did express optimism on this point.

Secondly, however, we must also ask whether there will not always be a need for someone to come from the outside to take a detached view of what is being done, to suggest possible alternatives and to ensure that all the necessary questions raised by attempts at curriculum planning and development are addressed and not, as we saw earlier is the danger, only those of a managerial or organizational kind. Few of us cannot profit from this kind of second opinion. Perhaps this is to be seen as a function of teachers from other schools as part of the process of moderation that should be an essential element in all assessment procedures. In this context, it is interesting to note the experience of a research team which has been seeking to support the professional development of early years practitioners through action research. For among the preliminary findings of the *Principles into Practice (PiP)* project has been the evident importance to practitioners of various forms of 'networking'. And it has also appeared that there may continue to be a need for someone acting as a professional consultant. As the report of Phase One of this project (Blenkin and Kelly, 1997:100) has said:

> While at the level of the individual settings it seems clear that action research by individuals is more likely to be effective, there is a growing and quite striking body of evidence emerging of the advantages to be gained from creating opportunities for those individuals to meet regularly to 'compare notes' with others pursuing their own action research in different settings. And regular 'conferences' of action researchers and the project team have become an increasingly significant feature of the work as it has progressed.

We noted earlier that the ideas of school-based curriculum development and of action research, as well as generating the change-agent within the school, have also given birth to various forms of 'curriculum support team' (Ball, 1981, 1983a, b). In fact, we have already seen the emergence of two quite different models of such curriculum development, the one relying on initiatives and support from within, the other responding to such from outside. We noted too that the provision of such support became a major focus for the work of the newly reconstituted Schools Council and also that some local authorities had created their own curriculum support groups.

It is also clear that the role of such support groups is not always an easy one (Ball, 1981, 1983a, b). To some extent they exist to respond to and support changes initiated within a school and this is not in itself necessarily a difficult task. Their main function, however, certainly at local authority level, is to prompt changes in schools which do not initiate these for themselves and this is obviously a much more difficult and sensitive task.

We have noted the importance of the organizational health of the school in respect of its likely receptivity to change and development. For those schools whose organizational health might be lower than one would wish, strategies must be developed for bringing about the qualities that will make curriculum development possible as well as that curriculum development itself. In short, it is necessary to go beyond Havelock's Problem-Solving model of change by identifying the problem for the consumer when he or she appears to be unable to recognize it for himself or herself. In cases of this kind the external curriculum developer or support team has a major role to play and it is clear that it is not an enviable one.

There is, then, still a role for the wandering expert in curriculum development. That role is to provide teachers with expert advice and the detached appraisal they cannot provide themselves and not to arrive hawking his or her own pet project, cobbled together in a place somewhat removed from the realities of any particular group of classrooms. His or her job is to follow and serve the teachers rather than to lead them into his or her own new pastures. He or she can only support curriculum development; he or she should no longer attempt to direct it.

The understandings which have developed from all of the work which has been undertaken in order to support curriculum innovation and development, not only in the UK but everywhere else, have had as their common denominator the centrality of the teacher to effective educational provision. Thus they have been predicated on the need to ensure that any proposed innovation, if it is to be successful, must start from an attempt to obtain the teachers' understanding, support and, indeed, approval. In the terms offered by Bennis *et al.* (1969) which we noted earlier, it must seek to promote change through 'empirical-rational' strategies, which attempt to demonstrate the validity and desirability of the proposed change, or through 'normative-reeducative' strategies, which try to persuade teachers of the value of what is proposed and to provide them with whatever new skills are needed to implement it. The alternative, as we also saw, is the adoption of 'power-coercive' strategies which simply set about implementing the change by enforcement, a policy which, if we have been right to claim that the teachers' commitment is crucial to effectiveness, cannot lead in the long term to genuine improvement. It may bring about change, but it cannot lead to innovation, in the sense of advance and improvement on current practice. The contrast again is between approaches to change which we might describe as 'ethical', concerned to promote genuine innovation and improvement, and those we might describe as 'technicist', seeking to bring about change for other, less worthy reasons.

In the light of this, it will be illuminating to conclude this exploration of strategies for curriculum change by considering the devices employed to bring about the major changes in the school curriculum which the last decade or so has seen, especially in England and Wales.

Changing the curriculum through centralized control

It might be argued that the plethora of official documentation with which schools have been flooded in recent years constitutes an attempt to adopt an empirical-rational strategy for change, although we have noted the intellectual inadequacies of much of this. And certainly there are elements of the normative-reeducative in the assumption of control over the training of teachers, both initial and in-service, as part of the attempt to ensure compliance with, rather than challenge to, government policies.

These strategies may be said to have had some success in persuading the general public that improvements in educational provision were occurring, and they may also have been effective in winning the support, or at least the acceptance, of the teachers themselves, especially those whose concept of their role has not been changed to any dramatic extent. Those teachers, however, for whom the new policies have involved a head-on clash with their own professional values, as, for example, those working in the early years of education and those who have been responsible for preparing them for such work, have not been, and could not be, won over by these devices. In these cases, nothing less than power-coercive strategies could be employed. And the adoption of such strategies has served to highlight that this is the underlying principle of the changes implemented at every level. Fundamentally, the concern is to change and control the system, whether this can be done by winning teacher support or not. The model of change is a centre-periphery model, and the hope and expectation is that the inadequacies of this model, as revealed by experience such as that of the Schools Council, can be offset by the application of the means of enforcement which the Schools Council lacked (and, indeed, would not have wanted). We must note, however, that, if we have been right to interpret earlier experience as demonstrating the centrality of the teacher to effective educational provision, then these strategies are fundamentally misguided and, while they might bring about a tightening of centralized control of what goes on in schools and even a temporary appearance of improvement, they can never lead to a raising of standards in any genuine educational sense.

Power/coercion, however, is the current mode, and, since this is a difficult tactic to employ in a supposed democracy, subtle devices have had to be found to enable the enforcers to operate it. We noted in Chapter 2 how the use of rhetoric and the legitimation of discourse has been used as one such subtle device. We must note here the equally plausible (although rather less subtle) manipulation through tightly framed systems of testing and inspection.

Testing and inspection

Nothing can be more plainly power-coercive than legislation, since the law, by definition, requires us to do as we are told or to suffer the penal consequences. And this is the point at which current policies for schooling in England and Wales began (although we shall trace in Chapter 7 a long history of preparatory build-up). Thus the 1988 Education Act, along with those minor acts which subesequently filled some of the emerging gaps, established the framework of centralized control and initiated the many changes which the last decade has witnessed. And we must note again that such an approach to change is technicist rather than ethical; it is conerned more with the mechanisms for bringing about change than with the niceties of the nature and worth of that change.

What is more interesting, and indeed more sinister, however, is the subtle strategies which have been employed since then, to bring about further changes without recourse to the overtly power-coercive device of legislation. In particular, in addition to the manipulation of thinking through control of language and discourse which we noted in Chapter 2, testing and inspection have come to be used as devices for implementing political policies without the need for overt dictation through legislation.

Assessment and evaluation, in the full and educational sense of these terms, will be the major concerns of our next chapter and we must leave a detailed discussion of them until then. We must briefly note here, however, the use that has been made of those processes which have masqueraded under these titles as strategies of centralized control and power-coercive change.

We will see in Chapter 6 the sophisticated form of pupil assessment which was recommended by the Task Group on Assessment and Testing (TGAT) (DES/Welsh Office, 1988) as the essential accompaniment of an educationally effective National Curriculum. In the event, what has emerged is a programme of simplistic testing at 7+, 11+ and 14+ and with it the publication of 'league tables' claimed to provide information of value to parents relating to the quality of provision in individual schools.

In reality, from the parent's point of view this information is worthless, as the parents' own responses to Ofsted's questions have revealed (unpublished Ofsted Report, 1998), and the only justification for this eleborate programme of testing (if indeed this be a justification) is that it provides a mechanism for ensuring that schools and teachers do what they are supposed to do and concentrate their attentions on the limited demands of the National Curriculum. We will argue in Chapter 8 that a national curriculum framed in much looser terms, guidelines rather than tight prescriptions, is likely to offer a much more effective route to quality of educational provision in a democratic context. In the meantime, we must note here that in England and Wales we have a far more prescriptive national curriculum than this, and that that prescription is imposed, maintained and reinforced by a system of testing, combined with the publication of the results of these tests. Again, we should note that the rhetoric surrounding these procedures is that of information to parents, quality control and the raising of standards. The reality, however, as every teacher knows, is very different.

It is further reinforced by the programme of regular inspections by Ofsted teams. These inspections are conducted according to criteria set by Ofsted itself, albeit in response to government requirements, so that effectively it is Ofsted which is controlling and directing the school curriculum on the government's behalf.

Furthermore, this process spares the government the potential embarrassment of further coercive legislation. It can merely issue 'guidelines', as, for example, the recent pronouncements of David Blunkett on homework. Such guidelines, as he informed us on that occasion, will not be given the force of law. They will, however, figure in the criteria employed in Ofsted inspections. They thus do not need the force and overt compulsion of law, if they are to be enforced on the ground in this covert but equally effective manner. What more evidence could one have of the forked-tongue character of 'edu-speak'.

Perhaps a more telling example of this has been the control which has come to be exercised over educational provision for the pre-school child. The function of Ofsted inspections is to ensure that schools are meeting the requirements of the 1988 Act and its subsequent legislation, albeit having more freedom than perhaps any government quango should have in its interpretation of those requirements. That legislation, however, specifically excluded provision for the pre-school, non-statutory stages of schooling, leaving teachers and other providers and practitioners at that level to pursue the kind of developmental curriculum which the evidence indicates to be the most appropriate for that phase of education.

The response to this was the publication by the Department for Education and Employment, in conjunction with the School Curriculum and Assessment Authority (SCAA) of documentation setting out what were called 'desirable outcomes for children's learning' (DfEE/SCAA, 1996; SCAA, 1997a). And these 'desirable outcomes' have become the criteria by which nursery schools are evaluated by Ofsted inspections and, more importantly for us in the present context, the devices by which these schools are being forced to change and to adopt a form of curriculum which both the experience of practitioners at this level (Blenkin and Kelly, 1997) and the research evidence (Blenkin and Kelly, 1996, 1997) indicate to be inappropriate and unsuitable.

Ofsted inspections have thus become a sinister and covert device by which the school curriculum is changed in accordance not only with legislation approved by Parliament but also with what are perceived to be the wishes of government as interpreted or even second-guessed by those who are prepared to act as political aides and lackeys. And their effect is not merely to undermine the morale of teachers but also to introduce an instability of policy which must threaten the quality of provision.

Assessment and evaluation, including evaluation by school inspections, when used for purposes other than those of a nakedly political kind, can contribute much to the promotion of educational quality. The potential and possibilities of the educational use of these procedures will be explored in full in Chapter 6, as will other threatening pitfalls. What we must note here in concluding this exploration of strategies for change is that that potential and those possibilities are lost when both assessment and evaluation become distorted for use towards ends which are essentially political.

Key issues raised by this chapter

1) What is the most valuable source of support for the professional development of teachers?
2) What implications are there for the quality of educational provision in the imposition of a common curriculum by power-coercive methods?
3) What implications does this also have for the development of the curriculum?

Suggested further reading

Blenkin, G. M., Edwards, G. and Kelly, A. V. (1992) *Change and the Curriculum*, London: Chapman.
Elliott, J. (1998) *The Curriculum Experiment: Meeting the Challenge of Social Change*, Buckingham: Open University Press.
Elliott, J. (1991) *Action Research for Educational Change*, Milton Keynes: Open University Press.

6

Assessment, evaluation, appraisal and accountability

In considering the related issues of pupil assessment, the evaluation of the curriculum and the appraisal of the effectiveness with which schools and teachers meet their responsibilities, we will again find ourselves pursuing two lines of enquiry. First, we will need to apprise ourselves of the insights and the understandings which have emerged from theorizing in these areas and from the practice in which much of that theorizing was based. And, second, we must again trace the loss of those insights and understandings which has resulted from the politicization of the school curriculum and the demise of serious intellectual curriculum debate, and which, as we saw at the end of Chapter 5, has led to a degeneration of pupil assessment into testing and curriculum evaluation into school inspections, with both attuned more to political than to educational ends.

Pupil assessment

Assessment is essential for effective teaching. All teachers, whether consciously or unconsciously, are continuously assessing their pupils, albeit usually in an informal way. For it is of the essence of good teaching that one should constantly be attempting to gauge the levels of pupils' learning in order to lead them on to further development. An understanding of the complexities of assessment is thus an important element in the teacher's professional armoury of skills.

In recent years, however, it has begun to loom larger than this, and it has become a central issue of debate because of the increased use of external forms of assessment as a major part of the policies and practices introduced with the National Curriculum. And this process, as we shall see, has changed the nature of assessment practice in schools, as the teachers' own assessments of their pupils have been overshadowed by those made through the externally framed Standard Assessment Tasks (SATs).

In particular, this practice has heralded a return to the outmoded habit of regarding assessment as a form of *measurement* rather than the essentially *judgemental* process which in reality it is. The term 'measurement' brings with it connotations of accuracy and precision, but it is plain to anyone who will look more closely at the matter that there is little accuracy or precision in most forms of educational assessment. And the degree of accuracy and precision varies inversely in relation to the complexity and sophistication of what is being assessed. It is easier to achieve when we are assessing relatively simplistic forms of attainment, but even then it is unlikely to be error-free.

And this feature of assessment becomes particularly crucial, and dangerous, when far-reaching decisions concerning a pupil's future, career or further educational provision are being made on the basis of such questionable data. The use of 11+ testing for the allocation of pupils to different forms of secondary education is the most infamous example of this. Hence, I have elsewhere (Kelly, 1992:5) described accuracy of measurement in education as 'a myth, a chimera, an attractive but totally fanciful conception', and have suggested that educational assessment

> must be recognised as being a highly imprecise activity at all but the most basic levels, and as being judgemental rather than metric in character, as requiring the making of sound professional judgements rather than of objective, mathematical measurements.
>
> (1992:5)

A second danger which we must note at the outset of our discussion is that of assessment coming to lead rather than to support curricular provision. As long ago as 1868, the Taunton Report was expressing a concern that any examination system would become directive of the curriculum and the same concern was voiced by the Beloe Report (SSEC, 1960). And it has long been accepted as a fact of secondary school life that the curriculum, especially in the upper school, is geared almost totally to the demands of external public examinations. This is one reason why the impact of National Curriculum testing has been less significant at that level.

This assessment-led or test-led form of curriculum has now been extended into the primary, the infant and even the nursery school, in spite of constant assurances from officialdom that assessment 'should be the servant, not the master of the curriculum' (DES, 1988:para.4; DES, 1989). In this context, it is not without significance that the first stage in the planning of the new policies, before the National Curriculum was itself designed, was the creation of a group to frame the assessment procedures – the Task Group on Assessment and Testing (TGAT).

We must further note that 'assessment, like evaluation, is not one but several things' (Eisner, 1993:224). It has a number of different uses, educational, administrative or political. Politically, as we have seen, it can be used as a mechanism for changing and controlling the curriculum. Administratively, it can be used to select pupils for different types and levels of schooling, the 'gate-keeping function' (Eisner, 1993:225), as with procedures for secondary school selection, or to grade them, often through the award of qualifications as with public examinations in schools and universities. Educationally, it can be used as a means of quality control, to maintain and/or raise standards, as a source of data for curriculum evaluation to improve the quality of provision, as a form of extrinsic motivation, and as a device for diagnosing the educational needs of individual pupils in order to plan the most effective curricular diet for them.

Two important things follow from this. First, it is crucial that the form of assessment we employ is matched to the particular purposes we have in mind. We will later note that this is equally crucial of evaluation procedures. And, second, there is again much scope for confusion, even distortion, if we do not make sure of this, if we are unclear of our purposes, if there is a mismatch between the purpose of the assessment and its nature, or if we seek to use one form to meet several disparate purposes. Hence it is important to begin by clarifying some of the different purposes to which assessment may be put.

Purposes of assessment

The major purposes of assessment are clearly set out by the TGAT Report (DES, 1988:para.23), and these are the purposes which it suggests that the National Curriculum assessment programme should be able to meet:

- *formative*, so that the positive achievements of a pupil may be recognised and discussed and the appropriate next steps may be planned;
- *diagnostic*, through which learning difficulties may be scrutinised and classified so that appropriate remedial help and guidance can be provided;
- *summative*, for the recording of the overall achievement of a pupil in a systematic way;
- *evaluative*, by means of which some aspects of the work of a school, an LEA or other discrete part of the educational service can be assessed and/or reported upon.

It is worth noting that the Report recommended that assessment should be summative only at Key Stage 4 (16+), at the point where, since the individual may be about to leave school or move on to further education, some summation of his/her achievements is likely to be valuable. At earlier stages, summative assessment was felt to be unnecessary, and possibly damaging. Summations are inappropriate before the end of a process; what is required in the course of it is evidence which will guide future planning – evidence either of positive factors in a pupil's progress (formative evidence) or of hindrances to that progress (diagnostic evidence).

> We recommend that the basis of the national assessment system be essentially formative, but designed also to indicate where there is need for more detailed diagnostic assessment. At age 16, however, it should incorporate assessment with summative functions.
>
> (DES, 1988:para.27)

The political decision, however, was that National Curriculum assessment should be summative at all stages (DES, 1989). And there could be no clearer indication that, as we suggested in Chapter 5, the main thrust of the assessment system is towards control of the school curriculum. For there can be no justification for summative assessment at 7+, 11+ and 14+ other than the desire to focus on the **evaluative** function of assessment, the evaluation of schools and LEAs through the publication of 'league-tables'. The argument that test results should be used '*summatively*' at ages 7, 11, 14 and 16 to inform parents about their child's progress' (DES, 1989:para.6.4) is again little more than rhetoric, since summative accounts are of little value to parents whose concern must be with future provision and support for their offspring.

Further, with that arrogance and lack of intellectualism characteristic of all the recent official documentation, we were told that the national system would achieve all of these purposes at the same time (DES, 1989:para.6.2) –

> The national assessment system will serve several purposes. It will be:
> **formative**
> **summative**
> **evaluative**
> **informative**
> helpful for **professional development**.

However, apart from the rather ludicrous appearance of this claim when seen in the context of the simplistic testing programme currently in operation, as the TGAT group indicated (DES, 1988:para.13), 'no system has yet been constructed that meets all the criteria of *progression, moderation, formative* and *criterion-referenced* assessment', so that it had seen its own task as being 'to devise such a system afresh' (DES, 1988:para.13). In the event, its recommendations went largely ignored (Black, 1993), as the simplistic nature of current practices illustrates.

Whether such a system could ever be devised, then, is an issue to which we are unlikely to see an answer in the foreseeable future. It is likely, however, that it could not, at least while assessment is defined in terms of testing. The main reason for this is that the summative function of testing can be defined 'only in relation to fixed, agreed and common notions of what all pupils must be exposed to and must learn' (Kelly, 1992:10). If we are to go beyond this, we need to explore the possibilities of more sophisticated styles of assessment. And it is to such an exploration that we now turn.

Styles of assessment

Criterion-referenced and norm-referenced assessment

Much has been made recently of the distinction between criterion-referenced and norm-referenced assessment. And the national testing programme is in this respect in tune with the recommendations of the TGAT Report in attempting to be criterion-referenced.

In criterion-referenced assessment the criteria of assessment, the standards of 'measurement', are derived from the knowledge to be assimilated. Hence, within each subject of the National Curriculum, we find attainment targets selected by reference to that subject and its profile components and defined in statutory orders. These attainment targets therefore constitute the criteria by which the testing is conducted. The object of the testing procedures is to ascertain the degree to which pupils have attained the targets set for them.

Norm-referencing, on the other hand, seeks to identify its criteria of assessment not from the bodies of knowledge to be assimilated but by reference to what is considered to be the norm, the average performance of children at any given age. Thus the comparison which is sought is between pupils of similar ages, not between levels of attainment within subjects and the individual's performance.

It has been claimed (Kelly, 1992) that both in theory and certainly in practice this distinction is difficult, if not impossible, to maintain. For it would be foolish to set attainment targets without reference to what might be considered norms of attainment; and, conversely, impossible to establish norms without reference to levels of attainments within areas of learning.

It must be noted, however, why it is important for those who have framed current policies to eschew all suggestion of norm-referencing.

For to acknowledge that the national testing system is norm-referenced, even though it clearly is, would be to concede that it is competitive and thus elitist, that in part its function is to grade and select. Again, we must note too that such norm-referencing must be an integral part of any system of testing which seeks to be summative. To pretend that it need not be is to attempt to conceal the political realities of current practice.

Ipsative assessment

It has been suggested, therefore, that a more useful and positive distinction is between both of these styles of assessment and that which has come to be known as 'ipsative' assessment. Here the central criterion of assessment is the individual's own previous levels of attainment. He/ she is assessed not against subject attainment targets nor against the performance of peers but against his/her own earlier achievements. It might be argued, therefore, that this style of assessment is related to that curriculum ideology we described in Chapter 4 as 'developmental', and that its absence from current practices is further evidence of the fact that the National Curriculum reflects a quite different ideology. It has been argued (Nuttall, 1989:55), however, that 'the very notion of progress through levels implies an ipsative framework as much as it does a criterion-referenced one'. If our concern with *progression* is serious, then our focus must be on the progress being made by each individual. Again, therefore, we see how the insistence on a summative function for assessment at every stage hinders, even invalidates, other more pupil-focused purposes.

What may be even more important is that, in considering an ipsative style of assessment, as in concentrating our attention on its formative and diagnostic functions, we find ourselves moving away from the notion than it can be achieved by the use of simplistic forms of external, 'pencil-and-paper' tests. If assessment is to have a genuinely valuable educational role, it must be more sophisticated than that. In particular, it must rely more on the assessments made by teachers of their own pupils. For these first-hand and personal assessments, if made with a proper professionalism, are of much more value in meeting the demands of formative, diagnostic and ipsative assessment. It is, however, the political demands for summation and for tighter external control of schools that has caused the rejection of teacher assessment or at least a subordination of its role to that of external tests.

Profiling

Discussion of the role which teacher assessment might play in supporting educational progress leads naturally to a consideration of that style of assessment known as 'profiling' which was gaining increasing favour and momentum until current policies took over.

Before the arrival of the current testing programme, there were numerous attempts to develop systems of profiling or records of achievement. The now defunct Inner London Education Authority (ILEA) pioneered a Primary Language Record which traced the linguistic development of pupils in a highly sophisticated manner. And, especially at secondary level, there were a number of profiling systems, seeking to create records of the achievements of individual pupils in a range of dimensions, both to produce positive profiles of those pupils in whose cases a record merely of public examinations passed would be unimpressive and to provide prospective employers with more useful information than examination grades. Indeed, so successful was this development that we were promised a national system of Records of Achievement, to be in place by 1990, this promise being subsequently withdrawn, ostensibly in order not to overburden teachers at a time when they were being required to meet the demands of the newly created National Curriculum and its testing programme, in reality because such an approach to assessment was not in tune with the policy of control through testing and inspection which was about to be put in place.

For profiling systems depend to a great extent on teacher assessment, ipsative assessment and even an element of pupil self-assessment, and only partly on testing and public examinations. They can of course include the results of externally imposed, standardized assessment tests, but they seek to embrace much more than that. The concern is that the profile be holistic, that it should provide a description and an account of all aspects of a pupil's achievement, that it be more than a largely meaningless aggregate of grades. The intention is that the profile be formative even at the final, summative level of school-leaving, in order to guide pupil, parents and potential employers towards a productive future for the individual. Thus, 'in principle at least they [profiling systems] take a rather more dynamic stance' (Torrance, 1989:187) than, for example, graded tests which 'are clearly tailored to a mechanistic, if not static, view of learning' (1989:187). They adopt a more open, evolutionary, democratic view of knowledge and learning than the National Curriculum permits. And they recognize the point we made at the beginning of this chapter that educational assessment is a matter of judgement rather than measurement, so that they seek to offer descriptions of a pupil's attainment and performance, along with professional comments on these, rather than merely recording grades or marks which are often largely meaningless.

They also acknowledge that there is an essential interplay between assessment and curriculum planning, especially if we are to avoid assessment-led planning. This again is something which escaped the notice of the architects of current policies when they began by establishing a body for planning the curriculum, the National Curriculum Council (NCC) at York and a body to plan its assessment, the School Examinations and Assessment Council (SEAC), at Notting Hill in London. Eventually, that nonsense was corrected, but the fact that this is how the planning began is further evidence of its lack of sophistication.

Graded tests

However, an approach to assessment which displays these characteristics, desirable as it may seem to be when viewed from an educational perspective, is clearly linked to a curricular ideology which leans more towards the developmental than those objectives or content models of curriculum which we considered in Chapter 3. It is thus inappropriate in the context of a curriculum which, as we saw there, is firmly rooted in both. We noted at the beginning of this chapter how important it is for the form of assessment to be matched to the form of the curriculum. In this respect at least, therefore, the architects of current policies have got it right and their technicist approaches to curriculum are matched by similarly technicist approaches to assessment. 'Planning and assessment are integral to successful teaching. Planning identifies learning objectives and assessment reveals how far children have acquired learning' (SCAA, 1997b:3). Again we note the lack of any concept of education which might go beyond the learning of preselected content or the achievement of predetermined objectives. We thus have further evidence of the underpinning ideology of this curriculum, whatever elaborate rhetoric is used to disguise this. For, as Harry Torrance (1989) has argued most persuasively, the choice existed for them between graded tests and profiling; and the choice they made indicates clearly the political considerations which carried the day.

Yet, there is convincing evidence, especially from other countries, that such an approach, while it might be effective in terms of establishing and maintaining central control of the curriculum, does not have the potential claimed for it to raise standards in any genuinely educational sense. In fact the opposite effect seems to be the more likely outcome.

> Much of the evidence from other countries suggests that attainment targets, when designed for a whole population of school pupils of a given age, are more likely to decrease expectations, have a harmful and restricting influence on teaching approaches, and generally lower educational standards rather than raising them.
> (Murphy and Torrance, 1988:105)

And Paul Black, who headed the TGAT group, in berating the use to which that group's work was put, or rather not put, recounts evidence gleaned from his work in the USA (Black, 1993:63–4):

> I have spent more than 2 of the last 4 months in the USA. The practice of assessment there is undergoing a rapid change. The use of short external standardised tests, almost always multiple-choice tests, has been widespread for several decades, and the technical expertise in developing these has reached a far higher level than anywhere else in the world. However, many of the States are now abandoning them, because it is evident that they have done almost nothing to improve education.

In part, the reason for this is that, as Robin Alexander (1984:36–7) pointed out, 'assessment via *formal* testing or other publicly verified procedures can only deal with very limited and specific areas of school work and is much less important than the continuous *informal* (even unconscious) evaluation of the pupil by the teacher'. Formal testing assesses levels of teaching and learning; it is far less effective in assessing *educational* progress.

All of this evidence, along with the experience which had been growing as a result of work on quite different lines, experiments with forms of assessment of a much more sophisticated kind, adds to the conviction that the true agenda for the curriculum planners who adopt and adhere to practices and policies which are outdated, ineffective and, indeed, educationally harmful is not the improvement of education but, as we have suggested, something more sinister – the control of the curriculum for purposes other than educational advance.

New approaches to assessment are badly needed. Educationally, the need is for forms of assessment which will be capable of providing everyone, parents and employers as well as teachers, with far more sophisticated and complex information about the progress of individuals through what is after all a highly complex process, that of becoming educated. Eisner (1993:226) has suggested, for example, that 'the tasks we use to assess students should reveal how students go about solving a problem, not only the solutions they formulate', and 'new assessment tasks should make possible more than one acceptable solution to a problem and more than one acceptable answer to a question' (1993:229). Similar claims were being made, for example by Jerome Bruner, two decades or more ago.

And forms of assessment, assessment tasks, have been developed which can offer this level of sophistication and this range of information. They can be seen, perhaps most extensively, within the projects sponsored by the Assessment of Performance Unit (APU), and in the Standard Assessment Tasks (SATs) which were initially developed (often by those experienced in and familiar with the work of the APU) for the testing programme at 7+, 11+ and 14+. These were rejected as being too complex. Their replacement by more simple forms indicates *ipso facto* that these must be correspondingly limited in their value. Sophisticated and informative schemes of assessment are available, then, but there is no will to use them. The choice of simplistic forms of assessment, however, the use of simple testing, has not been accompanied by any acknowledgement of the loss in value of the pseudo-information they provide. They continue to be regarded as reliable and as sufficiently informative to be used for the production of 'league-tables' and for the public identification and pillorying of 'failing schools'.

Finally, we note again that the only explanation of this can be that the prime purpose of the testing programme is not educational advance but curriculum control. The adoption of more complex forms of assessment would imply an acceptance of a more complex view of curriculum. New approaches to assessment would imply a different curriculum ideology, a competence-based rather than a performance-based modality (Bernstein, 1996). There was thus never any possibility that the proposals of the TGAT Report would be accepted. Their underlying curriculum ideology was incompatible with that of the new curriculum they were seeking to assess. And, as we have seen, there has been no political will to provide the kind of curriculum those proposals presupposed.

Again, therefore, the picture is one of, on the one hand, extensive development in both understanding and practice derived from that understanding, and, on the other hand, a rejection of that understanding in favour of practices which are often so limited as to be counter-productive to educational advance in anything but the most slender sense. And, further, again it is not always merely rejection; sometimes it is positive degeneration, as in the present case where assessment has become testing and its prime purpose to control the curriculum, what Patricia Broadfoot (1996) calls 'assessment for system control', rather than to secure educational advance or a raising of standards, except in a severely restricted meaning of that term.

Sadly, a similar picture will emerge when we now turn to consider what has happened to evaluation theory.

Evaluation theory

Most of that body of understanding which has come to be known as evaluation theory has been gleaned from attempts to evaluate existing curricular practices or, more often, innovatory curricula, such as those developed by the Schools Council, so that it has been generated as a by-product, albeit an essential by-product, of attempts at curriculum development – as the fourth element of that simple curriculum planning model of Ralph Tyler (1949) which we noted in Chapter 1. In short, it has been closely linked to the notion that the curriculum should be subject to continous evaluation as an essential element of continuous change and development.

There has often of course been the additional concern for 'value for money', especially, for example, in the evaluation of the Schools Council's projects, and, while it is clear that that brings a political flavour into the brew, it has until relatively recently been a slight flavour only. In the last two decades or so, however, in the United Kingdom, in the context of that politicization of curriculum which has occurred, that flavour has been intensified and the focus of curriculum evaluation has shifted from curriculum development to teacher accountability. It has come to be seen as nothing more than the measurement of teacher competence and school effectiveness, largely, perhaps entirely, through the assessment of pupil performance. Hence, as we shall see, the curriculum itself is no longer evaluated; what is called curriculum evaluation has become little more than an assessment of the teachers' effectiveness in 'delivering' it; and, as we have already seen, evaluation has thus degenerated into school inspections.

Thus some important distinctions, especially those between evaluation and assessment, have come to be blurred and we see yet again the kind of conceptual confusion, with all its unsatisfactory consequences for practice, which we have noted in several other contexts. Again too, therefore, it becomes necessary to reassert the insights and understandings which earlier research and experience generated.

What is curriculum evaluation?

Curriculum evaluation is clearly the process by which we attempt to gauge the value and effectiveness of any particular piece of educational activity – whether a national project or a piece of work undertaken with our own pupils. On such a definition, it might seem *prima facie* to be a relatively simple matter. However, as we saw in our earlier discussion of pupil assessment, the first complexity we must note is that which arises from an awareness of the variety of purposes that one can have in making an evaluation of anything, and the range of different conceptions one can have of such an activity, each of which may be perfectly suitable for some area of curriculum development. What might we be doing in evaluating a curriculum project or a particular activity? We might be doing no more than attempting to establish that the programme is in fact happening, since we have already commented several times on the gap that often exists between planning and practice. Or we might merely be attempting to ascertain if we have achieved what we set out to achieve. On the other hand, we might be endeavouring to compare a particular project or approach with other alternative methods, procedures or programmes in the same area. Is it really better than what it has replaced or than other new alternatives that are offered? Again, we might be concerned to do no more than to ascertain if it is acceptable to teachers and/or pupils (Schools Council, 1974a). Then again, we might be attempting to assess whether we have got our goals or our principles right.

In short, the purposes of any scheme of evaluation will vary according to the purposes, views, conceptions of the person or persons making the evaluation. We noted, when discussing the problems of dissemination in Chapter 5, that the conception of any curriculum project will vary according to the angle from which one views it, whether as planner, teacher, pupil, parent or whoever. Each will have his or her own conception or definition of the project (Shipman, 1972, 1973). For the same reason, each will have his or her own view of the purposes of evaluation and his or her own interpretation of the data which it produces. And so different people will make different uses of those data, some using them as a device for continuing course development, some for decisions concerning the allocation of resources, some for action of a more overtly political kind and so on.

Thus the selection of which information to collect, the range of purposes one may have in collecting it, the variety of uses to which it may be put and the range of the decisions it may lead to, make of evaluation 'a multi-faceted phenomenon encompassing a range of diverse properties' (Hamilton, 1976:11).

As with assessment, an important distinction which arises from the need to be clear about the purposes of our evaluation is the contrast between 'formative' and 'summative' evaluation (Scriven, 1967). 'Summative' evaluation is concerned with appraisal of the work, it is a form of 'pay-off' evaluation (Scriven, 1967) and is concerned primarily to ascertain if the goals of the course have been achieved. 'Formative' evaluation, on the other hand, is concerned to provide feedback (Scriven, 1967; Stenhouse, 1975) and thus a base for course improvement, modification and future planning. As such, it may occur post-course, but it is more likely to take the form of continuous in-course monitoring of both goals or principles and procedures. It will, therefore, involve a number of dimensions, since it will be attempting to assess the extent of the achievement of the purposes of the project and to discover and analyse barriers to their achievement (Stenhouse, 1975). It may also be concerned to contribute to a modification of those purposes themselves, and that takes us to a second important distinction.

For we must note that the questions which may be asked in any process of evaluation are of at least two logically discrete kinds (White, 1971). Some of them are empirical questions which, like the investigations of a body such as the Consumers' Association, explore the relative merits of a project or approach in terms of its costs, its effectiveness and so on. For questions of this kind we are looking, therefore, for relevant empirical data. Other questions, however, are asked in the process of evaluating a curriculum which are not of this kind but raise those difficult issues of value that we can never get far from in any discussion of education. These are the questions about ends rather than means, which ask whether the purposes of the activity are the right purposes, whether the experience being offered to pupils is of educational value, whether the curriculum is good in itself rather than merely being 'delivered' effectively. Here the concern is to evaluate the goals or the underlying principles of the curriculum itself and not merely the effectiveness of its procedures.

Thus we see that a number of distinctions have been made to reflect those different purposes that we identified earlier, so that we can observe the emergence of several different models of, or approaches to, curriculum evaluation.

It is also important to recognize that the model of evaluation we adopt must match the model of curriculum planning we have adopted (Tawney, 1973). Otherwise there will be mismatch and distortion. In particular, the adoption of a model of evaluation which is based on the prespecification of curriculum objectives will have the effect of distorting an approach to the curriculum which is procedural or developmental, not least because its criteria of evaluation will not reflect the purposes of the planners or the teachers. It will be comparable to seeking to discover how many goals Donald Bradman scored in his last test match at the Oval.

However, too often the assumption has been made, and continues to be made, that curriculum evaluation is possible only if curriculum objectives are prestated. Early discussion of curriculum evaluation certainly tended to be located well within the context of the simple behavioural objectives model of curriculum. Ralph Tyler, for example, is quite explicit on this point. 'The process of evaluation is essentially the process of determining to what extent the educational objectives are actually being realized by the program of curriculum and instruction' (1949:105–6).

A good deal of both the theory and the practice of curriculum evaluation, therefore, as we saw in Chapter 5 was the case with many of the Schools Council's projects, has been set within the context of an objectives-based curriculum model, and for this reason evaluation has been seen as centrally concerned to help with the framing and subsequent modification of objectives, the assessment of the suitability of the learning experiences to the achievement of the objectives set and the measurement of the degree to which the prestated objectives are being or have been attained. The demand for accountability to which we have already referred also tends to encourage the use of this kind of model, as we can see from current policies.

Thus, although there may seem to be a *prima facie* case for the prespecification of objectives if adequate procedures of evaluation are to be found, we must pause to ask whether evaluation becomes quite impossible if we are not prepared to start with a statement of objectives and, if it does not, what differences does this necessitate in our methods of evaluation?

Developed forms of curriculum evaluation

First, we might perhaps note a weakness in the simple objectives model approach. For, a proper evaluation requires a proper level of understanding of the process that is being evaluated (Stenhouse, 1975). A simple assessment of the attainment of objectives is concerned only with the success or failure of the programme; it is not concerned essentially with an understanding of it. It assesses without explaining (Stenhouse, 1975). Thus the value of such evaluation is limited, since it can offer little feedback, if indeed it offers any at all. It is seldom helpful to know in black-and-white terms whether a project or activity has succeeded or not. In fact, it will seldom be possible to make that kind of simple assessment. What is needed is a far greater complexity of data which can provide a basis for present and future curriculum development. This in turn implies the generation of evaluation procedures which do more than attempt to measure success or failure and which, in order to offer more, must be based upon a full understanding of the educational process itself. In short, we must note that evaluation, like assessment, must be seen as an act of judgement rather than of measurement.

And we must also note that, if we are dealing with an approach to education or a project for which the prespecification of objectives is deemed inappropriate, any evaluation based on such a model will be equally inappropriate, will add to the confusion and may have quite disastrous consequences (Weiss and Rein, 1969), not least in distorting the curriculum itself. We noted in Chapter 4 that many teachers, especially in primary schools, have felt that an objectives model is unsuited to their work. We saw too that some project teams have begun their planning from the belief that, at least for some areas of the curriculum such as the humanities or social education, an objectives model is not suitable. Any attempt, therefore, to evaluate the work of such teachers or such projects in terms of what are thought to be their objectives must fail, either by providing inadequate, unsatisfactory and irrelevant data or by persuading teachers to alter their approach to the work in such a way as to change its whole conception and scope or by distorting the work itself through a mismatch between the curriculum model and the evaluation model.

On the other hand, it must be recognized that without evaluation there can be no proper base for course development or, at the individual level, for the development and improvement of our own work.

Hence others, who have been engaged in curriculum development or teaching activities for which they have felt the prespecification of objectives to be unsuited, have recognized the necessity to design procedures by which these could be evaluated and have thus faced squarely the problems presented by the evaluation of a programme whose objectives cannot be stated in advance and whose evaluation procedures, therefore, must be based on a different, more sophisticated view of what the whole process of curriculum evaluation is. Thus a more sophisticated, developed view has begun to emerge from the work they have done. As we have seen in several other contexts, a rejection of the simplistic, product-based, aims-and-objectives target-centred approach to curriculum planning leads to major advances in our understanding of the complexities of the educational process – here in relation to curriculum evaluation.

We saw in Chapter 3 that a number of curriculum projects rejected the aims-and-objectives planning model as unsuitable to the developments they were concerned to promote. These projects, therefore, immediately encountered difficulties in evaluating their work, since it could no longer be evaluated simply in terms of its effectiveness in achieving its objectives. In this kind of context, evaluation had to go beyond an assessment of effectiveness and embrace also questions of value. The concern was not to assess the extent to which certain purposes had been achieved but rather to evaluate the aims and purposes themselves of such an approach to the organization of the curriculum.

Thus, for example, the Schools Council's Integrated Studies Project adopted a 'horizontal' curriculum model 'in which aims, learning experiences and material were developed concurrently' (Tawney, 1973:9). As a consequence of this, evaluation was seen not as a process for measuring the results of an experiment but as a device for continuously monitoring the project as it developed and constantly reviewing its aims, the packs of material that were produced and the practical problems that arose when it was introduced into schools. What emerged was not so much objective scientific data as a growing collection of experience and understanding of the issues and problems involved, which offered teachers, therefore, not a curriculum package as such, but a set of principles and a body of experience to which they could refer and from which they might profit in developing their own schemes.

The most interesting project from the point of view of evaluation procedures, however, is the Humanities Curriculum Project, to which we have already referred on several occasions. We saw in Chapter 3 that this project eschewed the idea of the prespecification of objectives more vigorously and more completely than any other. For, as we saw there, being concerned to encourage pupils of secondary age to explore issues within the humanities and through discussion of all kinds to reach their own conclusions, the project team saw from the outset that to prespecify learning outcomes would be to contradict their own first principle and to pre-empt the very questions they wanted to raise.

However, 'in an approach which is not based on objectives, there is no ready-made niche for the evaluator' (MacDonald, 1973:82). Furthermore, the team also felt it inappropriate to evaluate a curriculum project during its trial period so that, although Barry MacDonald, the project's evaluator, was appointed during the developmental stage of the project, his job was to prepare evaluation procedures for use after the project was firmly established in schools.

Both of these factors combined to present a particularly difficult set of problems in evaluation (Stenhouse, 1975), difficulties which were acknowledged but which nevertheless were regarded as being there to be overcome. 'The evaluation then had to cope with an attempt at creative curriculum development with variable components, obvious disturbance potential and a novel approach' (MacDonald, 1973:83).

To meet these difficulties, Barry MacDonald adopted a 'holistic' approach. 'The aim of that stage [i.e. during the trial period] was simply to describe the work of the project in a form that would make it accessible to public and professional judgement' (MacDonald, 1973:83). It was not possible to define in advance what data would be significant, so that all data had initially to be accepted. 'In view of the potential significance of so many aspects of the project, a complete description of its experience was needed initially, as was awareness of a full range of relevant phenomena' (1973:83). Selection within and between such data could be made only later when the criteria of such selection began to emerge from the continuing experience. 'Evaluation design, strategies and methods would evolve in response to the project's impact on the educational system and the types of evaluation problems which that impact would throw up' (1973:83).

In this spirit the work of the thirty-six schools which experimented with the project was monitored, all possible techniques being used to collect a wide variety of data. Then attention was narrowed to eight schools which became the subjects of detailed case studies. The procedure appears to have been entirely justified since this method resulted in the acquisition of data and a recognition of phenomena that would never have been expected or envisaged in advance of the project's arrival in the classroom (MacDonald, 1973).

Furthermore, there also emerged from this holistic approach a number of principles of significance for curriculum planning as a whole rather than merely for the evaluation of this particular project, principles which reflect in an interesting way some of the general points that have recently been made about curriculum development.

For example, it emerged very clearly that, as we saw in Chapter 5, what actually happens when a project is put into practice varies considerably according to the local conditions prevailing in each school, whereas more simple evaluation procedures tend to assume that there is or should be very little variation between schools. Furthermore, the variations in the reaction of different schools led to the conclusion that the judgements of the teachers in them are crucially important, every bit as important as those of the project designers, in making decisions concerning the curriculum of any individual school. It also became obvious that a gap often yawned between the conception of a project held by its developers and that held by those implementing it in the school.

And it became apparent that, as we have just seen, curriculum innovations and, indeed, all educational activities have many unexpected but clearly valuable results, many 'unintended learning outcomes', and that these are not, and cannot be, allowed for in simple evaluation procedures or, as we saw in Chapter 3, in simple objectives-based planning models.

What was learnt from these processes of evaluation was seen, then, not so much as contributing to some statement of the project's effectiveness but as providing information for 'consumers', those who have the responsibility of making the decisions concerning the curriculum. Four main groups of these were identified – sponsors, local authorities, schools and examining boards and the task of evaluation was seen as to provide them with the kind of understanding of the problems of curriculum development that would help them to make their decisions (MacDonald, 1973).

The same general approach was adopted by those who proposed the notions of evaluation as 'portrayal' (Stake, 1972), as 'illuminative' (Parlett and Hamilton, 1975) and as 'responsive' (Hamilton, 1976). Portrayal evaluation is seen as an attempt not to analyse the results of a project in terms of its prespecified goals but to offer a comprehensive portrayal of the programme which will view it as a whole and endeavour to reveal its total substance. Similarly, the primary concern of illuminative evaluation is 'with description and interpretation rather than measurement and prediction' (Parlett and Hamilton, 1975:88). Such an approach to evaluation has three stages: 'investigators observe, inquire further and then seek to explain' (1975:92). As a result of this threefold procedure an 'information profile' is put together which is then available for those who need to make decisions about the project.

> Illuminative evaluation thus concentrates on the information-gathering rather than the decision-making component of evaluation. The task is to provide a comprehensive understanding of the complex reality (or realities) surrounding the project: in short, to 'illuminate'. In his [or her] report, therefore, the evaluator aims to sharpen discussion, disentangle complexities, isolate the significant from the trivial, and raise the level of sophistication of debate.
>
> (1975:99)

> 'Responsive' evaluation too seeks to respond 'to the wide range of questions asked about an innovation and is not trapped inside the intentions of the programme-builders'.
>
> (Hamilton, 1976:39)

What has emerged, then, as a result of the work of projects of this kind is a new and more sophisticated model of curriculum evaluation – a process model – which does not content itself with attempting to measure the results of one project in simple and often consequently unhelpful terms but sets out to provide continuous feedback to all of those concerned with the planning and implementation of this particular project and of curriculum development generally. Its concern is to disclose the meaning of the curriculum as much as to assess its worth (Stenhouse, 1975), and, in order to do this, it attempts to document 'a broad spectrum of phenomena, judgements and responses' (Hamilton, 1976:38). Such a form of evaluation is essentially formative and its main concern is to guide the continuing development of the curriculum. Furthermore, the aim will be to do this not only in relation to one particular project but to offer illumination for curriculum development as a whole. The holistic approach to curriculum evaluation implies that we do not restrict ourselves to a narrow canvas, in any sense.

Thus curriculum evaluation becomes part of curriculum research. As Lawrence Stenhouse (1975:122) said, 'Evaluation should as it were lead development and be integrated with it. Then the conceptual distinction between development and evaluation is destroyed and the two merge as research.' In general, all evaluation procedures see all curriculum planning and approaches as hypotheses to be tested (Taba, 1962), but the holistic view sees evaluation as part of a continuous programme of research and development, and recognizes that the curriculum is, or should be, a dynamic and continuously evolving entity. It thus encourages the adoption of a more sophisticated model not only of curriculum evaluation but also of curriculum planning and one which may be more suited to the notion of education as a process whose ends cannot be seen beyond itself.

Not only is it possible, then, to make an evaluation of a non-objectives curriculum; it also seems to lead to a more fully developed view of the role of evaluation in curriculum development. The procedural principles which we suggested in Chapter 4 provided a better basis for an educational activity than prespecified objectives can and should be monitored, and this monitoring will give us continuous feedback in our efforts constantly to modify and improve our practices. Again, as we also saw in Chapter 4, such a model reflects much more accurately than a simple means-end model what happens in practice when we make an evaluation of any educational activity. For we are seldom content merely to measure outcomes and, when we do, we experience uneasy feelings that we have somehow missed the educational point of the activity. And indeed we have, since we have failed to evaluate the goals of the activity and have obtained no data upon which to make judgements concerning its educational worth. Genuine education cannot be evaluated by reference to its outcomes but only by its processes.

One final point needs to be made about this approach to curriculum evaluation. We have seen that its concern is not to make decisions but rather to provide information for decision-makers. It is thus a highly suitable form of evaluation for school-based curriculum development and equally for the evaluation, and self-evaluation, of the work of individual teachers. In fact, the emergence of these more sophisticated techniques of evaluation itself contributed much to that shift towards school-based development, and, indeed, to action research and the notion of 'the teacher as researcher', which we noted in Chapter 5.

It thus highlights the crucial role of the teacher in any properly effective form of curriculum evaluation and it reinforces the point we made earlier that evaluation theory is as important to the individual teacher for the making of those day-by-day, minute-by-minute evaluations of his or her own work as it is to project directors or others concerned with monitoring or developing the curriculum on a national scale. Thus the teacher must be involved in evaluating his or her own work, since, without that, it is difficult to know how that work could ever improve; and there is much in what has been learnt about evaluation from the work of large-scale projects which can add to his or her understanding, offer insights into the complexities of educational evaluation at any level and provide techniques which can be used in each individual school or classroom.

For this reason it is important that teachers should continue to be provided with techniques and understandings which will enable them to evaluate their own work as professionals, even if they are discouraged from evaluating that of those who currently seek to control them in that work. Action research of some kind is essential for professional development, as is the notion of 'the teacher as researcher'.

For the same reason, it is important not to lose sight of what we have learned about teacher self-appraisal, about the involvement of pupils in curriculum evaluation through processes like the 'triangulation' of the Ford Teaching Project (FTP) and about school self-evaluation. The FTP suggested that subjectivity of evaluation might be avoided if the accounts which teachers gave of their work were to be checked by reference to other sources. The team thus developed a procedure which it called 'multiple interview' or 'triangulation' in which accounts were obtained not only from the teacher but also from the pupils and from an independent observer.

And, in this connection it is worth adding a brief comment on some of the schemes which emerged for school self-evaluation (Elliott, G., 1981; Elliott, J., 1981; Rodger and Richardson, 1985). Such a development is certainly highly desirable, although it now has a much more limited effect on the curriculum and, indeed, the quality of individual schools than it might have had, and it certainly represents what is potentially a more likely means of raising standards than the evaluation of schools conducted from the outside by the agents of Ofsted. It was an attempt to move away from these grosser, more simplistic forms of evaluation to something more sophisticated, to formative approaches, to evaluation with a qualitative rather than a largely quantitative emphasis, to process evaluation and especially to a proper involvement of the teachers themselves in the activity.

For to avoid over-simplification and to achieve the breadth of understanding necessary to make a useful evaluation of the wider aspects of the curriculum, any external evaluator needs to get inside the curriculum. Any evaluator needs to understand the complexities of what he or she is evaluating or judging and that kind of understanding can seldom be satisfactorily achieved from outside the activity; some attempt must be made to get on the inside and to evaluate what is to be evaluated on its own terms. Again, experience of Ofsted inspections suggests that these do not always attempt this but are often content to make their evaluations not in the terms of the curricular offerings themselves but according to the political criteria they are increasingly required to apply. This must, therefore, cast doubt on the *educational* value of those exercises.

This clearly leads us to a consideration of the political dimension of evaluation.

The politicization of curriculum evaluation

What has been said so far reveals the major strides which have been made in our understanding of curriculum evaluation, along with its relation to curriculum planning, development and, indeed, implementation, over a considerable period of time and through a process of painstaking research, both empirical and conceptual. It will also be clear that this research has taken place in a context in which the main concern has been with educational advance and improvement. It is important now to consider what is currently occurring in today's rather different context, not only because this will reveal perhaps the best evidence we have of the fact that those current policies choose to ignore the lessons of such research and the understandings and insights it has led to, but also to identify the implications of these policies in respect of curriculum evaluation and their consequent impact on the experiences children will have in schools.

The politicization of the processes of curriculum evaluation, like that of pupil assessment, and, indeed, of all other aspects of curriculum planning, has led, as it must, to an arresting of the development of our understanding of the process, a loss of important professional expertise and thus a reduction in the quality of educational provision. It might be argued further that there has been not only an arresting of this developmental process but, worse, a return to less enlightened practices, a degeneration in both theory and practice.

For this process of politicization has led to a blocking of progress towards 'democratic' forms of evaluation and a corresponding embracing and adoption of forms which are 'bureaucratic' and even 'autocratic' (MacDonald, 1975).

These distinctions are offered by Barry MacDonald from a recognition that evaluation is a political activity and the styles he describes represent several different ways in which that activity can be carried out. 'Bureaucratic evaluation is an unconditional service to those government agencies which have major control over the allocation of educational resources. The evaluator accepts the values of those who hold office, and offers information which will help to accomplish their policy objectives' (1975:133). This definition describes most effectively the current practices of Ofsted. 'Autocratic evaluation is a conditional service to those government agencies which have major control over the allocation of educational resources. It offers external validation of policy in exchange for compliance with its recommendations' (1975:133). Nothing could more clearly define the current role of the Teacher Training Agency (TTA).

'Democratic' evaluation, on the other hand, is defined as

> an information service to the community about the characteristics of an educational programme. It recognises value pluralism and seeks to represent a range of interests in its issue formulation. The basic value is an informed citizenry, and the evaluator acts as a broker in exchanges of information between differing groups . . . the evaluator has no concept of information misuse . . . The key concepts of democratic evaluation are 'confidentiality', 'negotiation' and 'accessibility'. The key justificatory concept is 'the right to know'.
>
> (1975:134)

It will be clear that this is the only form of evaluation that will facilitate that kind of continuous adaptation at the level of the individual school and the individual teacher which this book is concerned to argue is the only route to the proper development of the curriculum. If the curriculum is to develop in any genuine sense, it must be evaluated by procedures grounded in principles of this kind. It will also be clear that it is a form of evaluation which requires the fullest participation of the teachers themselves.

It will be equally plain, however, that in the United Kingdom we have experienced a significant shift in the style of educational evaluation and in its main forms and purposes.

For, this is a form of evaluation which raises important political questions concerning the control of the curriculum and its decision-making processes. The major thrust of 'process' forms of evaluation is identical with that of school-based forms of curriculum development, since its direction is away from external control and evaluation towards the view that the teachers themselves must have a central involvement in both processes. It thus raises important questions about who should conduct the evaluation procedures.

It will now be clear why this form of evaluation, like the curriculum model which spawned it and its matching approaches to assessment, has been rejected by those who have planned the current system of school evaluation. They do not favour this form of curriculum, and they do not want teachers or schools themselves to be involved in a process of evaluation which might lead to changes in the curriculum being offered. For all of these are inimical to direct, centralized control.

This in turn has led to a further crucial form of deterioration. For what has been lost in this shift from 'democratic' to 'bureaucratic' and 'autocratic' systems of evaluation is that major dimension of curriculum evaluation which we noted earlier, the evaluation of the value, the merits and the goals of the curriculum. For these latter forms of evaluation, at least as they are currently practised through school inspections, focus entirely on the effectiveness of the 'delivery' of the centrally determined curriculum, and no questions are asked about its merits. Indeed, there is every discouragement to ask or address questions of this kind. Yet, if we are to make a genuinely *educational* evaluation, we need to ask questions, which again are value questions, about the worth (or value) of the activity or the innovation, not merely those methodological questions which relate to the effectiveness with which teachers 'get it across'. We need to explore not only whether the curriculum is being 'delivered' effectively but also – and more crucially – whether it is *worth* 'delivering'. And we need to do this in order to effect justifiable change and improvement. This important distinction is being lost altogether in current policies and practices, whose question marks do not go deep enough. And so there is no longer any basis for change, development or improvement in what is offered, except at the level of methodology.

This is illustrated most clearly by the the fact that a major, perhaps **the** major, source of data for the evaluation of schools and teachers is now pupil assessment. For data gleaned from assessments of pupil performance can tell us nothing about the worth or value of the kinds of performance we make our central concern or thus of the curriculum which pupils are being offered (although they might, as a by-product, tell us much about the reaction and the response of many pupils to that curriculum). Thus, an approach to evaluation which restricts itself to a concern with the assessment of pupil performance, while it may tell us much about the effectiveness of schools and teachers in 'delivering' the National Curriculum, will offer no evidence at all which might have a bearing on whether that curriculum is worth 'delivering' or, indeed, about whether the attainment targets set for the assessment programme are reasonable, let alone valuable. Again, therefore, we must note that what we have here is a return to those simplistic forms of evaluation whose inadequacies have been fully exposed and which, as we have seen, because of those inadequacies had been supplanted by more sophisticated techniques of a kind designed to support the continuing development of the curriculum. And again we note that the thrust is political rather than educational, and that the prime concern is with teacher appraisal and accountability rather than with curriculum development or improvement.

In fact, it suggests, as we saw in Chapter 5, that the evaluation procedures, based as they are on testing and inspection, are to be used more for the control of the curriculum than for its development, more for manipulating the education system than for raising its quality or its standards. And it reflects a major shift from what, as we saw earlier, has been described as a 'democratic' style of evaluation to that which has been called 'bureaucratic' or even 'autocratic' (MacDonald, 1975).

Thus we have seen **curriculum** evaluation replaced by **school** evaluation. And the responsibility for it has been placed in the hands not of professionals, the teachers themselves and others who seek to understand their work, but of inspectors who in general make their evaluations not in a judgemental style, according to their understandings of the process they are seeking to evaluate, but mechanically, by the application of criteria provided for them by the political system they have chosen to serve. The process again has become almost entirely technicist rather than ethical, and, as we saw with pupil assessment, summative rather than formative; and it has become, as we saw in Chapter 5, a device for curriculum control and school/teacher accountability rather than for curriculum development or improvement.

> To the extent that evaluation goes beyond the mere gathering of information about students, and teachers, and proceeds not only to publicising that information, but also to interpreting it authoritatively against certain standards – to that extent evaluation does become an obvious and major instrument of control and intervention.
>
> (Weiler, 1990:444)

Standards, we are told, are to be raised, but there is no longer any evaluation either of what these are, whether the standards concerned are appropriate ones, or even of whether the curriculum in place is the best we could devise for achieving this, in particular whether it is indeed better than what it has replaced.

There has thus been a shift in curriculum research in recent years, from the kinds of enquiry which this book is seeking to advocate to a style which is perhaps best epitomized by what has come to be called the 'school effectiveness movement'. And we must shortly consider some further implications of this shift.

First, however, we need to consider the implications of what we have discussed so far in relation to assessment and evaluation for teacher appraisal and school/teacher accountability.

Teacher appraisal and accountability

The first point that needs to be made about teacher accountability is that it must be accepted rather than opposed. It is of the essence of life in a democratic society that no one should be unaccountable for his or her public actions; that is a privilege enjoyed only by those who hold power in totalitarian states.

'Public accountability, however, has to be clearly distinguished from political control. Its concern must be to ensure the best possible practice not to control that practice' (Kelly, 1995:131). A second important point, therefore, which emerges is that, in addition to being perhaps the most essential ingredient of democracy, accountability is also essentially *post eventum* (Downey and Kelly, 1979). It makes neither practical nor logical sense to endeavour to make someone accountable for his or her actions before he or she has performed them. A fundamental feature of the concept of accountability is that it comes into play after someone has had the freedom to exercise professional judgement and take whatever action he or she has deemed appropriate. In the context of teaching, therefore, accountability cannot be interpreted as entailing giving in advance an account of what one intends to do, although it has been interpreted by many people in this way and has thus been seen as adding its weight to those demands for the prespecification of teaching objectives.

Indeed, this has been a major feature of those schemes of accountability which have been introduced in many areas of the USA (Hamilton, 1976; Atkin, 1979) and which have been taken as the model for similar schemes which have been advocated and introduced into the United Kingdom. By 1974 nearly forty states in the USA were attempting to establish a legal base for demanding the accountability of teachers (Hamilton, 1976) and a major characteristic of their projected schemes was a concern with outcomes or outputs (Atkin, 1979), their focus being on 'management by objectives', 'programme budgeting' and even 'performance contracting', a system by which outside agencies are paid to work with teachers to raise the achievement levels of pupils (Atkin, 1979). In short, the emphasis is on achieving increased external control over education by intervention at the beginning, rather than by permitting teachers to exercise their professional judgement and calling them to account when they have done so.

Models of accountability

It is clear, then, that demands for teacher accountability can be interpreted and implemented in a number of quite different ways, so that the crucial question becomes not whether teachers should be accountable for their work but how this is to be achieved. In other words, we must seek for the most suitable model of teacher accountability.

In broad terms, two major models of teacher accountability can be identified. One of these is that instrumental, utilitarian, hierarchical, bureaucratic model that we have just suggested has been widely adopted in the USA. This is the model which Lawrence Stenhouse (1975:185) described as the 'systematic efficiency model'. The second might be described as the intrinsic, democratic or professional model.

The instrumental, bureaucratic model

The main feature of the first of these models is that it holds the teacher accountable to the public as taxpaying providers of the resources he or she is expending (Sockett, 1976b). It is a crude model, whose major focus is on the economic issues of resource allocation and value for money, and whose central concern is thus with the results obtained for the money spent. It is for this reason that it views the teacher as accountable to those who decide on the allocation of resources, that is, the government at local or national level, rather than to parents, pupils, employers or professional peers. It is also for this reason that it stresses the achievement of prespecified performances and thus adds its support to the adoption of the objectives model of curriculum planning, to target setting (Atkin, 1979). The main means it adopts to assess teacher competence is setting tests which are administered but not designed by the teachers concerned (Sockett, 1976b), and the future provision of resources is decided by reference to the results of these tests, a system of 'payment by results'. Its main characteristics then are that it is instrumental, economic and political.

The basic assumptions of this model are also worth noting (Elliott, 1976). For it assumes, firstly, that teachers are concerned to bring about only a limited range of outcomes – teaching rather than education; secondly, 'that achievement scores can be used to assess the causal effectiveness of what teachers do in classrooms' (1976:49); thirdly, that teachers can be praised or blamed, rewarded or punished, especially through the allocation of resources, on the basis of these causal evaluations; fourthly, that the teachers themselves have no rights of participation in such evaluations. Lastly, it also adopts a model of the teacher as a technician responsible for, and thus accountable for, no more than the 'delivery' of a curriculum whose objectives or targets have been determined by others.

In the light of earlier discussions in this book, it is not difficult to identify the inadequacies of this model nor the reasons for its growing current political popularity. To begin with, it trails with it all those difficulties associated with the objectives model of planning which we discussed in Chapter 3. In particular, it encourages the acceptance of simplistic educational goals by suggesting that what cannot be measured cannot be taught (Sockett, 1976b), for the model cannot be used to assess educational goals which cannot be defined in behavioural terms or clearly prespecified. It thus threatens to 'destroy schools as places where *education* goes on' (Elliott, 1976:51). Secondly, it substitutes teacher accountability for teacher responsibility or, to express this differently, it gives teachers responsibility without freedom (Stenhouse, 1975). This in turn has serious effects on teacher morale. Thirdly, the kind of data that this form of accountability produces does not help in any way with decisions as to how the performance of individual schools or teachers can be improved (Sockett, 1976b). In other words, it does not reveal why children have scored badly on the tests, merely that they have. The reasons why they have done badly are quite crucial, since it may be that these would justify the allocation of additional resources to the school, as was once felt to be the case with those schools in the United Kingdom decreed to be in Educational Priority Areas. It is for this reason that it has been claimed that one effect of this model of accountability may be to 'benefit the dominant middle class sectors of society to the disadvantage of minority communities' (Elliott, 1976:50), since if a school performs badly, even where this is directly attributable to the social class background of its pupils, this kind of scheme is likely to lead to a reduction in its resources, whereas social justice might be felt to require the opposite. In fact, it might be argued that its real purpose is to cut the costs of education rather than to improve its quality.

The intrinsic, democratic model
In contrast, a major characteristic of the intrinsic, democratic, professional model of accountability is that it is 'for adherence to principles of practice rather than for results embodied in pupil performance' (Sockett, 1976b:42). It thus eschews all links with curriculum planning by prespecified objectives, and suggests rather, or at least makes possible, the adoption of a 'process' or competence-based model of planning. For it is a model which is based on a recognition that educational value resides in the teaching-learning process itself rather than in its outcomes (Elliott, 1976), so that,

whereas the hierarchical model assumes that decisions concerning what is valuable in education are to be taken outside the school, this model recognizes that such decisions must be made within it, as part of the process of education itself. It also acknowledges that teachers have rights as a profession (Elliott, 1976) and that they must be regarded as autonomous professional people. Thus it accepts that teachers have a 'right of reply' or of direct involvement themselves in the accountability process, and that any action consequent on the evidence gleaned in that process must be reached after consultation with fellow professionals and not in total independence of their expert opinion. It concedes, therefore, that teachers should be accountable not only to the agencies of government but 'to a variety of "audiences" in society' (Elliott, 1976:51), 'to diverse constituencies rather than to the agglomerate constituency of the public alone' (Sockett, 1976b:42), and that among this diversity of audiences, or constituencies, must be included the teaching profession itself. The form of evaluation it recommends, then, is not the simple summative form of 'measuring' pupil performance associated with the instrumental model, but rather an illuminative form designed to provide information for this diversity of agencies.

This model also encourages an acknowledgement of the fact that teachers can in justice be held accountable only for those things which it lies within their powers to affect. Their work will be constrained by many factors beyond their control – not only the out-of-school experiences of their pupils, their social background, their exposure to the influences of the media and so on, but also the allocation of public resources and all those other constraints which we will identify in Chapter 7. It will also be apparent that those who are responsible for these factors – parents, local authority officials, politicians and, indeed, society as a whole, including, not least, those responsible for the media and the uses to which these are put – must take their share of accountability for pupils' attitudes and thus for their educational performance.

The major difficulties with this model clearly stem from its complexity. It has the merit of recognizing that education is a far more sophisticated activity than the advocates of the other, cruder model appear to think, but along with this must be accepted the difficulties of devising suitable and workable schemes for its translation into practice. These difficulties are virtually identical with those associated with the more sophisticated forms of curriculum evaluation which we explored earlier, and focus particularly on the problems of evaluating activities which are concerned with adherence to principles rather than the attainment of outcomes and those concerning the competence of teachers to evaluate one another's work. The solution to these difficulties, however, is to recognize the complexities of education and work towards similarly sophisticated techniques of evaluation and accountability rather than to reduce the work of teachers to the simplistic levels that existing techniques can 'measure'. Schemes of accountability, like all forms of evaluation and assessment, must follow and support the process of education rather than governing and controlling it.

What will also be plain, however, is that current political policies for education are reflecting the same kind of shift in relation to teacher accountability that we noted earlier in the context of evaluation. Evaluation, as we have seen, is now primarily concerned with the accountability of schools and teachers, and accountability itself, being directed centrally at the performance of schools and teachers, is focused increasingly on teacher appraisal and school inspections. In both cases too, this is accompanied by a change of model, a return to simplistic forms, an emphasis on the objectives-based, instrumental approaches to education, evaluation and accountability, whose concern is with political control rather than with educational development or improvement, and with checking teacher competence rather than supporting teacher development.

It is possible to find systems of teacher appraisal which have as their central concern teacher development, but there is now no area of the education system, from first schools to higher education, which is free of the need to appraise teachers and schools against externally imposed criteria of appraisal. In addition to the attainment targets of the National Curriculum assessment programme, we have already noted the 'desirable learning outcomes' against which nursery schools and teachers are evaluated – at least at the time of writing. 'Performance indicators' have been established for the evaluation of the work of university institutions, and these provide a basis for deciding on levels of funding and resourcing. Furthermore, these are procedural rather than process-oriented, instrumental rather than 'intrinsic', quantitative for the most part rather than qualitative, and are thus more likely to impose criteria of evaluation and accountability on institutions than to help them to develop their own.

It is thus difficult, if not impossible, to see any current system of teacher appraisal, in any kind of institution and whatever its stated philosophy, as anything other than a political act whose aim is to increase external control rather than to raise internal quality. And, just as we saw that this is accompanied by a shift from a 'democratic' to a 'bureaucratic' or 'autocratic' style of evaluation, we must note here the strong tendency for it to be associated also with a move from a 'democratic' to a 'utilitarian' or 'bureaucratic' form of accountability.

Indeed, there can be no place for the former in what, as a consequence of the 1988 Education Act, has become a completely bureaucratic education system in which all decisions of any consequence or significance are made by the politicians and their aides.

Finally, we should note that, as is inevitable when the focus is on control rather than development, these procedures for appraisal and accountability are not directed, except in a largely peripheral sense, at the professional development of teachers. Their main thrust is punitive. We hear much about the sacking of 'incompetent' teachers and the closure of 'failing' schools, after a brief period allowed for them to bring themselves into line with the Ofsted criteria of evaluation. Advisers have become inspectors, and the stick has replaced the carrot as the preferred motivational device. This constitutes perhaps the final evidence that the system of accountability now in place is bureaucratic rather than democratic.

The rhetoric of current policies has made much of 'teaching quality' (this was in fact the title of a White Paper issued in 1983); indeed the increased external control of educational institutions has been justified on that ground; the reality is that evaluation, accountability and teacher appraisal are no longer to be conducted in a manner which will facilitate the advancement of education in the full sense, even though they might raise 'quality' in a utilitarian, 'value for money' sense and maintain or even improve standards in the limited meaning given to that term by those outside the teaching profession and in the official documentation which has accompanied the introduction of these new policies.

Implications for educational research

As was suggested earlier, these changes also have far-reaching implications for educational research – its extent, scope and, indeed, nature. And it would be remiss to conclude this chapter without some reference to these implications.

The link between evaluation and research in education, as in any other sphere, is a close one. Both are concerned to discover more about the activity and, certainly in the case of those forms of evaluation which are aimed at curriculum development, both are directed at the improvement of practice. Thus we noted earlier Lawrence Stenhouse's vision of a time or phase when 'the conceptual distinction between development and evaluation is destroyed and the two merge as research' (1975:122).

We saw too in Chapter 5 that this view is also reflected in Stenhouse's notion of 'the teacher as researcher'. For what this essentially requires is that teachers should develop appropriate skills in the art of self-evaluation and that they should use these skills to make continuous appraisals of their own work as a basis for its continuing development. We also noted there how the idea of 'action research' had grown from similar assumptions about the teacher's task and the most effective ways to promote the professional development of teachers. We saw that this view of educational research had arisen at least in part from a dissatisfaction with traditional approaches and especially with their failure to explore educational practice from the inside. We must note also Elliot Eisner's criticism of these approaches on the grounds 'that we have distanced ourselves from the phenomena that should be central to our studies, that we employ models that have been designed to deal with other than educational phenomena, and that we reduce what is a rich source of data into a pale reflection of the reality we seek to study' (1985:262). The central purpose of action research has been to bring the researcher from the outside to the inside of the activity, in order to ensure both that he or she understands that activity with all its many nuances and that his or her research efforts make a worthwhile contribution to improving the practice of those directly engaged in the activity (Ebbutt, 1983), rather than, as has too often been the case, actually inhibiting that practice (Kelly, 1981). It is not difficult to see how the related notions of 'action research', 'the teacher as researcher' and 'research based teaching' merge into a concept of educational research as a process which requires the continuous monitoring of any educational activity by the teacher, supported by whatever contributions can be made by a 'sympathetic third party', with the prime intention of improving performance and developing teaching skills.

If we now draw together the issues explored in our consideration of strategies for curriculum change and development in Chapter 5 with our review of evaluation theory in this chapter, we can see that what emerges from both is the view that real curriculum development must rest in the hands of the individual teacher; that it is not a general but a particular matter; that, if it is to be influenced for the better by anyone else, that other person must first get on the inside of the particular situation; that evaluation, if it is to be effective in improving the quality of any teacher's work, must, in a fundamental sense, be self-evaluation through some form of action research, perhaps supported from outside the school, but not directed from the outside by the imposition of guidelines and checklists; that every evaluative activity, if it is to promote development (including, perhaps especially, professional development) and improvement, must be formative rather than summative, descriptive rather than prescriptive, illuminative rather than directive, 'democratic' rather than 'bureaucratic'; and finally, that accountability and appraisal must take forms which match this concept of research and evaluation, they too must be 'democratic' and must support educational development rather than inhibit it.

We must also note, then, that if, as was suggested above, current policies are taking us back to more simplistic notions of educational evaluation and to more politically grounded forms of accountability, they must lead to more limited views of educational research. Certainly, the shift to greater centralized control of the curriculum must have the effect of reducing, if not eliminating altogether, the scope for action research as we have seen it has been defined and developed and for any notion of the teacher as researcher, since it effectively reduces teachers' freedom to make any really significant changes in their curricular offerings whatever their own research or evaluation of these tells them.

We must note too that what we are being offered in lieu of genuine research is publications from official quangos. In particular, Ofsted is offering us reports based on its inspections, general statements on aspects of schooling revealed by its inspections, as though these represented the results of genuine research or were even comparable with the kind of independent surveys once carried out by HMI. These reports tells us little more than how schools might measure up more closely to the political criteria applied by the new breed of inspectors. They are evaluations made simplistically against the narrow templates devised by the quangos themselves. Genuine research is open, has no political agenda and is characterized by question marks which go much deeper than this.

Again we can see, therefore, that it is not only in relation to evaluation and accountability that the focus has shifted from educational advance to political control; it is in the associated area of educational research too.

Finally, we must note that, for these reasons, current research at the national level, even that which has the appearance of political independence, has begun to reflect this same shift of focus. We have already noted that most funded research does not direct its attention to the worth or the value of the National Curriculum but contents itself with monitoring the effectiveness of its 'delivery', albeit with a view to enhancing that effectiveness. Hence, within educational research, the flavour of the month, indeed of the decade, has been the 'school effectiveness movement'.

The 'school effectiveness movement'

The school effectiveness movement offers us the classic illustration of what is being said here about the current limitations on educational research.

This style of research, like most of the other developments we have noted, has been a recent phenomenon not only in the United Kingdom but throughout much of Europe and the USA. And at first glance it appears to be forward looking and to reflect an optimism about the potential of education in a free society. For it is based on the belief that 'schools can make a difference' (Chitty, 1997), that children are not locked forever into the limitations imposed by their inborn IQ, as the traditional view of intelligence seemed to suggest, but that, as Lord Boyle as Minister of State for Education said in his preface to the Newsom Report (1963), 'the essential point is that all children should have an equal opportunity of acquiring intelligence'.

First impressions, however, often mislead, and a closer examination of the assumptions of this movement lead one to a rather different interpretation of its role and of its value. For, while it has drawn our attention to a number of features of schools which appear to promote their effectiveness, inevitably it is less helpful in advising on how ineffective schools might be improved, and it suffers from that weakness we have just identified in post-National Curriculum research generally of not recognizing, or at least not acknowledging, the problematic nature of curriculum, even though it must be the curriculum and its development which are crucial to *educational* effectiveness.

Earlier studies, perhaps most notably that of Rutter *et al.* in their account of *Fifteen Thousand Hours* (1979), had sought to identify the key characteristics of the successful school, and these are not unrelated to those studies which considered the organisational health of schools, especially in order to discover those features which rendered them most receptive to curriculum change and development (Bernstein, 1967; Halpin, 1966, 1967; Hoyle, 1969b). All of these 'findings', however, have been shown to be far more uncertain and controversial than was first thought. In spite of that, indeed even after acknowledgment of it, a recent report to Ofsted by a team at the University of London Institute of Education (Sammons *et al.*, 1995) has confidently listed eleven key characteristics of the effective school, characteristics which may be seen as little more than 'an elaboration and refinement' of earlier studies (Elliott, 1996:205).

These characteristics are (1996:8 [abbreviated]):

(1) Professional leadership
(2) Shared vision and goals
(3) A learning environment
(4) Concentration on teaching and learning
(5) Purposeful teaching

(6) High expectations all round
(7) Positive reinforcement
(8) Monitoring progress
(9) Pupil rights and responsibilities
(10) Home-school partnership
(11) A learning organisation – school based staff development.

A thoughtful examination of this list of characteristics will reveal the major difficulties with this approach to educational research. In particular, it will raise questions at the point where attempts are made to move from description to prescription, from attempts to describe school effectiveness to attempts to advise on policies for school improvement, and especially to provide inspectors with criteria of evaluation, which are likely to be applied with little sophistication or professional judgement. For, apart from 'the number of platitudes' it contains (Elliott, 1996:206), such as the suggestion that the good school is one which concentrates on teaching and learning, several other weaknesses are apparent.

First, as Clyde Chitty has pointed out (1997:55), 'it places too much emphasis on the notion of progressive school management as the dynamic of change'. And, further, it suggests that, if these are the key characteristics of an effective school, all schools might become effective by adopting them. Thus description edges into prescription and school effectiveness into school improvement.

Second, and consequentially, as Chitty also points out (1997:55), the movement 'fails to take full account of the characteristics of the education system as a whole'. For example, 'even adopting all the practices revealed as "effective" will take certain schools only so far if they are locked into a local or national system where selection and polarization are taking place' (1997:56).

Above all, this movement fails to recognise the school curriculum as problematic. It takes for granted that everyone knows what the goal of school effectiveness is, and thus denies the possibility that improvement in the quality of educational provision might be brought about by curriculum change rather than enhanced managerial efficiency. It is concerned, as Lawrence Stenhouse (1975:69) once said of systems theory, 'with efficiency, rather than with the truth' and displays 'an emphasis on value rather than on values'. In other words, we must note again the failure to acknowledge any conceptual distinction between 'education' and 'teaching', or to make explicit the underlying concept of education to which it is committed, 'one emphasising the transmission of systematically organised academic knowledge, i.e. knowledge organised through the academic disciplines' (Elliott, 1996:206), requiring a content-based, performance-based form of curriculum. And of course in doing so it effectively rules out alternative concepts and ideologies, so that it can be seen as 'an attempt to redefine the field of school research in a way which denies the legitimacy of dissenting voices' (Elliott, 1996:200).

It is for this reason that it was suggested earlier that this style of research epitomizes the degeneration of educational research in recent years. For it reflects that damaging shift of focus from ends to means, from questions of value to those of methodology, from the ethical to the technicist, which we identified in our earlier discussion of the politicization of educational evaluation. And it is for this reason that it is a form of research which has come to be welcomed by those responsible for that process of politicization. For, to the uncritical, it has a plausibility which is very attractive, since it suggests that 'if only teachers could get a proper professional grip on themselves, then schools could reduce inequality, provide unlimited opportunity and reverse the declining national economic competitiveness for which they are largely responsible' (Fielding, 1997:13, referring to Davies, 1994). However, as Fielding goes on to say (1997:13), 'school effectiveness is not merely a supporter of the political status quo, it is an active agent of its continued development'. And, in support of this claim, he quotes Stephen Ball (1996), 'Quality and effectiveness are not neutral mechanisms. They do not simply improve education, they change it. What education is, what it means to be educated are changed.'

The school effectiveness movement, then, can be seen as an attempt to bring about a shift of focus for educational research which, if not checked, will ensure that research takes its place alongside, assessment, evaluation and inspection as another mechanism for control and for the promotion of what is essentially 'a right wing political and social agenda' (Chitty, 1997:57). For, 'in what is often a limited vision of schooling and society, the blame for underachievement and pupil disaffection can be neatly shifted from society at large with its structural inequalities to individual schools and teachers' (1997:57).

Again, therefore, one is forced to the conclusion that, whatever the political rhetoric, the reality is that the immediate future will see little improvement in the quality of education and no advance, in fact possibly even a regression, in the levels of our understanding of educational theory and practice.

Like all things human, educational assessment, evaluation, accountability and research can be used for good or ill, to promote educational improvement or to inhibit it. There is every sign that the pendulum has now swung towards the latter end of this scale.

We can see, then, that what has happened is that the school curriculum has been reduced to a narrow concern with 'standards'. It is these 'standards' that the new procedures for both assessment and evaluation by inspection are concerned to 'measure', and it is these 'standards' that educational research is expected to raise. Since, however, the systems for both assessment and inspection are simplistic, the 'standards' which they 'measure' are conceived simplistically too. And, since the school curriculum is now both assessment-led and inspection-led, that curriculum itself has been forced into a simplistic form, focused on these narrow concerns to the loss, detriment and even exclusion of much of that dimension of the curriculum which may be seen to convert schooling into *education*. Thus Mark Twain's famous advice that we should not let our children's schooling interfere with their education is being ignored.

It is possible that some of those who spout the rhetoric of raising standards, and even embrace and support current policies and practices with equanimity, do genuinely believe in what they are saying and doing. If so, the evidence of this and previous chapters would seem to suggest that they are seriously misguided. Those who recognize it as rhetoric but spout it anyway and support the process of imposing the policies and practices it conceals are seeking seriously to misguide the rest of us. In either case, the effect, if not always the intention, is that assessment and evaluation through inspection, supported by politically correct forms of educational research, have become devices for the centralized control of schooling and the bureaucratic accountability of schools and teachers rather than for raising standards in any sophisticated and genuinely educational form.

How this state of affairs has been brought about will be the main theme of Chapter 7.

Key issues raised by this chapter

1) What additional information becomes available for schools, teachers or parents from Standard Assessment Task testing and/or Ofsted inspections?
2) How far do these constrain and control provision for pupils/ students?
3) What are the essential characteristics of forms of assessment, evaluation and research which will genuinely support educational improvement?

Suggested further reading

Broadfoot, P. M. (1996) *Education, Assessment and Society*, Buckingham: Open University Press.

Blenkin, G. M. and Kelly, A. V. (eds.) (1992) *Assessment in Early Childhood Education*, London: Chapman.

Gipps, C. (1994) *Beyond Testing: Towards a Theory of Educational Assessment*, London: Falmer.

Norris, N. (1990) *Understanding Educational Evaluation*, London: Falmer.

7

The politicization of the school curriculum

It is worth noting first of all that education is essentially a political activity, that the education system is the device by which an advanced society prepares its young for adult life in the society, a formalization of the role played in primitive societies by all or most of the adult population. The political context, then, is a major element in any scheme or system of education, and one without reference to which such a scheme or system cannot be properly understood, or, indeed, planned.

It is for this reason that most of the major educational theorists or philosophers have also been, or even have primarily been, social and political philosophers. Plato, for example, offers us his theory of education only in the context of his political theory, introducing his whole discussion of education with the words 'These are the kinds of people our guardians must be. In what manner, then, will we rear and educate them?' Clearly, his main concern was with the social or political function of education; and we must note that this has been true also of many of the major figures who have followed him – Locke, Rousseau, John Stuart Mill, Dewey and so on.

At the practical level, this is reflected in the importance attached to schools and teachers in revolutionary times and by totalitarian governments. Control of the school system has been seen as a close second in terms of importance to control of the media of communication in most revolutions; and it has also been a major concern of leaders of major national movements, such as Lenin and Hitler. In this connection, it is worth noting that the idea of a national curriculum which was mooted in the United Kingdom in the 1930s was rejected at that time because it smacked of totalitarianism. We should also note the interest in education which has long been shown by religious bodies. It would be a mistake to assume that such interest has always been prompted by charitable intentions and never by a desire to propagate particular religious creeds and tenets. Few can be unfamiliar with the Jesuits' claim about what can be achieved through control of the early years of schooling.

Education and politics, then, are inextricably interwoven with each other, so that one cannot productively discuss curriculum issues in a political vacuum.

Direct and indirect political influences

We must begin, however, by distinguishing direct political intervention from influences of an indirect, less overt and thus possibly less effective kind. And we must remind ourselves that, even before the advent of direct political intervention in the school curriculum, there were many indirect constraints within which teachers have always had to work. For it must not be assumed that the former respect for teacher autonomy implied complete freedom or licence for them to do as they pleased. Autonomy is always relative; and teacher autonomy may even be regarded as a myth (Maclure, 1968).

Among the more influential of the constraints we may identify are the influence of tradition, which always tends to favour the *status quo*, and the need to respect the preferences of parents, again usually for provision of a kind they can recognize from their own school days. There are also the ever-present constraints imposed by the administration of the school system, both nationally and locally, and, indeed, those arising from the internal structures of each individual school and its 'micro-politics' (Ball, 1987). Above all, we must never forget the inhibitions which have always been recognized as deriving from the system of external examinations and testing, at 11+ as well as at 16+.

Direct intervention, however, until recently in England and Wales, had been confined to organizational changes and had barely touched the curriculum itself. The state has pronounced, and indeed introduced legislation, on the establishment of compulsory schooling, on the progressive raising of the minimum school leaving age, on access to grammar schools and support for children granted such access, on the provision of secondary education for all and on the provision of this through the creation of comprehensive forms of secondary schooling. All these organizational changes do, of course, have implications for the school curriculum, but it has been left to teachers and other educationists to draw these implications, and, on occasions (as with the raising of the school leaving age in 1972), money has been made available to help teachers and others to explore the curricular consequences of the legislation. There have been no direct injunctions, however, in relation to the school curriculum (except for the requirement of the 1944 Education Act for the regular provision of religious education for all pupils).

As a result, the development of the curriculum has been left to influences of an indirect kind. Thus one can identify in the development of education in the United Kingdom a number of competing influences. In particular, one can see a conflict or tension between political/economic forces and idealistic or philosophical theories. One can recognize the influence, on the one hand, of notions like that of a 'liberal education' and 'progressivism' and, on the other, that of a concern with the inculcation of 'the basic skills'; one can see tensions between liberalism and vocationalism, between egalitarianism and elitism, between the Crowther Report's two purposes of education – education as a national investment and education as the right of every child (CACE, 1959). One can see the emergence of the three distinctive curricula of tripartism and the contrasting view that all pupils should have access to the same kinds of educational provision. And one remembers Raymond Williams's (1961) view of the three main general influences on the development of education in the United Kingdom: that of the 'old humanists', concerned with the transmission of the traditional cultural heritage; that of the 'industrial trainers', who looked to education for little more than a trained workforce; and that of the 'public educators', who sought a new form of curriculum to reflect the new philosophy of mass education.

Hence the curriculum can be seen as the battleground of many competing influences and ideologies. And, in practice, at least until recently, the actual curriculum in schools in the United Kingdom has not reflected one faction or ideology but an unhappy, and probably unsatisfactory, amalgam of many, as each source of influence or pressure has had a little, but not an exclusive, effect on its form and content. Thus a rather unsatisfactory compromise has usually emerged, in which one can see the conflicts and the tensions between these competing claims and influences, which might be broadly polarized as a conflict between the claims of society and those of the individual, the vocational and the liberal, the economic and the humanitarian, a national investment and the right of every child, the instrumental and the intrinsic, what education *is for* and what it *is*, elitism and egalitarianism, and perhaps, in general, between the possible and the desirable, between reality and idealism.

The history of the development of education in the United Kingdom reveals a constant swinging of these pendula; and the actualities of the curriculum as a result always represent some attempt at achieving a compromise view. One can also see that the degree to which the more liberal, idealistic influences prevail or predominate depends to a very large extent on the degree of freedom enjoyed by teachers in curricular matters, since teachers have on balance tended to choose their profession because of certain ideals they hold about children, people and human potential, their salary scales having always been such as to provide ample evidence of their total lack of economic acumen. And so, as we shall see later, the political moves to press the school curriculum in the opposite direction, towards what is possible within the constraints imposed by the resources made available, towards the best economic return for the investment of those resources, have inevitably been accompanied by a major reduction in the extent of teachers' control of curriculum planning. The rhetoric has been that of improved standards and quality; the reality has been that of increased political control. The dominant ideology has indeed begun to dominate.

The early historical context

From the beginning of the school system in England and Wales, schools wishing to qualify for public funding had to demonstrate their efficiency, and this was monitored by His/Her Majesty's Inspectors, a body which came into being in 1839.

This control of elementary schooling was strengthened by the Revised Code (1862), and the 'payment by results' policy then instituted on the recommendations of the Newcastle Commission (1861), persisted until the last decade of the century. Even that extension of educational provision and broadening of curriculum which followed the passing of the Education Act of 1870 was subject to similar funding policies. Thus, while there was no direct control of the curriculum, indirect control was exercised through procedures for student assessment and school evaluation. And, as Matthew Arnold (1908:113) said of that time, 'making two-thirds of the Government grant depend upon a mechanical examination, inevitably gives a mechanical turn to the school teaching, a mechanical turn to inspection'. *Plus ça change . . .*

Successive codes at the end of the eighteenth and beginning of the nineteenth centuries led to the introduction of alternative forms of curriculum and the abolition of the annual assessment of pupils. 'Having for thirty three years deprived the teachers of almost every vestige of freedom the Department suddenly reversed its policy and gave them in generous measure the boon which it had long withheld' (Holmes, 1911:111). And the transfer of responsibility for educational provision to Local Education Authorities (LEAs) reinforced this policy of devolution.

One can even detect a concern to avoid uniformity of provision, so that, instead of directives, schools and teachers are provided with regular issues of 'Handbooks of Suggestions', and there is little evidence of any concern to dictate even the subjects to be taught, let alone the content of those subjects. The 1926 Code, for example, makes no mention of any particular subject – possibly, as John White (1975) suggests, through fear of what a possible future Labour Government might do with powers to dictate the curriculum. And, in this context, it is important to remember that the 1944 Education Act, the work of the wartime coalition government, offered no directive in relation to the curriculum other than the compulsory inclusion of religious education and a daily act of worship.

Thus the way was open for experiment and change, and the influence of the so-called 'Great Educators' and of 'progressivism' generally began to be felt. Certainly, this is a feature of the major reports which were published during this time, from the Hadow Reports (1926, 1931, 1933), through the Newsom Report (1963) to that of the Plowden Committee (1967).

In the early years of this period, this influence had less effect at the level of practice. A major reason for this was the continued restrictions created by the examination system. For, although there was now no regular testing of pupils for funding purposes, grammar and technical schools still had the task of preparing their pupils for public examinations. And in the primary sector, even before the 1944 Act separated this off from the secondary, there was the ever-present responsibility of preparing pupils for secondary school selection, the tripartite form of which was strongly endorsed by the Hadow (1926), Spens (1938) and Norwood (1943) Reports, first by way of the 'scholarship' and then by the 11+ examinations. And so, although more development can be seen at this level than in the secondary curriculum, even there progress was limited. Thus Denis Lawton (1980:22) has said that 'from 1944 to the beginning of the 1960s may be seen as the Golden Age of teacher control (or non-control) of the curriculum'.

The 1960s, however, saw two contradictory developments. First, it saw the comprehensivization of secondary education and consequently the abolition of the 11+, at least in its more competitive form. And, conversely, it saw the beginning of serious questioning of the wisdom of allowing this degree of curriculum control to teachers. The cynic might resolve this apparent contradiction by suggesting that teachers were permitted this degree of control, this level of autonomy in curriculum planning just so long as they did not use it, and that the challenge came when, in the context of the freedom conferred by comprehensivization, some teachers did begin to effect major changes. In 1968, Stuart Maclure was able to speak of 'the English myth of the autonomy of the teacher' (1968:10), but by 1985, Janet Maw was drawing our attention to the fact that 'it is inadequate to dismiss the notion of teacher autonomy as simply a myth . . . It influenced the whole style of the curriculum development movement in this country, and it had a powerful (though haphazard) impact on teachers' conceptions of their professional responsibilities and their willingness to engage in the realities of curriculum change. In other words, the belief in the teachers' autonomy had an impact on *practice* at all levels' (1985:95).

In fact, prompted by the Newsom (1963) and the Plowden (1967) Reports, spurred too by the planned raising of the school leaving age to 16+ in 1972, and taking a lead from the work of several research and development bodies (most notably the School Council), significant changes were occurring in the curricula of both primary and secondary schools. At secondary level, this period saw the advent of new subjects on the secondary curriculum, new combinations of subjects (humanities, for example, and other forms of Integrated Studies), and new reconceptualized versions of traditional subjects (Modern Mathematics, Nuffield Science, Geography for the Young School Leaver and Classical Studies). And at primary level, the Plowden Report gave a new impetus to the move towards 'progressivism' and 'child-centredness'. The evidence shows that none of this was as widespread as it might have been, and much of it was not as successful as one would have hoped. Nevertheless the shift was sufficiently significant for Basil Bernstein (1967) to write about open schools for an open society, and to do so in a manner that suggests one could detect a clear movement towards both. However widespread the practice, then, there can be discerned an important shift in the climate of educational thinking and perhaps a movement within the profession to a greater use of the autonomy it then enjoyed. Nor is it unreasonable to see this greater use as directed at ends such as equality of opportunity for all pupils, regardless of class, race, gender or disability, and a focusing of attention on 'the development of the individual – not in isolation from society, but as a member of a social and cultural collecive, the continued health – social, cultural and economic – of which depended centrally on the quality of life of each member' (Edwards and Kelly, 1998b:4). The shift at the level of thinking about education, and, increasingly at that of practice, was towards Bernstein's competence model of curriculum (1996).

And so it comes as no surprise to note the parallel emergence of political challenge to this autonomy, prompted perhaps in some cases by a genuine worry that 'standards' (as narrowly defined) were falling, largely by the fact that the kind of curricular provision which the teachers were fashioning in this way was expensive, but also in some areas by a concern at the implications of a society in which all had been educated to think for themselves. The key feature of education policy and practice, then, in the 1960s and 1970s was the parallel development of freer competence-based approaches to curriculum and of the beginnings of a political movement to stifle these and establish an unchallengeable performance-based curriculum at every level of education.

The challenge can be seen to begin in the early 1960s, when Sir David Eccles, as Minister of Education at that time, spoke of the 'secret garden of the curriculum' and declared an intention to open that garden to more public scrutiny, 'to make the Ministry's voice heard'. 'Of course, Parliament would never attempt to dictate the curriculum, but, from time to time, we could, with advantage, express views on what is taught in schools and in training colleges' (quoted in Chitty, 1990:5)

One result of this stated intention was the proposal to establish a Curriculum Study Group, a 'commando-like' unit to make raids into the curriculum. However, the professional opposition to this was so strong that the successor to Sir David Eccles, Sir Edmund Boyle, on the advice of the Lockwood Committee, recommended the establishment of the Schools Council for Curriculum and Examinations, which, as we saw in Chapter 5, came into existence in 1964 and was from the start under the control of the teaching profession itself and thus largely a politically independent body. It is clear, as Denis Lawton (1980) has shown, that that was not the end of the matter, and that the intention to wrest curriculum control from the teachers continued to be pursued, and those attempts, as we shall see shortly, slowly became more overt, particularly as we moved into the 1970s, an acceleration of events which was prompted to a considerable extent by the economic effects of the oil crisis of 1973/4.

The ambivalence we have noted, the parallel development of a competence based view of curriculum within the profession and pressure for a move to a performance base from the politicians, is illustrated most interestingly, and effectively, in the official literature of the time. In particular, that literature reveals a tension between HMI, as representative of the professional view, and the civil servants of DES, promoting an instrumental view of the curriculum on behalf of their political masters and mistresses, 'a lack of consensus within the DES itself, between the political/administrative view (the civil servants) and the professional (Her Majesty's Inspectorate)' (Maw, 1985:96). Both in tone and in content, this tension is most apparent. Up to as late as 1980, HMI were offering us a view of the curriculum, framed in terms of individual entitlement. 'We have to ensure that the curriculum does everything possible to help pupils to develop as individuals' (DES, 1977c:1). The same document speaks of 'the responsibility for educating the "autonomous citizen", a person able to think and act for herself or himself, to resist exploitation, to innovate and to be vigilant in the defence of liberty' (1977c:9). And it suggests that this can only be attained through a curriculum framed in terms of 'areas of experience', the famous 'eight adjectives' it offers as an alternative to school subjects –

aesthetic/creative, ethical, linguistic, mathematical, physical, scientific, social/political and spiritual. And a similar ideology of curriculum was to be seen in *A View of the Curriculum*, published in the HMI *Matters for Discussion* series in 1980. Indeed, many HMI, individually as well as collectively, were still at this stage advocating 'progressivism' and 'child-centredness' in primary schools.

These statements from HMI compare most favourably, not only in content but also in the intellectual quality of the arguments they mount in support of that content, with a document like *A Framework for the School Curriculum*, which was published, also in 1980, by the DES. In terms of sheer banality and intellectual impoverishment, this has no rival in 2000 years of discussions of education. However, its task was to set out the political view, the instrumental, performance-based, approach to the school curriculum. And this it sought to do in a very basic form, listing what it saw as the esssential subjects to be included in that curriculum, and outlining the merits of each, almost entirely in instrumental terms. It was seen at the time from within the profession as the typical, uninformed outpouring of administrators who lack all understanding of the nuances of the educational process. It was in fact something rather more sinister than that; it was the first major shot across the bows of the competence-based curriculum, an early attempt to replace personal empowerment with vocationalism as the prime concern of the school curriculum.

A feature of the 1980s was the rapidity with which this conflict between HMI and DES was resolved. HMI were brought to heel very smartly, and it is impossible to tell, without looking closely at the small print, what is the precise source of subsequent documentation. Perhaps the best illustration of this is the HMI *Curriculum Matters* series, to which we have referred before, and which illustrates very clearly how far HMI had been brought into line with the official ideology, how completely their professional independence had been surrendered, so that it came as no surprise when they were later ousted by a very different form of Inspectorate, as we shall see later.

We must now trace the major landmarks in this shift in curriculum ideology and policies of which the events we have just considered were the early indications.

The shift to direct intervention and control

It was suggested earlier that, while there is a sense in which the whole social context of curriculum planning can be described as political, it is also possible, and indeed necessary, to identify more overt forms of political influence and pressure; in short, to note the point at which such pressure changes from being an influence on curriculum development to being a deliberate attempt to exert control over it. It was also noted that a change of this kind has occurred in England and Wales during the last few years.

We must now consider some of the ways in which those general influences which we discussed earlier have become sharpened up by recent political developments to the point where their impact on education has become more clearly overt, direct and significant and where the degree of autonomy and of responsibility exercised by teachers has become correspondingly more limited. In short, we will be tracing the development of some of these influences into agencies of direct control.

We noted earlier that, perhaps particularly because of the easing of the constraints imposed by the examination system, significant changes in school curricula began to be observed in the 1960s and especially the 1970s. These significant changes in the school curriculum can be seen as reflecting several aspects of what Lawrence Stenhouse (1980a) has called the 'curriculum development' or the 'curriculum research and development' era in British education. This was an era when attempts were being made to incorporate some of the things we were learning about curriculum development, especially through the work of the Schools Council, into the realities of curriculum practice in schools. In other words, this was a time when our knowledge of the complexities of education and of curriculum planning was being markedly extended by research of many different kinds and in many different contexts, and this was leading, quite properly, to the emergence of more sophisticated approaches to educational and curriculum planning. We were beginning to understand more clearly what it means to claim that education entails more than the mere acquisition of knowledge; we were questioning the sanctity of traditional divisions of this knowledge into subjects; we were becoming aware of the inadequacies of curriculum planning based on the achievement of simple behavioural objectives; we were learning more about the problems of educational equality, or rather educational inequality; and in particular we were coming to appreciate how far such inequality is a function not so much of society or even of the education system as of the curriculum itself.

A growing awareness of all of these factors, then, along with a concern to act on our increasing knowledge and understanding of them, was pushing the curriculum in directions other than those in which those who are concerned primarily with the economic or political role of education in society wished it to go. For what underpins these factors is a concern with education as a process of individual development, which can be promoted only by curriculum provision tailored to the requirements of individual pupils rather than the kind planned to force all through the same programme, by an educational diet designed to suit each person's unique intellectual metabolism rather than the offering of the same food to all, whether it helps them towards healthy educational development or nauseates them. In turn this leads to a move away from traditional forms of academicism; educational experiences can take many forms and are certainly not confined to what can be gained from studying traditional school subjects. And what seems most obviously to count as an educational experience is more likely to be found in areas which comprise what we call the humanities (the etymology of the word itself would seem to support this claim) or social studies than in the study of science and technology. This is the substance of that leaning towards 'idealist' approaches to schooling which, we noted earlier, is displayed by most teachers and is thus a significant effect of teacher autonomy in matters of curriculum.

In short, one can detect at least the beginnings of an ideological shift – from a prime concern with society's needs to a favouring of those of the individual, from the rhetoric of educational equality towards its realities, from the economic to the social function of schooling, from education as the transmission of knowledge to education as individual development, and from the notion of the teacher as instructor to a clearer view of the teacher as educator.

Two further factors can be seen as adding to the complexities of this movement. The first is the accelerating rate of technological advance and the consequent view that the educational system needs to be able to respond continuously to this. The second is the continuing economic recession, which has not only created a desire for schooling to be used to promote, above all else, economic productivity, but has equally and perhaps more significantly led to a reduction in the level of resourcing of education (as of all other social services) and thus to an ever increasing demand for 'value for money'. To put it rather simply, and perhaps crudely, there had been less concern with the resources and energies teachers were devoting to the promotion of educational equality, education as development, the 'social service' dimension of educational provision, when the state could afford this as well as the other, more economically useful, things that schools were doing and can do. But that 'golden age' (if it had ever really been such, except with hindsight and by comparison with the present) was about to end.

It is worth noting also that this general trend can be discerned in most of the 'developed' countries throughout the world (Kennedy, 1995), and for the same reasons.

An increased rate of technological advance, along with a reduction in the resources made available to education (again a change paralleled in other social services), has resulted, therefore, in a move towards the increased external control of the school curriculum and of teachers, and a corresponding loss of teacher autonomy. That shift towards a more liberal view which we noted just now has had to be arrested. The movement has had to be reversed, away from the view of education as a social service, away from the Crowther Report's view of it as the right of every child regardless of return, towards the view of education as a national investment, towards an emphasis on its economic function, towards a curriculum framed solely in terms of subjects and with an emphasis on those subjects whose major contribution can be seen to be utilitarian. Lawrence Stenhouse's (1980a) era of 'curriculum research and development' has given way to an age of accountability, 'the fashion has swung from "curriculum reform" to "educational accountability"' (1980:259); and the period which Maurice Kogan (1978) describes as 'the onset of doubt', from 1964 to 1977, has become his 'struggle over curriculum and standards'.

This is a development whose major landmarks it will be interesting and enlightening for us to trace.

Major landmarks in the move towards central control

Denis Lawton (1980) argues with some conviction that the movement to establish greater central control over the school curriculum began immediately after the failure to establish the commando-style Curriculum Study Group in the early 1960s. That movement began to reveal itself in overt forms in the late 1960s and gathered increasing momentum throughout the 1970s and 1980s.

One of its first manifestations was the publication of a series of 'Black Papers' on education in 1969 (Cox and Dyson, 1969a and b). The contributors to these publications, in Jeremiah fashion, inveighed against all the forms of educational innovation we mentioned earlier as emerging in response to a growing concern within the profession for improvements in quality and the increased understanding of education and curriculum which was becoming available through various forms of research. These innovations, they claimed, were leading to a serious decline in educational standards, and, on their definition of educational standards, perhaps they were. In reality, it was the very concept of what might constitute educational standards which was changing. For them, however, since this was resulting in significant changes from traditional patterns of schooling, it had to be unacceptable. Individual contributors to the Black Papers attacked the comprehensivization of secondary schools with its concomitant 'destruction' of the grammar schools, the introduction of mixed-ability classes, the spread of informal approaches to teaching in primary schools with their emphasis on 'play' (a vastly misunderstood concept) and corresponding lack of attention to what they called 'the basic skills', although these they never clearly defined. In general, the claim was that all such developments were leading to a lowering of educational standards. And this was asserted with no apparent recognition of the need for evidence to support such a claim, for some conceptual clarification of notions such as that of 'standards', or even for an acknowledgement of the research evidence which had led to the innovations in the first instance. In fact, the lack of any kind of respect for the basic principles of intellectual debate and argument has been a major feature of this movement from the beginning, and it continues to chime very oddly in the claims of those whose prime concern is stated to be the raising of academic standards.

Scaremongering, however, has never relied on evidence or logic or any aspect of rational argument. Its basic premise is that if you frighten people sufficiently they will begin to support your alternative, usually reactionary, policies.

The first group formally to board this bandwagon was the Confederation of British Industry (CBI) which itself began to assert that schools were not doing enough to encourage high standards in what it also called, but again never clearly defined, 'the basic skills', nor were they giving enough attention to *applied* forms of both the arts and the sciences. The cry now was not merely that educational standards were falling but that the economic function of schooling was being neglected.

This of course does represent a redefinition, albeit never made explicit, of what we might mean by educational standards; a redefinition, moreover, in terms of economic utility rather than of the intellectualism or academicism of the Black Paper writers. It thus represents perhaps the earliest evidence of what the purpose and the flavour of increased central control of the curriculum was to be. For the criteria by which schools and teachers are to be judged, evaluated and held accountable are clearly to be criteria derived not from their conceptions or definitions of their tasks as professional educators but criteria based on the expectations of people outside the schools and the teaching profession, those who see themselves as 'consumers' and/or as 'providers' and, in either role, as having the right to dictate policy. Developments since that time, up to and beyond the 1988 Education Act, can be properly understood only if viewed and recognized in those terms.

These critics were soon to have what they regarded as the most effective ammunition possible for their battle against curriculum development and innovation. In 1974 events at the ILEA's William Tyndale School were made much of by the press and were seized upon by the critics as overwhelming support for the criticisms they had been offering, the fears they had been expressing and the assertions they had been making about where teacher autonomy would take us. The same lack of concern for scholarship which had permitted them to make their earlier assertions without proper evidence now allowed them also to blow this piece of evidence up to something totally disproportionate to its significance. The events at William Tyndale School were in many respects highly unsatisfactory; they showed up many people, not least the ILEA inspectorate, in a very poor light; they did reveal what the abuse or misuse or injudicious use of teacher autonomy could lead to. What they did not do was offer evidence of a nationwide problem; they had no significance at all for the work of those tens of thousands of schools where teachers were exercising their professional autonomy to the best of their ability in what they saw as the best interests of their pupils. That, however, was the interpretation placed on them by those who wished to see things in that light.

At the very time when the William Tyndale affair was continuing, the nation suddenly found itself in the throes of the crisis created by the Oil Producing and Exporting Countries' (OPEC) decision to raise dramatically the price of oil. This event had an immediate impact on many aspects of the nation's economy. Its significance for education was not so readily apparent. The consequent economic recession, however, was bound to lead to major reductions in the resourcing of the education service and to those demands for 'value for money' referred to earlier. In fact, the education budget continued to expand in real terms until as late as 1977 (Kogan, 1978), but the problems of the economy soon caught up with it and, as we saw earlier, this became another element in the tale being unfolded here.

There followed a series of events which can be seen as leading remorselessly to the level of central control of education encapsulated in the 1988 Act.

In 1974 the Manpower Services Commission was created with a clear brief and the necessary resources to develop schemes to correct what was seen as a mismatch between the qualities and skills displayed by school leavers and the needs of employers. Its focus was on the further education sector of schooling, a sector increasingly seen as embracing the age group from fourteen to eighteen, and successive schemes, such as its Youth Opportunities Programme (YOP), Youth Training Scheme (YTS) and Technical and Vocational Educational Initiative (TVEI) led to a progressive separation of training from education which resulted in 'the creation of a separate group of worker-pupils' (Ball, 1984a:15), and thus in the emergence of a new form of tripartism in which 'a clear technical-vocational stream is being established alongside the academic stream within comprehensive schools' (Simon, 1985:227) and in which 'it is likely that the intention is that this stream should bifurcate into a higher and a lower level, the majority focusing on more strictly vocational activities in the latter' (1985:227).

One can thus see the place of this development in the scheme of things we are describing here and, in particular, its significance for the redefinition of education and educational standards in instrumental, utilitarian and economic terms.

In the following year, 1975, the Assessment of Performance Unit was established. There is no doubt that ultimately this Unit's work made a significant contribution to curriculum development (Kelly, 1987), but there is equally no doubt that that was not the object of its creation and that it must be seen as a further milestone on the road to greater centralized control of education and of the curriculum. For its main task was to monitor standards and to identify the incidence of underachievement in schools and, while there is no suggestion here that its concern was to be with any redefinition of standards in vocational or economic terms, it can be no coincidence that its initial attention was directed towards what were later to become the core subjects of the National Curriculum (DES, 1987a) – mathematics, language and science – or that a major subsequent concern was design and technology. There is no doubt that it was set up to act as a watchdog over the curriculum nor that it was viewed in that light, in spite of its many efforts to carve out for itself a more positive role in curriculum development. Its establishment thus represents another step towards centralized control.

At about this time, too, events were occurring in teacher education whose implications were to prove far-reaching. Miscalculations in the Department of Education and Science had led to a massive over-production of newly qualified teachers in the early to mid-1970s as school rolls fell dramatically. There was much unemployment among teachers, especially those who had just completed their initial courses, and clearly there was a need for tighter controls of entry to such courses. It was an opportunity to raise entry qualifications for the profession and it was used as such, first to create an all-graduate profession and later to make additional requirements for such qualifications as GCE 'O' level mathematics and English language passes for all new entrants.

It also offered, however, seemingly sound pretexts for intervention of a more direct kind in the work of institutions offering courses of teacher education. To reduce the number of students on such courses, colleges had to be 'diversified' (have their attentions switched to courses other than teacher education courses), merged with one another or with other institutions of higher education to make viable units, or even, in many cases, closed altogether. Decisions of this kind were to a large extent left to be decided at local level, but they ultimately depended on the allocation of student numbers by the Department of Education and Science. The Department thus gained effective control over the system through the distribution of these numbers and it is no great step, as subsequent events have shown and as we shall see in due course, from that kind of control to control over the nature and content of the curriculum of these courses. The need to reduce the number of teachers in training, therefore, was the thin edge of a wedge whose effects in prising open not only the colleges and departments of education but also the schools and, subsequently, the universities and polytechnics were to prove very far-reaching indeed.

There followed a series of events which made overt and public the drive towards greater central control. For most people the first indication of this came in the autumn of 1976 with a famous speech by James Callaghan as Prime Minister, at Ruskin College, Oxford, in which he mounted a direct attack on the teaching profession for failing to respond to the needs of society by permitting too many people to spend too much time studying subjects which he deemed to be not directly productive in commercial and economic terms. Too many sixth form pupils were studying humanities subjects and thus too few were studying science and technology. This perceived imbalance was leading to a similarly unsatisfactory pattern of study in universities and other institutions of higher education. This was seen as a result of allowing teachers at all levels too much 'say' in the planning of the curriculum, so that one obvious solution to the problem was to be found in a reduction of teacher autonomy and a corresponding increase in external control, particularly from the centre.

While this may have come as a surprise to many people, to some it was expected. All that was in that speech, and indeed much that has followed since, had been foreshadowed in 1976 in a supposedly confidential 'Yellow Book' which contained detailed plans for the achievement of greater central control of the curriculum. And, also in 1976, a report of the House of Commons Expenditure Committee had propounded the view that the Department of Education and Science did not have enough control over expenditure on education or, rather, that it contributed nothing to national planning of education beyond the allocation of resources. Policy-making was largely in the hands of local education authorities, which for a variety of reasons, some of them party political, did not always arrange the distribution of resources in accordance with policies of which central government would entirely approve. One of the recommendations of this report was for the establishment of a permanent group, with a significant lay membership, to offer an independent view on the planning of the education service at the national level.

Nothing that has happened in subsequent years can be understood as anything more than an attempt to put right these perceived deficiencies by this kind of device, by strengthening the control of central government over all aspects of educational policy and spending, and increasing the lay, and especially the industrial and commercial, involvement in educational planning.

The 1944 Education Act, by not laying down any requirements for the school curriculum (other than the necessary inclusion of religious education), had created, or perpetuated, a triangular form of control of both education and the curriculum, the three corners, or sides, of that triangle being central government, the local education authorities and the teachers themselves (Lawton, 1980). This was now being regarded in some quarters as a serious deficiency, so that calls began to be heard for a common, centrally determined curriculum – at least for secondary schools – for the reformation of and increased powers for governing bodies and for a corresponding reduction in the influence of the teachers in matters of curriculum. This was subsequently extended to include policies for reducing the powers of local authorities in all areas of educational provision, for the 1988 Education Act gave the Secretary of State unprecedented powers of control and, by reducing the roles not only of the teachers themselves but also of the local authorities, effectively replaced that triangular form of control with a set of mechanisms which are largely unidimensional.

The declaration of James Callaghan at Ruskin was followed by the so-called 'Great Debate' which was conducted through all the media and stage-managed by Shirley Williams, Secretary of State for Education and Science in that Labour government. Ostensibly, the point of this was to make education a matter of public concern and discussion. Its real purpose can be seen only as a step towards increased centralization of control.

This debate culminated in the publication in 1977 of a Green Paper (DES, 1977b), which set out an interventionist strategy based on several major proposals of a specific kind for, amongst other things, the establishment of a national curriculum, performance testing of pupils and the appraisal of teachers. In the same year, Circular 14/77 required local education authorities to produce detailed statements of their curricular policies, and this requirement was naturally and immediately passed on to schools, which suddenly found themselves faced with the task of preparing and producing curricular statements at a level of detail they had in most places never experienced before, for which, one must admit, few were prepared and of which fewer, sadly, were capable.

The year 1977 also saw the publication of the Taylor Report (DES, 1977a) on the government of schools, a report whose main recommendations, as we saw earlier, were that governing bodies of schools should be given increased powers, especially in relation to the school curriculum, and that there should be increased representation of parents on all such bodies.

Also at about this time began to appear that plethora of official documents on the school curriculum, emerging from Her Majesty's Inspectorate and from the Department of Education and Science, which we noted earlier.

The first piece of the legislation which was to translate these discussions and proposals into official policy was the 1980 Education Act, which gave more power to local authorities in the matter of controlling the curricular provision of their schools, although at the same time requiring of them statements of their own general policies in this area, and also increased the powers of parents, not only by translating into statutory form some of the recommendations of the Taylor Report concerning membership of governing bodies, but also by giving them increased scope for the choice of schools for their children and, as a corollary to this, requiring schools to make public their curricula and their achievements, especially their results in public examinations.

Attention then turned to less prominent, although equally important, aspects of educational provision. As we saw in Chapter 5, the Schools Council was reconstituted in such a way as to remove that control by teachers over its finances which we suggested in Chapter 5 was so crucial to its work. This move effectively put an end to all open, teacher-controlled research in education. The money available through this channel for research (never, it must be said, a very large sum) was now to be spent according to policies generated by administering committees on which politicians and industrialists were to have effective control. It was no surprise, and not much more of a loss, therefore, when, with effect from 31 March 1984, all public funding of the Council was withdrawn and it was thus effectively killed off. It was immediately replaced by the School Curriculum Development Council (SCDC), which was essentially a political rather than professional agency, and which looked remarkably like that Curriculum Study Group which we saw Sir David Eccles had failed to establish in the early 1960s.

In the early 1980s the Council for the Accreditation of Teacher Education (CATE) was also established, again a political agency with a very strict and detailed brief to review all courses of initial teacher education and to approve only those which conform to specifically laid down criteria. These criteria were mainly quantitative, but they revealed a clear underlying policy, since they included requirements such as that all four-year undergraduate courses leading to qualified teacher status must devote at least two of the four years to the study of a 'curriculum subject', even for students preparing to teach nursery age children – a clear example of the simple subject-based view of the school curriculum which pervades all current official policies. They required too the setting up of advisory committees to oversee the planning of courses in all institutions preparing teachers for entry into the profession, and these committees were to include representatives from commerce and industry and from the employers of teachers as well as from the teachers and teacher-educators themselves. We noted earlier how, in response to the need to control entry to the profession, at least in numerical terms, the Department of Education and Science had taken to itself the power to allocate target numbers for admission to teacher-education courses in all institutions. We can see here how that power was extended to encompass control over the content and the curricula of such courses since, if they were not accredited by CATE in terms of their content and curricula, they were allocated no target figures and no resources, so that they would wither and die. The work of CATE has now been taken on by the Teacher Training Agency (TTA), a body which has made much of its role in establishing a 'national curriculum for teacher training', in spite of the fact that such a national curriculum has long been established through the initial work of CATE.

Not only then, with the demise of the Schools Council, is there now little politically independent research in education, there is also no more politically independent initial teacher education. Teachers are not to be encouraged to ask the kinds of question about education and the school curriculum which our earlier chapters have tried to show are so important and which the work of the Schools Council and the courses provided in many colleges and departments of education had been prompting them to address. Their professional responsibilities are no longer to be regarded as extending that far. What they are to teach is now decided for them; how they are to teach it is to be their only professional concern, and even here they are subject to ever-increasing political dictation.

This development was reinforced by the 1986 Education Act, which not only extended the work of the 1980 Act by further increasing the powers of governing bodies and the level of parental representation on them, but also introduced new arrangements for the funding of the in-service education of teachers (INSET). These arrangements effectively placed control of the funding of all INSET work in the hands of the Department of Education and Science, to which all local education authorities had to submit their proposals for approval for funding. In practice, this has resulted in most of the available money being devoted to short courses, often of a largely practical kind, or to school-based 'Baker days' – opportunities for the staffs of schools to explore together aspects of their curricula. And, while one does not wish to denigrate such provision, one must acknowledge that its corollary is that very little money is now being made available for teachers to attend courses of a more rigorous or more intellectually demanding kind in institutions of higher education, so that again it is that critical and analytical review of education and curriculum which such courses seek to provide which is being lost.

The slow disappearance of this element from INSET provision has reinforced the loss of free, professionally controlled research and the reduction of opportunities in initial courses of teacher education for the development of properly critical professional attitudes, and it has taken the profession inexorably back to an era of much reduced professional responsibility and thus of greatly limited professional opportunities. That element of job satisfaction, which has attracted so many people to the teaching profession and which has been seen as compensating, at least to some extent, for low salaries and the total absence of any of those 'perks' that people of comparable abilities in almost any other walk of life enjoy, has disappeared very quickly indeed, so that one wonders what, if anything, will continue to attract young people into teaching and one is not surprised to learn of the increasing difficulties of recruitment which have been experienced for the last decade or more.

The process which this section has endeavoured to describe reached its culmination in the Education Act of 1988. The pieces of the jigsaw were all finally put together and, if the picture was in any way obscure before, it then became complete and clear. There is a subject-based, centrally determined National Curriculum; its core subjects are mathematics, English and science, to which 30 to 40 per cent of curriculum time should be devoted, although at primary level 'the majority of curriculum time . . . should be devoted to the core subjects' (DES, 1987a:6); in addition 'the foundation subjects should comprise a modern foreign language, technology, history, geography, art, music and physical education' (1987a:6). There is a programme of national testing at four key stages during the period of compulsory education – 7+, 11+, 14+ and 16+. To this has now been added 'baseline testing' at 5+.

Local education authorities must prepare and submit to the Secretary of State for approval a formula by which they will allocate resources to the schools within their jurisdiction. These schemes must also show how responsibility for managing each school's budget is delegated to its governing body. Governing bodies also have greatly increased powers in respect of the appointment, suspension and dismissal of school staff. And they have the right to apply to the Secretary of State for grant-maintained status, in short to 'opt out' of the supervisory control of their local authority and 'go it alone' with direct funding and supervision from the Department of Education and Science. There is also machinery for the establishment of city technology colleges, whose normal running costs are met by central government but whose capital costs are shared between the Secretary of State and whichever commercial organization has offered to put up the money to establish each such college. A significant number of schools will thus become independent not only of local authority funding but also of local authority control (and, consequently, support).

Finally, although it is not our direct concern here, it is worth noting, since it reflects those general trends we have been identifying, that the Act also contained many clauses designed to ensure much greater centralized control over higher education. There were new arrangements for the funding of universities, polytechnics and colleges through funding councils containing a significant non-professional element. Local authorities lost direct control over polytechnics and other colleges of higher education currently within their jurisdiction, and here too, as in the case of the financing of schools, they were required to obtain the approval of the Secretary of State for schemes for the delegation of budgetary responsibility to governing bodies of all but the smallest colleges. Furthermore, at least half the members of such governing bodies had to be representatives of employment interests.

The trends, then, are virtually complete: direct central control, subject-based curricula, an emphasis on economically productive subjects, increased involvement of industry and commerce in the management of the educational institutions of all kinds, and a much reduced professional role for teachers at all levels from the nursery to postgraduate studies. And the whole shebang managed, directed, controlled and steered by a succession of quangos.

Events since 1988

At first glance, it might appear that the most significant development since the 1988 Act itself and its implementation is the revision of the

National Curriculum by the Committee chaired by Sir Ron Dearing. This revision, however, was cosmetic only (Kelly, 1994), since the committee's brief was to do no more than to slim down an overlarge curriculum, to simplify the administration and especially the testing arrangements and to review the ten-level attainment scale (SCAA, 1993). Thus, while the content to be transmitted was reduced, the ten-level scale simplified and the testing procedures rendered so simplistic as to be educationally largely valueless, no change was made to the essence of the performance-based curriculum which the 1988 Act put in place.

Perhaps the most significant aspect of the Dearing Report (SCAA, 1993) was the embargo it placed on all further change for period of five years. For this provided official confirmation of the fact that we have a curriculum which is planned as static and monolithic, and that the notion of curriculum development has, as we suggested earlier, been jettisoned. No matter what social and technological changes occur, even at a time of the most rapid change humankind has seen, there must be no change in the school curriculum.

However, the most significant event in the period since 1988 is the replacement of HMI by a non-ministerial government office, the Office for Standards in Education (Ofsted). This quango, headed by Her Majesty's Chief Inspector, now a government executive, has the task of managing the national scheme of regular school inspections by independent Registered Inspectors (RI). HMI, now massively reduced in number, are no longer the front-line inspectors, their role now being to supervise the monitoring process carried out by others, and to advise and support schools which are deemed by those others to have weaknesses and inadequacies.

They have been replaced by a 'powerful and independent Inspectorate', as it has been described by the DfEE (1992:para.1.13), which aims to inspect every school once in every four years. It consists of people, including lay-persons, who have been 'Ofsted-trained' (i.e. schooled in the predefined criteria by which they must make their evaluations), and inspection teams, each of which must include one lay inspector, are chosen on a value for money basis on tender to Ofsted.

One significant aspect of this is that it represents a policy of raising standards and bringing about school improvements not by advice, guidance and support but by rigorous external evaluation and the related threat of exposure to public censure. Reports on all schools are published and are available on the Internet. Furthermore, the focus is on schools rather than on individual teachers, and, while those teachers might be relieved that they are not to be personally subject to this kind of process, it must be a matter for regret that their professional development is no longer a concern to the inspectorate. Indeed, Ofsted inspectors have been officially warned not to 'allow discussions about the work and its evaluation to stray into giving on-the-spot advice, nor adopt an advisory role in any part of the inspection' (Ofsted, 1995:31). Thus sticks are preferred to carrots; it is assumed (despite all the evidence to the contrary) that schools will improve when under threat rather than in response to encouragement; and the advisory role has been converted very positively into an inspectorial one.

The process is, therefore, technicist, managerial and, consequently, deprofessionalizing, even dehumanizing, and certainly demoralizing (Jeffrey and Woods, 1998). It represents a colonization of schools and teachers, personally as well as professionally (Jeffrey and Woods, 1998), of a kind which is far from likely to enhance the quality of their work, except in so far as that work is conceived, as we have seen on several occasions that it is, in very narrow terms.

And so, again, we need look no further for corroborating evidence in support of the claim made in Chapters 5 and 6, that the prime purpose of the new inspectorial system, whatever, the accompanying rhetoric, is control rather than improvement.

A second, less overt but equally significant, development which can be seen to have occurred since 1988 has been the growing influence of those pressure groups which have come to be known collectively as the New Right. These 'think-tank' groups, closely linked to the Conservative government and especially to Mrs Thatcher, as its leader and Prime Minister, came increasingly to dominate such debate as there was about the school curriculum and its purposes in the period leading up to the 1988 Act, mainly by shouting down all opposition, a prime example of 'discourse of derision' (Ball, 1990).

Some differences of emphasis can be discerned between these groups, but a general ideological similarity binds them together. Their demands, particularly as voiced by the Centre for Policy Studies and the Hillgate Group, are for a return to 'traditional values', i.e. 'basic skills' and traditional subjects; a reassertion of traditonal moral values and standards, especially a respect of British institutions and religion; an end to 'child-centredness'; schooling as the transmission of facts rather than as an exercise in enquiry and exploration; regular summative assessments of pupils in support of parental choice of schools; and in general an opening up of the school system to the free play of market forces.

The nuances of difference within these views reflect divergence of degree only, and those nuances are well summed up in the ideologies of curriculum which Denis Lawton (1989:7) identified, and which we noted in Chapter 3. First, there are the 'privatizers' who would leave education entirely to market forces and the ability and willingness of parents to pay for their children's educational provision. Second, the 'minimalists' or 'segregators' believe that the state should provide only a basic schooling for every child and leave it to parents to purchase any extras they might wish for or to opt out of the system entirely. Third, there are the 'pluralists' who want a sound state system but one which is based on a meritocratic view of educational opportunity, a system which would select out the ablest pupils regardless of social background or ability to pay. These, he suggests, favour the metaphor of 'the ladder of opportunity'.

All of these can be seen as gradations of a common view, a view which he contrasts with that of the 'comprehensive planners', whose preferred metaphor is that of the 'broad highway', and who want to see the state providing a good education for all and one which would be focused on individual empowerment and competence. This of course is the very group whose defeat and demise we have been tracing.

The main features of these developments

A simplistic concept of 'standards'

The stated concern of these developments, which have led inexorably towards not only direct intervention in the school curriculum but also a very tight control over it, has been with educational 'standards'. In principle, such a concern is unexceptionable. However, as anyone who has given a moment's real thought to this issue will have quickly come to appreciate, 'standards' in education are very difficult to define, one person's view of 'standards' often being very different from another's not only in terms of their levels of expectation but also, and much more importantly, in terms of their definition. One person's concern may be with whether children have learned to read, to write, to perform mathematical computations or to understand technology; another may be far more concerned with whether they have learned to think, to explore all things critically or to appreciate art of all kinds.

It is necessary, therefore, for any discussion of 'standards', and consequently, and more crucially, any attempt to implement policies concerned to improve educational 'standards', to recognize the problematic nature of this concept and to begin from some attempted analysis or clearly stated definition of what these 'standards' might be or at least what they are taken to be in the context of the policy being pursued. It is intellectually dishonest, or at best inept, to fail to acknowledge this and to act as though it is not necessary to do any more than assume a consensus on such a contentious issue. It is even more unacceptable to adopt or assume that 'scientist' view of education, the inadequacies of which were explored in Chapter 1, and treat 'standards' as though they had some objective status which anyone of right mind can 'discover'. These kinds of approach must lead, as in this case they have done, to a view of educational 'standards' framed in highly simplistic terms.

In particular, they have led to a view of educational 'standards' in terms of traditional subjects and traditional subject-content, education as what the Hadow Report (Board of Education, 1931:para.75) criticized as 'knowledge to be acquired and facts to be stored'. We saw in Chapter 3 some of the problems associated with the notion of curriculum as content and, in particular, with the criteria for the selection of such content. Those problems are not recognized in current policies, which here again ignore several decades of debate, discussion and research in this area.

This unquestioning acceptance of a traditional, indeed outmoded, view of subjects and their role in education has further consequences which we must briefly note. It leads to the same kind of academicism which once underpinned the tripartite system of secondary education, a view of education as access to high-status knowledge – that taught in the grammar schools or, nowadays, in the city technology colleges. One consequence of that view must be, as it was in the days of tripartism, an elitist system – that new form of tripartism we referred to earlier – which clearly offers differentiated curricula, one version for those who have the ability, the motivation, the interest or the ethnic and social background to handle this form of academic curriculum, and another version for the rest, designed to prepare them for less demanding jobs and, since these continue to be few and far between, planned also with some notion of social control in mind, the 1990s version of 'gentling the masses'.

Hence there must be frequent testing and assessment. We must have a means of identifying which children will benefit from the academic curriculum and which must be offered something less. We must identify weakness from the earliest possible stage. It is no longer enough to apply selective procedures at eleven-plus; we must also apply them at five-, at seven-, at fourteen- and at sixteen-plus.

And all of this reflects a view of education with a quantitative rather than a qualitative emphasis, a concern with how much of the content-based offering children can absorb rather than with the quality of the experiences they can he offered by their years of compulsory schooling. It is very little different, therefore, from the approach to education which the Hadow Report (Board of Education, 1931) also criticized (and suggested was a thing of the past), an approach concerned solely 'to secure that children acquired a minimum standard of proficiency in reading, writing and arithmetic, subjects in which their attainments were annually assessed by quantitative standards' (1931:16).

Instrumentalism

A further major feature of these developments is the emphasis on technology and on the resultant demands of the economy. The education system is now seen almost totally as a national investment and not as one of the welfare state's social services (or at least, in respect of this latter function, is being increasingly deprived of resources in the same way as the other social services). Thus the emphasis is on what schooling is *for* rather than on any notion of education having some kind of value for its own sake. This is most apparent in the vocational stress which is being placed on educational provision at all stages from the nursery to the university. But it is more important that we recognize the general instrumentalism which is its natural, if not inevitable, effect. It would be foolish to condemn out of hand the vocational aspects of schooling, or even of higher education, and to hanker after an educational system in which all was the pursuit of knowledge for its own sake. Clearly, all educational institutions have a duty to help their pupils or students towards the attainment of productive and satisfying careers. There must be a concern, however, at the extent to which the attempt to do that can lead to an instrumentalist philosophy being displayed in all aspects of schooling, so that nothing can be valued, or its inclusion in our curriculum justified, or, as is most often the case, the expenditure of resources on it approved or made possible, except by reference to what it will lead to. For, by that criterion, much that is valuable (some might argue most valuable) in our culture will be lost from our curricula, and thus ultimately from that culture.

Commercialism

Another feature of the developments we are reviewing and one which also reflects that instrumentalism we have just noted is that prevalence of industrial models and imagery in much of the official pronouncements on the curriculum which we discussed in Chapter 2. We are offered a factory, or even factory-farming, view of schools and schooling, an analogy which leads us to the instrumentalism of commerce. And it is worth remembering Elliot Eisner's comment that metaphors 'shape our conception of the problems we study' (1982:6).

Nor does this remain at the level of analogy or metaphor. There are many aspects of current policies which not only use the imagery of commerce but move us positively towards the notion of schools and other educational institutions as commercial enterprises, which must compete with each other. The right now granted to schools to 'opt out' of local authority control is one such example; the invitation to industrial and commercial sponsors to subscribe financially to the establishment of city technology colleges, which can be created, we are told, only if such financial sponsorship is forthcoming, is another. Perhaps the most striking example, however, is the progressive reduction in the financing of universities and other institutions of higher education, which are now funded at such a level that they cannot maintain anything like an adequate level of resourcing for their teaching activities without engaging in extensive money-making activities, not only through raising research funding and academic endowments, but also through such things as subletting their buildings, including offering them as holiday accommodation, and the development of profit-making courses for students from abroad. Indeed, a recent report has suggested that all public funding of universities should cease and that they should be required to become completely self-funding and thus commercially viable, most notably by the charging of full-cost fees to all students, whether from home or abroad. A major step towards this has already been taken through the requirement that home students must now contribute substantially to their own fees.

We thus have here clear indications of what Thatcherism or the ideology of the 'New Right' means for the education service at all levels. The Thatcherite philosophy is that of paying one's own way, of no free 'hand-outs', of survival by one's own abilities, particularly the ability to pay for what one needs. It is manifested in the increased privatization of housing, in policies for a major shift in the National Health Service towards private provision and, in general, in a running-down of government funding of all social services. There is no reason to hope or expect that the education service should be any exception to this consistently applied policy. And the developments we are tracing here reflect the application of this philosophy to the provision of education. It is well summed up in the advice given by Sir Keith Joseph, as Secretary of State for Education, that 'schools should preach the moral virtue of free enterprise and the pursuit of profit'.

An increased emphasis on management

This pattern of commercialization has been matched by an increased emphasis on the management of the system and of individual schools.

Substantial sums of money have been made available to offer headteachers and other senior teachers opportunities for managerial training, through attendance at approved courses. One can have no objection to such teachers being offered facilities for the improvement of their managerial skills. Indeed, one might claim that too often in the past teachers in senior positions have conspicuously lacked such skills. However, we must note again that the emphasis in such courses has been on industrial models of management and one might further argue that there has been a notable neglect of what might be seen as the specific and peculiar concern of educational management – management of the curriculum, its development and its implementation, in forms which reflect educational rather than commercial emphases.

This trend towards industrial forms of educational management has been matched by and reflected in the move towards the increased involvement of industry in the control of education. A major feature of the new structures for overseeing and planning educational provision has been a significant increase in the number and proportion of representatives of industry on all major planning bodies – on all of the national quangos – the School Curriculum Development Council (SCDC), the National Curriculum Council (NCC), the School Examinations and Assessment Council (SEAC), the School Curriculum and Assessment Authority (SCAA), the Qualifications and Curriculum Authority (QCA) and the Teacher Training Agency (TTA) – on all Ofsted inspection teams, on the new funding bodies for higher education, on the governing bodies of all educational institutions, schools and colleges, and on the top-level planning committees of institutions of higher education.

And there has been a corresponding weakening of professional influence and control. We have noted how the control exercised by the teachers themselves in curriculum matters has been progressively eroded. It is worth noting too that the developments, outlined in the last section, in the area of teacher education have considerably reduced the potential influence on curriculum development from that quarter. And the independent role that Her Majesty's Inspectorate was once said to play in education, offering advice to the makers of policy from an independent professional perspective, is no longer in evidence. Members of the national inspectorate, now much reduced in number as we have noted, are no longer heard to offer any comment on national policies, either publicly or to the politicians and civil servants themselves, and their role is now better understood in terms of the implementation of policies decided upon with little reference to them than in terms of the maintenance of any kind of independent professional stance.

We must note finally the reduced influence of local authorities on the curriculum of the schools. The National Curriculum inevitably reduces that influence but, as we have seen, the powers now granted to individual schools to undertake their own financial management, and even to 'opt out' of local authority control altogether, weaken it even further. It is now at least technically possible for local authorities to disappear altogether. If they do so, or where they do so, control of the schools for which they were once responsible will revert to the Secretary of State. We have already seen a number of examples of 'failing' schools being taken out of the control of their local authorities and managed centrally.

Effectively, therefore, it adds up to tight and all-pervasive control from the centre.

The premises of direct intervention

There are a number of assumptions which underlie these policies and practices and we must end our analysis of these by briefly identifying them.

The first of these assumptions is that the education system is deficient and 'we must identify the deficiencies in the system and those who operate it, and devise ways of circumventing them' (Holt, 1987a:7). We have noted that throughout the process of development which has been described, from the publication of the Black Papers through to the present day, a major element in the 'debate' has been criticism of standards and especially of the teachers responsible for those standards.

We must also note, however, that deficiency, like beauty, and like the notion of 'standards' itself, is in the eye of the beholder. And we have seen that the deficiencies identified have been deficiencies only in relation to the view of schooling and its purposes held by those identifying them – the failure to meet the needs of the economy, for example, or to maintain the traditional academicism, or to promote 'the basic skills'. The deficiency, then, is more a failure on the part of teachers to meet the expectations of others than to attain the professional goals they have set for themselves.

A second assumption or premise of current policies and practices, therefore, which arises from this is that it is not the role of teachers to make judgements of this kind. Teachers are, or should be, merely operators, passive agents, technicians rather than professionals, whose task it is to carry out the policies made for them elsewhere and by others, to instruct children in those things their political masters wish to have them instructed in; 'they become not people, but functionaries –

"educational personnel'" (Holt, 1987a:7). Whether, in reality, teachers can be thus operated by remote control is another question, but it is certainly a premise and an assumption of current policy that they can and should be. The 1988 Act took from teachers responsibility for the *what* of the curriculum but left them with the freedom to decide on the *how*. Again, it might be argued that this is a distinction which cannot be made in practice. What is perhaps more important is the evidence that increasingly since 1988 even their responsibility for teaching methods has been continuously eroded, especially in key areas such as the teaching of reading and of number.

A third assumption, related to this, is that the curriculum can be planned, developed and implemented nationally by central agencies. The model is that which we saw in Chapter 5 has been called a centre-periphery model, and we also saw there how ineffective this approach has been when it has been tried elsewhere. This is yet another of those lessons we learned from research, experience and reflection which is currently being ignored.

It might of course be argued that the attempts, such as those of the Schools Council, at dissemination of innovation lacked the support of legislation, which the implementation of the National Curriculum does not, but what we know about the centre-periphery model's deficiencies and the problems of power-coercive strategies, allied to the point we have just made about the difficulty of operating teachers by remote control, suggests that this may make little difference.

Certainly, there is a growing body of evidence from the attempts of other countries to conduct their education systems in this way that it is a model which is seriously deficient and which does not work. In a country which has led the world in some aspects of educational provision it is sad that we should now be committed to a system which most other advanced societies are currently rejecting. The Japanese, for example, after many years of experience of this kind of subject-based national curriculum, have decided that it is too rigid and inflexible and are currently attempting to move towards more individual and personal forms of educational provision. It is worth noting, however, that one of the problems they face in this attempt is the lack of any tradition or research background of the kind such a development will undoubtedly require.

A fourth assumption or premise which lies behind attempts to move towards the centralized control of the curriculum is that educational planning is a scientific exercise, that education is an applied science and can thus be both studied and planned scientifically. Attempts to study society in this way and to produce scientifically based plans and prescriptions for social change were abandoned long ago, and for very good reasons. And we saw in Chapter 1 some of the fundamental flaws in this kind of approach to the study of education. The attempt to resurrect this as a model for educational research and planning is yet another example of the primitive nature of the underlying thinking of current policies – indeed of the lack of any depth of thinking. For attempts to denigrate the notion that teaching is an art and to insist on viewing it as a science reflect the kind of lack of conceptual subtlety we discussed in Chapter 1. For they fail to distinguish teaching as instruction from teaching as education. Or perhaps they merely reflect again that unwillingness to see schooling as anything more than an instrumental activity.

These, then, are the underlying assumptions of the educational policy whose emergence over the last three decades we have been tracing. Inevitably, in our discussion of them we have been led to many criticisms. Some of these criticisms are clearly directed at the underlying ideology of these new policies which have developed and which are encapsulated in the provisions of the 1988 Education Act and subsequent policies and practices. As such, therefore, they might be written off as mere manifestations of the irritations and concerns of those who adopt a contrasting ideology.

Others, however, are mounted not from the point of view of a different ideology but from a concern at the unsatisfactory nature of the thinking which underlies these policies and especially of the degree to which they ignore, in a manner which would be recognized as totally unacceptable in any other sphere, all the many advances in our understanding of the complexities of curriculum planning which this book is endeavouring to outline. It may be worthwhile to end this chapter, therefore, with a brief survey of the main features of this process of de-intellectualizing the educational debate and thus of effectively writing off any notion of curriculum studies as a productive undertaking of the kind we sought to define in Chapter 1 and have attempted to illustrate in subsequent chapters.

The de-intellectualization of the curriculum debate

Perhaps the most serious general problem with current policies is the limitations they are placing on debate about education, and on independent research which might help us better to understand the educational process, in its own right and not merely as a means for instruction in economically useful skills. The development of a worthwhile system of education requires such a debate and it needs to be able to respond to whatever understandings such debate generates. Central control inhibits, indeed seeks entirely to stifle, the kind of debate that is needed, and certainly to prevent the translation of the understandings it may offer into policies or practice.

Several things follow from this. First, we have seen that it leads to a deterioration in the intellectual quality of much of what is said and published about education. In so many respects, the present policy represents a return to an earlier, more primitive era, when our understanding was far less than it is, or could be, now. Historians of education will tell us that the National Curriculum is to all intents and purposes the curriculum recommended by the Board of Education in 1902 and that we have gone back to the era of 'payment by results'. Curriculum theorists will draw our attention to all the lessons which current policies ignore – lessons about attempts at the scientific study of curriculum, about approaches to dissemination, about how the curriculum actually changes or can be changed and, perhaps above all, lessons about the very different approaches to education and curriculum which recent years have seen emerging – especially from the literature about primary education, a field whose distinctiveness current policies do not begin to appreciate. Philosophers will alert us to the simplistic, undefined, unanalysed and consequently too often muddled concepts with which the official literature abounds – not only concepts of education and curriculum but also more specific concepts such as 'standards', 'progression', 'continuity' and even 'subjects' – and the concomitant failure to acknowledge the problematic nature of such concepts. Logicians will point to the internal contradictions and the unquestioned assumptions with which these same publications, and even the legislation itself, abound. Sociologists will comment on the failure to appreciate the central role of the teacher in education and curriculum development and the lack of wisdom of attempts to deny his or her developed professionalism, to see him or her merely as 'a carrier of knowledge with transmission skills' (Goddard, 1985:35) and to take the profession back to the days when teachers were mere instructors and education was something not many children were privileged to receive.

In general, then, the most serious effect of these policies has been to de-intellectualize the work of that profession which, above all others, should be concerned with the maintenance of intellectual standards. All the other difficulties which have emerged from our discussion stem from that basic weakness.

Above all, however, we are contemplating a picture of an education system and a national curriculum which is not only a sorry kind of baggage to be trailing into the next millennium, but also raises important and wide-ranging questions about the state of our society and especially the justification of its claims to be a democracy. For the picture which this chapter has painted is fundamentally characterized by a progressive loss of freedom – the academic freedom of the university community, the professional freedom of the teacher and, most of all, the intellectual freedom of the pupil. The implications of this go far beyond the school curriculum. For they have serious repercussions on the nature of society as a whole. In a democratic community, freedom is not to be equated with licence, but the alternative is not oppressive control. And in a democratic society, while professionals must not expect to pursue their professional concerns with little or no accountability, they are entitled to expect to be allowed to play a proper part in the planning and execution of policies and practices within their areas of expertise. A society which does not permit this is seriously compromising what might be seen as fundamental democratic values.

The question to which we must turn in our final chapter, then, is whether the kinds of policy and practice this chapter has described and analysed are consonant with the democratic context in which they are located.

Key issues raised by this chapter

1) What are the implications of external imposition of a curriculum for the quality of children's learning?
2) If the curriculum is a battleground of competing ideologies, is the only solution to yield that battleground to one of those ideologies?

Suggested further reading

Lawton, D. (1992) *Education and Politics in the 1990s: Conflict or Consensus?*, London and Washington, DC: Falmer.
Lawton, D. (1994) *The Tory Mind on Education 1979–1994*, London: Falmer.

8

A democratic national curriculum

Perhaps nothing sums up the dramatic changes that we have seen in attitudes to the school curriculum in the United Kingdom during the last twenty years so well as the fact that the concluding chapter of the first edition of this book, published in 1977, was called 'A Common Curriculum', that of the second edition in 1982 'The Whole Curriculum', that of the third edition in 1989 'The National Curriculum' and now the fourth edition concludes with 'A Democratic National Curriculum'. For this reflects a somewhat sorry progression from an open discussion of the issues, *via* an exploration of one possible solution framed in terms of the educational considerations which that exploration raised, to a consideration of what became the chosen solution – a set of policies and practices whose thrust is essentially political, utilitarian and economic – and finally to a questioning of whether the implementation of those policies and practices has any legitimacy within the context of a supposedly democratic society.

A major topic of discussion throughout the 1970s was the notion that there should be a centrally determined common curriculum in all schools, as there is in most other countries. The main aspects of that theoretical debate we shall look at shortly. Towards the end of that decade, especially as a result of the survey of secondary schools carried out by Her Majesty's Inspectorate (DES, 1979), which revealed, among other things, programmes of study for many pupils in the upper reaches of those schools which seemed to lack overall coherence, there emerged a growing awareness of the need to view and plan the curriculum as a whole and a concern with the notion of curriculum balance. All that theorizing about curricular issues has now been overtaken by those accelerating political policies whose main features have been a recurring underlying theme in previous chapters, so that we now have a centrally determined core of 70 per cent of the school curriculum – in primary as well as in secondary schools, in spite of the fact that a comparable HMI report on that sector (DES, 1978) produced nothing like the same critical evidence. And it does appear, as we have noted before and will see again later, that both the National Curriculum itself and the translation of it into the realities of school subjects and testing programmes owe more to those political pressures than to the theoretical debate which they have largely ousted.

This chapter, then, will attempt several things. Firstly, it will explore that theoretical debate, considering the case for and against the idea of a common curriculum and examining the associated concept of curriculum balance. It will do this partly to provide a theoretical base from which to evaluate the actualities of the National Curriculum now in place, but also because the arguments offered continue to provide the same kind of culmination of the theoretical discussions of the early parts of this book as they did in 1977, 1982 and 1989. Secondly, the chapter will explore the political case for a common curriculum and show how it reflects a quite different approach to schooling and one that owes nothing to that theoretical study of the curriculum of which this book has attempted to provide an overview. Indeed, we shall see that in several fundamental ways it represents a rejection of that study. It will be argued that that study must continue if we are not to lose our hard-won appreciation of the potential and the possibilities of the kind of education which becomes attainable through curricula which are properly framed by people who understand the complexities of curriculum planning. And, finally, we will consider the appropriateness of these policies and practices within a supposedly democratic society.

The chapter will, therefore, highlight that tension and conflict which have been present throughout our earlier discussions, and will thus offer a summary as well as a culmination of those discussions.

It is perhaps worth reminding ourselves from the outset that the United Kingdom was an exception in allowing its teachers and headteachers the degree of freedom over the curriculum of their schools that they enjoyed before 1988. Legally, until 1988, there was no binding requirement on any school to include any particular subject or activity in its curriculum other than a weekly period of religious instruction. This freedom contrasted most markedly with the procedures in other countries, most of which lay down, in varying degrees of detail, essential requirements for the curriculum of all schools. There are, of course, variations in the degree of control. Not all countries, for example, specify the number of hours to be devoted to each area; some leave rather more time for optional areas of study; there is some variation in the extent of the control that is exercised in relation to different age groups of children; and sometimes more than one common curriculum is established to cater for children declared to be of different intellectual abilities. On the other hand, in some countries, such as Greece, the degree of centralized control extends even to the approval of text-books (Moutsios, 1998). Whatever the details, however, the principle of central control over what are seen as the most important areas of the curriculum is well established and almost unquestioned.

In the United Kingdom, as we have seen, the tradition had been very different, and the idea that there should be a common curriculum for all pupils is a comparatively recent one, the realities of this as expressed in the National Curriculum dating only from the 1988 Education Act.

The case for a common core to the curriculum

Broadly speaking, three kinds of argument are produced in favour of the idea of a common curriculum, all of which we have touched upon in earlier sections of this book. First of all, we have the philosophical or epistemological arguments which base their recommendations for both the idea and the content of a common curriculum on those rationalist views about the nature of knowledge and of culture which we noted in Chapters 2 and 3. Second, we have certain social or sociological arguments which develop their case from the idea of equality of educational opportunity and the consequent need for all pupils to have access to the same educational diet. Finally, we have those very different political or economic arguments which claim that the school curriculum should be planned in such a way as to ensure that all pupils have the opportunity to develop to a certain standard the skills and knowledge which will enable them to meet the demands and to contribute to the continued growth of a technological and industrial society. This last line of argument we will return to later.

The argument from the nature of knowledge

The first kind of argument, then, is based on that objectivist and rationalist view of knowledge which we examined in some detail in Chapter 2, and it claims that, since certain kinds of knowledge have a status and value superior to others they have a prior claim for inclusion in any curriculum that is to be regarded as educational in the full sense. On this kind of argument any pupil whose curriculum excludes him or her from any of these areas of human knowledge and understanding is being offered an educational provision that is by definition inferior or is not receiving an education in the full sense at all.

An important variant of this same argument is the one we also noted in Chapter 3, the claim that it is the task of the school to transmit the culture of the society, so that the curriculum must be designed to convey what is worthwhile in that culture to all pupils – what, as we saw there, Matthew Arnold once called 'the best that has been thought and said'.

This kind of consideration has formed the basis of the cases that have been made on academic grounds for a common core to the curriculum (Lawton, 1969, 1973, 1975; White, 1973), and it is based on those particular views of knowledge and of society that we considered earlier in this book and on the belief that it is possible to establish some kind of value system that will enable us to choose what is worthwhile in knowledge and in the culture of the society.

It is worth noting further that, whatever doubts we may have over the underlying epistemology, the case made here is at root a moral one, based on a concern with equality of entitlement, a desire to ensure that everyone has access to the kind of curriculum which will promote their development as human beings.

The argument from the principle of equality

It is from the same basic moral stance that the second form of argument begins. The social or sociological arguments for a common curriculum start, as it were, from the opposite end of things. For they begin by considering some of the implications of *not* offering a common form of education to everyone. These arguments were to a large extent prompted by attempts to base education on the interests of children, to try to make school work meaningful and relevant to them by planning it in relation to their experience of their own immediate environment, thus generating the kind of low-level differentiated curriculum for which we noted in Chapter 5 the Schools Council was criticized. The suggestion made by the Schools Council's Working Paper No. 11, for example, that we might base the education of pupils in part on the experience to be gained from a study of 'the 97 bus' (Schools Council, 1967) was particularly effective in sparking off this kind of reaction. For it was claimed that an approach such as this can lead to a form of social control every bit as sinister as the imposition of one culture or one set of values on all (White, 1968, 1973). If a child's experience is to be limited to his or her own culture, his or her own environment, what he or she is already familiar with before he or she enters school, then there is a real risk that he or she will be trapped in that cultural environment and given little opportunity of gaining experience outside it.

Furthermore, if we once concede that two or three curricula might be generated to meet two or three broadly different kinds of need, we are almost certainly accepting implicitly the idea that Plato made quite explicit, that education in the full sense is capable of being achieved only by some gifted people and that the rest must be offered something inferior, which can only be some form of indoctrination or 'education in obedience' (White, 1968). We thus have, it has been claimed, a 'curriculum for inequality' (Shipman, 1971), and this is regarded as being unacceptable in a genuinely democratic society.

There is no logical connection, however, between the idea of education for all and that of a common curriculum, nor do demands for educational equality imply that all must have the same educational diet. As the Plowden Report (CACE, 1967) asserted, there is no incompatibility between the idea of equality of educational opportunity and variety of educational provision. And, as Mary Warnock (1977:26) has pointed out, 'there is a difference between claiming that everyone has an equal right to education and saying that everyone has a right to equal education'. To promote genuine entitlement a curriculum must not only be common to all it must also be 'genuinely suitable for all, not suitable only for the middle class or the most academic' (1977:84). Originally, therefore, the ideal of education for all, as it was expressed in the 1944 Education Act, was interpreted as requiring not that all should have the same educational provision but that the content of education should vary according to such considerations as age, aptitude and ability.

In practice, however, so long as the curriculum was conceived in terms of subjects and subject-content, and especially while this conception was aggravated by the selection of pupils for a bipartite or tripartite system of secondary schooling, inequalities of educational provision gave increasing cause for concern to those committed to the principles of democratic equality. The introduction of comprehensive forms of secondary schooling was intended to address this problem, but such problems cannot be resolved by organizational changes alone; they require appropriate changes in the curriculum. And so, many saw the introduction of comprehensive secondary education as implying a need for some commonality of educational provision. Thus we find the claim being made that, if justice and fairness are to be attained and the ideal of education for all achieved, all pupils should have access to the same areas or bodies of knowledge and learning – a common curriculum which will avoid the exclusion of pupils from their proper entitlement on any but the most extreme grounds.

Some problems and difficulties

Let us now consider some of the problems and difficulties raised by these arguments for a common curriculum, problems and difficulties which, as we shall see, are both theoretical and practical.

First, in so far as many of the arguments offered in support of the idea of a common curriculum derive from certain views about the nature of knowledge and of values, we need do no more than remind ourselves of the difficulties of this kind of argument which we examined in some detail in Chapter 2, and again in Chapter 3 when we were discussing this same question of the basis upon which we can decide upon the content of the curriculum. For we noted then that there is a variety of positions one can take on this issue of the nature of knowledge and that among the least convincing of these is that which claims some kind of objective status for knowledge. Even less convincing, we claimed, are those arguments which attempt to demonstrate the superiority of certain kinds of knowledge and human activity over others. If we were right to argue there that there is no firm foundation upon which we can establish the prior claims of some areas of human knowledge and activity to be included in the curriculum, then that same argument has even more force in the context of proposals to establish a common curriculum for all pupils on this basis.

This becomes immediately apparent when we ask what is to be the content of such a common curriculum. For even if we agree in principle that some of the arguments for a commonality of basic educational provision are strong, such agreement immediately breaks down when we come to decide what such basic provision should consist of. What is it that all pupils should be introduced to as part of their education? Those proposals that have been put forward for the content of such a curriculum are far from indisputable. For they are derived, as we have seen, either from a particular view of the nature of knowledge or from some idea of what is valuable in the culture of society or some attempt at combining both of these considerations (Lawton, 1969, 1973, 1975; Thompson and White, 1975; White, 1973). There is probably no single activity that will have universal support in its claims for inclusion in a common core of the curriculum.

The converse of this is also true. For just as there will be minority views opposed to the inclusion even of those things that have almost universal acceptance, there will also be minority interests that will be vociferously demanding the inclusion of those things that they themselves happen for personal reasons to be committed to. A good example of this is the demand for the inclusion of religious instruction of some kind in the common core. Once the principle of a common core curriculum is accepted, such idiosyncratic demands will proliferate and thus render its implementation almost impossible.

Thus the establishment of a common curriculum must founder on the practical issues of what should be included in it and who shall decide on this.

To these problems that derive from the difficulty, even the impossibility, of establishing any universally accepted criteria for judging the relative worth of different kinds of knowledge, we must add the further difficulties that are raised by the criticisms of the content of the curriculum which have been made by many sociologists (Whitty and Young, 1976; Young, 1971). For, as we have seen, their claims that all knowledge must be recognized as being socially constructed lead not only to an awareness of the lack of such objective criteria; they also raise further issues of a more sinister kind concerning the likely results of imposing a common system of knowledge on all pupils, as we saw when discussing the 'politics of knowledge' in Chapter 2.

For, as we saw there, it is argued that knowledge is socially constructed, that culture is impossible to define and that many cultures can be identified in a modern pluralist society. It is also argued that to impose one body of knowledge, one culture, one set of values on all pupils regardless of their origins, their social class, race or creed is to risk at best offering them a curriculum that is irrelevant, meaningless and alienating and at worst using the educational system as a means of effecting an inhibiting form of social control.

Such a process, it is claimed, results in the attempt to introduce children to areas of knowledge that they find irrelevant to their own lives and meaningless in relation to their own experience and thus encourages them to reject what they are offered, so that it leads not to education but to disaffection and even alienation from both the content of education and society itself. Further, as an attempt to impose a particular value system on pupils, it is difficult to defend such practice even from the charge of indoctrination, so that such a system is not only inefficient and counterproductive, it is also open to criticism on moral grounds.

Thus we have the strange situation that the idea of a common educational provision which is argued for on grounds of equality, justice and fairness is opposed most vigorously for precisely the same reasons by those who see the imposition of knowledge as a form of social control and as a source of alienation and disaffection.

We are, therefore, presented with yet another dilemma, or rather with evidence that we are faced by a debate about means rather than ends. For on both sides we have a commitment to the ideal of educational equality and entitlement, but we are faced with a head-on clash on the question of how such an ideal is to be achieved, whether by insisting that all pupils have access to the same knowledge or by tailoring educational provision to suit their individual needs. This is a point we must return to later.

First, however, it will be helpful if we spend a little time considering the associated concept of a 'balanced' curriculum, since a major feature of the arguments of both the factions we have just referred to is a concern that all pupils should be given a 'balanced' set of educational experiences. And, indeed, it is a major claim of the National Curriculum for England and Wales that it is providing this.

A 'balanced' curriculum

Without closer consideration, the use of the term 'balance' appears to bring with it those connotations of scientific exactitude which we have seen on other occasions and in other contexts to be spurious and misleading in any debate about education. The notion of balance in physics is precise and can be expressed as a mathematical formula, for it is a function of the weight of the objects in balance in relation to the distance of the forces they exert from the fulcrum around which they exert them. It would clearly be a mistake to look for this kind of precision in any educational context and we must recognize that the use of such terms in education is figurative and that any promise of exactitude they seem to offer is spurious. Like all other such notions, that of balance in education must be recognized as relative, taking its meaning almost entirely from the value system of the person using it. In short, we will all have our own view of what constitutes a balanced curriculum and what that view is will in turn depend on what we see as the fundamental principles of education. We must begin, therefore, by recognizing this and noting once again the essential and problematic value element in all educational debate.

This notion does bring several elements into the debate, however, which take us a good way beyond the idea of a common curriculum. For, in the first place, the demand that the curriculum be balanced requires that we view it and plan it as a totality and not in the piecemeal fashion hitherto adopted. The dangers of the piecemeal approach to curriculum planning within subjects emerged clearly and disturbingly from the survey of secondary education in England conducted twenty years ago by Her Majesty's Inspectorate (DES, 1979). It became apparent from that survey that the 'options' system employed by most secondary schools for their fourth- and fifth-year pupils was resulting often in a curriculum for some individual pupils which few would or could describe as balanced, whatever their notion of education. And so the survey went on to argue that 'teachers need a view of the school curriculum as a whole . . . if they are to coordinate their pupils' learning and provide them with some sense of coherence in their programmes' (1979:42).

A second element, which also emerged from this survey, is that the need for balance must be recognized not only within education but also between education and the other demands that the schools must respond to. For the criticism offered of some of the work reviewed was not only based on the fact that it represented an imbalance in educational terms, by losing opportunities, for example, 'to enlarge experience and understanding', but also that it failed to achieve a balance between educational and vocational considerations. This suggests, therefore, a further dimension to the notion of curriculum balance, that in planning the curriculum we should be looking not only for a balance of educational experiences for each individual, but that we must also be aiming for a balanced response to the conflicting claims of the interests of the individual and those of society, of the needs of the individual for both personal and vocational preparation. It suggests too that we must strive for balance between demands for the development of the pupil's capacities and those for the learning of certain bodies of knowledge, which might be deemed necessary, and between the need for specialization and that for breadth of study and experience. The balance we are looking for, then, is that of the juggler rather than that of the scientist, the engineer or the architect.

In fact, it is a more delicate notion than that, since the juggler, although needing to keep many balls in the air at one time, must achieve this by adherence to certain scientific and mathematical principles. These are not the principles that apply to calculations of educational balance. For here 'balance should not . . . be thought of in terms of equal quantities; the balance referred to here is a judicial balance rather than a mathematical one' (Schools Council, 1975c:27).

Again, therefore, we must remind ourselves that the notion of balance in education must be loose, flexible and relative – again a matter of judgement. If we do so, we can recognize that it not only introduces into the debate an acceptance of the existence of competing interests whose demands have to be accommodated to one another. It also introduces the idea of the need for individual interpretation and reveals precisely why we should concede a good deal of freedom in curriculum matters to local authorities, to schools, to teachers and even to individual pupils. For it makes clear that successful educational planning must always be of an *à la carte* rather than a *table d'hôte* kind, and that a balanced education, like a balanced diet, must be suited to the needs of the individual organism.

It suggests too the need to be tentative rather than dogmatic in educational planning, and thus illustrates what is the root inadequacy of the plan to establish a common core to the curriculum. For, in a somewhat paradoxical manner, the introduction of the apparently precise term 'balance' into the educational debate brings connotations of inexactitude, imprecision and the need for individual interpretation. For a common curriculum, even in the form proposed by educationists, would in practice result in a very unbalanced curriculum for a majority of pupils, as we suggested earlier.

Common processes and principles

What lies at the root of the problem is the attempt to specify precisely the subjects and the subject-content of which our common, balanced curriculum is to consist. The alternative, the solution to the problem which we are proposing, is to see external guidance as taking the form not of directives or specific statements of subjects or subject content, but rather of broad principles or guidelines. And it is this that points us towards the desirability of adopting that 'process' or 'developmental' approach to curriculum planning which we discussed in Chapter 4. For it suggests that the basis of educational planning should be certain broad principles which are susceptible to individual interpretation and which provide a basis for the selection of appropriate content, rather than lists of subjects or lists of goals or aims to be translated into step-by-step hierarchies of objectives or attainment targets. 'The true balancing agent lies not in the subject content but in the methods and approaches of the teacher and his [or her] inter-reaction with the pupils' (Petter, 1970:43; Schools Council, 1975a:18).

For the major error committed by the advocates of a common core curriculum is one that can be detected also in the work of most educational theorists. For almost all of them, from Plato onwards, having set out their educational principles, have immediately translated these into prescriptions for subject content, and have thus failed to recognize that education consists of learning *through* subjects rather than the learning *of* subjects. A number of problems follow from this kind of misconception, some of which we noted in earlier chapters, but the major difficulty it presents is that it denies the possibility of interpretation and adaptation to individual needs and circumstances.

If we are to make this possible, and thus to resolve the problem we noted earlier of the conflict between pressures for external control and the requirements of internal development, we have to recognize that what is or should be common to everyone's education, what is essential to it, what constitutes a balanced educational diet cannot be defined by listing subjects but only by listing broad procedural principles. In the same way, and for the same reasons, what constitutes a proper nutritional diet cannot be defined merely by listing foodstuffs but only by establishing broad dietary principles to be translated into individual prescriptions to suit the requirements of each separate and unique physical constitution. We would rightly look with some suspicion on a doctor who prescribed the same diet or medicines for all his or her patients. We must begin to view educational prescriptions in a similar light, and to recognize that variations in methods of delivery do not reflect the necessary degree of differentiation. It is not how you take your pills that matters; it is what pills you take.

Broad procedural principles, then, are the only basis for curriculum planning and for planning a common curriculum, as some exponents of the primary school curriculum suggested a long time ago (Board of Education, 1931). For it is by reference to these, as we saw in Chapter 4, that choice of subjects and of content is made; that objectives are chosen when they are chosen; that those objectives are modified and changed; that the value of 'unintended learning outcomes' is gauged; and it is by reference to these that the content of education can be varied to meet the needs of individual schools, teachers and pupils, with no loss of educational value or validity.

We are likely to find too that agreement is easier to attain at this level than at that of subjects or subject content. For the question to be asked is what it means to be educated, and few would wish to argue against the propositions that it means, for example, to have learned to value some activities for their own sake; to have learned to think for oneself; to have developed the ability to view the world critically; to have acquired understanding; to have achieved this in a number of fields; to have gained insight into several areas of human experience; to have been assisted to develop emotionally, aesthetically and physically as well as intellectually; and, in general, to have developed capacities and competences of a number of kinds. Few would want to argue too against the proposition that education must prepare the individual to take his or her place in society with all that that entails. For these reasons, few have raised serious objections to the eight adjectives which, as we saw in Chapter 7, Her Majesty's Inspectorate offered to 'identify 8 broad areas of experience that are considered to be important for all pupils' – aesthetic/creative, ethical, linguistic, mathematical, physical, scientific, social/political and spiritual (DES, 1977c).

Two things are worth noting here in relation to this important suggestion. The first is that it reflects a view of education and an approach to curriculum planning very much in line with that process or developmental approach we explored in Chapter 4, and that, for that reason and because, as we saw there, such an approach requires more rather than less teacher autonomy and less rather than more external control and direction, it has now disappeared from official publications on the curriculum, all of which have now returned to a combined content/objectives model, as we have seen.

The second point which we must note is highly germane to our discussion here, for these proposals for a curriculum framed in terms of eight 'areas of experience' became the basis for the 'entitlement' curriculum, which was the subject both of a subsequent HMI publication (DES, 1984b) and of an attempt to translate it into practice in six local authority areas.

In short, thinking – even at the official level – was moving towards the view that a common curriculum was needed to provide genuine entitlement, real equality of educational opportunity for all pupils, but that the best way to avoid the charge of indoctrination and those problems of alienation and disaffection which we saw earlier do, and must, arise when this is interpreted in terms of common subjects or a common body of curriculum content to be imposed on all, is to define that common curriculum in terms of common 'areas of experience' or processes, to produce a set of curriculum guidelines rather than what is in effect not so much a common curriculum as a common syllabus. In this way we might hope to ensure entitlement without uniformity, quality in diversity, a genuine equality in difference.

The solution to that theoretical dilemma we noted earlier which is posed by the concern with equality of entitlement would seem to lie in a move from the notion of education as transmission and curriculum as content, the problems of which we saw in Chapter 3, to that view of curriculum as process and education as development we explored in Chapter 4. Agreement on broad common principles should be the aim. The interpretation of those principles and decisions as to how they apply to individual schools and individual pupils must be left to the individuals concerned. This is precisely the approach to curriculum which was recommended for primary education by the Hadow Report (Board of Education, 1931) and reinforced by the Plowden Report (CACE, 1967), and which has now effectively been halted by current policies which are diametrically opposed to it.

It is at this level, then, that we might succeed in achieving some kind of agreement about what should be common to the curriculum of all pupils. We must, however, resist the temptation to translate these immediately into subjects or bodies of knowledge-content, since it is this that creates not only controversy but also some of the confusions and resultant inadequacies, as we noted earlier.

We must also resist the temptation to see these principles as aims and to translate them into hierarchies of curriculum objectives. For we must remember that, as was stressed in Chapter 4, the distinction between principles and aims in curriculum planning is very much more than a semantic one; it is quite fundamental. And we must bear in mind that, as we also saw there, to translate aims into objectives is to be committed to an approach to curriculum planning which again is diametrically opposed to and incompatible with that which translates them into procedural principles.

It is important, then, to treat principles as principles, to recognize that they are fundamental to planning that is to be educational in the full sense, to acknowledge that, while permitting a degree of centralized control, they also invite that complementary degree of local interpretation which we have seen is essential not only for the satisfactory education of every pupil but also for the continuing evolution of the curriculum itself.

The failure or refusal to appreciate the force of this case for the planning of education in terms of broad common principles which are then open to individual interpretation is the most salient feature of current political policies as they have been codified in the 1988 Education Act, especially in its National Curriculum and in the practices adopted for its implementation.

We must now briefly consider, therefore, the arguments for the National Curriculum, or rather we must attempt to identify its major concerns, since 'rationale is not in general its strong suit: it gives every impression of having been written by people used to issuing orders with no questions asked' (White, 1988:114).

The political case for the National Curriculum

We should perhaps note very firmly at the outset that none of those theoretical arguments we considered earlier plays any part in the case for the new National Curriculum. In fact, it is worthy of comment that the implementation of the legislation setting up this National Curriculum has not only reflected a disregard for all research evidence, whether empirical or conceptual, but also a very positive and deliberate rejection of this, and displays what can be described only as an anti-intellectual stance towards curriculum theory and planning. 'Political energy from the centre has focused educational debate upon economic questions . . . New initiatives depend on a ruthless slander of previous efforts rather than research and evaluation; argument proceeds by political assertion, not the accumulation of evidence' (Barker, 1987:8–9).

And so, there has been no suggestion anywhere that its content has been selected on the basis of a rationalist view of the intrinsic value of certain bodies of human knowledge (Peters, 1965, 1966; White, 1973), or a concept of rationality as divisible into several forms of understanding (Hirst, 1965) or 'realms of meaning' (Phenix, 1964), or a carefully thought-through policy for the achievement of equality of educational opportunity, or even a theory, whether carefully thought out or not, of what might constitute a balanced curriculum. The case for the inclusion of the core subjects of mathematics, English and science is clearly derived from considerations of social and economic utility. The 1988 Education Act also speaks of 'a balanced and broadly based curriculum' which in addition to preparing pupils 'for the opportunities, responsibilities and experiences of adult life' also 'promotes the spiritual, moral, cultural, mental and physical developments of pupils at school and of society'. However, the subsequent definition of the curriculum in terms of 'knowledge, skills and understanding' and 'matters, skills and processes' makes it plain that a developmental curriculum, such as we explored in Chapter 4, which might make possible the promotion of those many varied aspects of development, is not what is envisaged, but rather the emphasis is on the acquisition of knowledge-content. And the assessment programme reinforces this interpretation, as we saw in Chapter 6. The realities must be seen through the rhetoric.

Fundamentally, therefore, the case is an instrumental one (Kelly, 1990, 1994), concerned primarily, as we have noted on several occasions, with what education is *for* rather than with what it *is*. And schooling is seen as largely, if not entirely, concerned to ensure vocational success for the individual pupil (or for some individual pupils) and economic and commercial success for the nation. This instrumental, vocational, commercial flavour comes through very clearly in the 'consultative document' which was offered as the only real attempt to explain and justify the National Curriculum (DES, 1987a). For, as we saw in Chapter 7, the imagery of that document is that of the market-place, of commerce and industry. It is a factory farming view of schooling.

The Crowther Report (CACE, 1959), in an attempt to explicate the egalitarian philosophy of the 1944 Education Act, spoke of the 'burdens and benefits' of the education system, and in doing so it identified 'the two purposes that education serves' (1959:54) – as 'a national investment' and as 'one of the social services of the welfare state', as 'the right of every boy and girl', a right which 'exists regardless of whether, in each individual case, there will be any return'. It went on to say (1959:55), 'We have made no attempt to disentangle these two purposes of education'. The 'philosophy' behind the present legislation, although never made explicit, is located very firmly at the national investment end of this spectrum and in those ideologies of the New Right which we have seen Denis Lawton (1989, 1994) has so clearly identified.

We must not appear to be claiming that the economic health of society should be of no concern to those planning the school curriculum or that they should totally ignore the vocational interests of pupils. We have, or should have, left behind those simplistic polarities of the individual and society or liberal and vocational education. What is apparent, and disturbing, in these current policies is that there is no awareness that different educational purposes require different forms of planning and, in particular, that while the instrumental, economic and vocational aspects of schooling may well be properly served by the adoption of a content and/or objectives model of planning, other kinds of educational purpose necessitate other kinds of approach. The fact that the whole of the National Curriculum is framed in terms of its content and explicated in the form of curriculum objectives means that in its entirety it becomes instrumental and must inevitably fail to achieve, except by accident, those more subtle developmental goals we saw just now it also sets itself; for these require more subtle developmental approaches to the curriculum of a kind that the Act does not allow or, indeed, acknowledge.

We must also note that, as a corollary of this basic instrumentalism, this kind of curriculum must also be elitist in its effects, even if it is not elitist in its intentions (Kelly, 1990, 1994). We noted earlier that any curriculum framed in terms of a common content to be offered to all pupils whether they regard it as congenial or not, whether it reflects their own cultural background or not, must inevitably lead to the alienation and disaffection of some pupils, and to different levels of response to the content offered – differences which in no sense are a result of differences in 'ability', however that is defined. In this connection, we must note too that, even if it does not itself contribute to law and order problems in the young (and it may well do so), it can do little to obviate them and it renders it difficult to implement other measures which might (Kelly, 1998).

We suggested, therefore, that such an approach cannot offer a route to equality of educational opportunity. The case for this form of National Curriculum, then, must be seen as including, if not a positive commitment to an elitist system – although Kenneth Baker as Secretary of State, did in a televised interview publicly justify it on the grounds that 'people are naturally competitive' (they are naturally aggressive and lustful too) – then certainly an acceptance of such a system as an inevitable outcome of policies framed in this way. Again we see the effective influence of the New Right.

This point links closely with our former one in another way too. For elitism is a *sine qua non* of competitive commercialism, to which there is little point if all are to end up with equal shares. Both the instrumentalism and the content base of the National Curriculum, then, must take the education system away from that egalitarian road the 1944 Education Act, with its declared aim of achieving 'education for all according to age, aptitude and ability', set it on.

The most important conclusion we must draw from all of this, however, is that the National Curriculum reflects an educational policy and a view of the school curriculum which is at odds with most of those developments in curriculum theory which the earlier chapters of this book have attempted to explicate. And, if we have been right in arguing that curriculum development is possible only if full account is taken of the understandings and insights which we have in recent years acquired through studies of the curriculum of both an empirical and a conceptual kind, the implications of such a National Curriculum for curriculum development are serious and profound. It is to an exploration of some of these, then, that we must now turn.

The National Curriculum and curriculum development

There would seem to be four important general developments in our understanding of the theory and the practice of curriculum planning, change and development which studies during the last two or three decades have led to, and which have been thoroughly explored in the earlier chapters of this book. These all imply an enhanced rather than a reduced role for the individual teacher in both the planning and the implementation of curricula suited to the educational needs of pupils.

First, there is that increase in our knowledge and understanding of how children's minds develop which, as we saw in Chapter 4, has come from the work of Jean Piaget, Jerome Bruner, Lev Vygotsky and those many others who have taken forward the approach to the study of child psychology which they initiated. The important point about this work, as we saw there, is not that it compels us to adopt an approach to schooling which is based on it – no one could validly argue for that – but that it has revealed to us the potential and the possibilities of a form of education based on that kind of understanding. It has thus both extended our range of choice in curriculum planning and made it necessary to explain and justify the choices we make. Thus it is more than reasonable to ask for an explanation and a justification of the choice made by the architects of the National Curriculum not to take advantage of these insights and to go for a different, even outmoded, kind of approach to the planning of the school curriculum.

Secondly, we have seen that, allied to this increase in our understanding of how children develop, there has emerged a curriculum model which is a reaction to the perceived limitations of those models whose prime concern has been with either the content of the curriculum or its objectives, a model whose emphasis and starting point are the processes of education and their translation into procedural principles (Stenhouse, 1975), a model which in more recent times has been developed to reveal how those insights of the developmental psychologists might be adapted to the realities of curriculum planning and practice (Blenkin, 1988; Blenkin and Kelly, 1988a, 1996). We explored all the many dimensions of this debate about curriculum planning models in Chapters 3 and 4. The conclusion reached there was that planning by statements of content or by lists of 'aims and objectives' is severely limiting in terms of what it enables us to do in education, while taking clearly declared procedural principles as the base opens up far greater possibilities and also reflects more accurately the realities of any educational situation.

What is important here, however, is not the conclusion we reached but rather the fact that again this development opens up the range of choices available to curriculum planners, and thus, again, makes it necessary for anyone planning a curriculum at any level, but especially a nationally imposed curriculum, to explain and justify his or her choice of curriculum model. It is important too to note that the adoption of a process or developmental model places far more dependence on the autonomous, professional judgement of the individual teacher.

The third major advance in our understanding of the curriculum is that which emerged from our discussion of strategies for curriculum change and development in Chapter 5. For we saw there how the experience of twenty years of planned dissemination by the Schools Council had produced extensive evidence of the difficulties of bringing about change from outside the school, of some of the explanations of this, and of the need for any kind of curriculum change or development to be approached and tackled from the inside, and for any research intended to be supportive of such development to be a genuine form of action research. In short, we saw that the only genuine changes in the school curriculum, changes in the 'actual' rather than the 'official' curriculum, in the 'received' rather than the 'planned' curriculum, are those which result from developments which are school-based.

Again, the important point to note is the emphasis this places on the role of the individual school and of the individual teacher, on the concept of 'the teacher as researcher', as 'reflective practitioner', along with the doubts it raises about the effectiveness, in real terms, of any kind of attempt to manipulate the actualities of the school curriculum from outside. Syllabuses can be laid down centrally; tests can be conducted regularly to see how effectively those syllabuses are being taught;

frequent inspections can be carried out to ensure that schools are doing what is required of them; but how far this will influence children's education, as opposed to their acquisition of knowledge, is less easy to predict. Education is an interactive process, and the quality of that interaction must always depend on the professional capability of the individual teacher. It cannot be brought about by remote control, even when that control has the backing of the law of the land. That is the lesson of those attempts at changing and developing the curriculum which we considered in Chapter 5. Again, therefore, it is legitimate to ask for explanations and justification of the decision by the architects of the National Curriculum to ignore that lesson.

Fourthly and finally, a further major development in our understanding of the complexities of the curriculum and its planning is that which has emerged from those advances in assessment and evaluation theory which were outlined and examined in Chapter 6. There are several things of note there. First, we noted the sophisticated techniques of assessment and evaluation which have been developed to match those more sophisticated approaches to education to which we have just made reference. Secondly, we saw that these have included a concern with evaluating all aspects of the curriculum, and especially with attempting to make judgements of its worth and not merely of the effectiveness of its 'delivery'. Thirdly, it was emphasized too that this kind of evaluation necessitates our collecting data which go well beyond the mere assessment of pupil performance. And lastly, we concluded again that the teacher himself or herself had to be seen as central to this process, since in this context too we recognized the importance of action research and of the notion of 'the teacher as researcher'.

Again, therefore, we note that these developments are ignored in the new policies for education; indeed, we saw in Chapter 6 a shift in the style both of evaluation and of accountability towards a more bureaucratic or autocratic style as part of that general move towards more centralized control whose other aspects we traced in Chapter 7. Again too, however, we must acknowledge that the development of more sophisticated techniques and, indeed, different forms of evaluation and accountability have opened up the range of choices available to educational planners and thus here too have made obligatory some kind of explanation and justification of the forms adopted.

Two general points emerge, therefore. The first is the increased range of choice which has been made available to curriculum planners by all these developments, and the consequent need to explain and justify choices made. It is at best intellectually dishonest to make, and to implement, policy choices without explanation or justification. The second is the centrality of the teacher to that form of education which stresses development, which is based on processes, which requires school-based curriculum development and leads to, and indeed necessitates, democratic forms of evaluation and accountability. And it is of course this second factor which explains, even if it does not justify, the choice of approach made by the architects of the National Curriculum, whose prime concern is with centralizing control of the curriculum rather than with its continuing development as an instrument for promoting an individually tailored, 'bespoke' rather than an 'off-the-peg' education for all pupils. Indeed, it will be clear that all the evidence points to the fact that this kind of educational provision is incompatible in every respect with centralized control.

There is no doubting the need for improvement in the education system, so that criticisms of the new policies should not be interpreted as implying that one thinks that all was well with the old. Indeed, it would go against everything that has been said in earlier chapters not to acknowledge and, indeed, proclaim the necessity for continuous development. What is highly depressing about current policies is that they are designed in such a way as to arrest that process of development, and that they do not capitalize on the possibilities for improvement which can be found in that extended understanding which this book has attempted to outline. For there is a base there for developments of a kind which might not only enhance the life experiences of a majority of pupils, nor only ensure greater equality of educational experience; they might also contribute more to the needs of the economy than that narrowly conceived utilitarianism and vocationalism which we have seen to be the core of current policies.

These are developments, however, to which the teachers themselves are central and of which increased scope for the exercise of professional judgement is a *sine qua non*.

The central theme of this book, then, has been that the task of the teacher, at least of the teacher *qua* educator, cannot, and indeed should not, be defined in the kind of technicist and mechanistic terms that current policies imply, that education in the full sense can proceed only if teachers are able to make professional judgements on a much larger scale, and that any attempt to inhibit them in the exercise of this kind of judgement is likely to rebound to the disadvantage both of education and of their pupils.

Furthermore, it has also been argued that it is only through the exercise of this kind of judgement that curriculum development of any meaningful kind can proceed. If this is true, it reinforces what was said earlier in the book about the variations in interpretation that there will be of any curriculum imposed from outside; it suggests too that such an approach will bring out the saboteurs; it has already offered irresistible temptation to cheating and many forms of 'scam'; it raises the question whether, as a result, the imposition of a common curriculum is not likely to lead to less efficient rather than more efficient teaching; it also must cause us to reflect that if the central factor in curriculum development is thus rendered largely ineffective, the overall effect will be the ossification of the curriculum.

It is also likely to lead to the ossification of curriculum theory and curriculum research. Indeed, one has wondered constantly throughout the exercise of revising this book what the purpose of that exercise might be in the context of a National Curriculum which discourages debate of any depth about curricular issues and, as we have seen, denies and negates all the recent advances in curriculum theory and research, a policy which I have suggested elsewhere is comparable to denying doctors the advantages of transplant surgery. It will be worth our while, therefore, to consider next some of the implications of current policies for curriculum theory.

Implications for curriculum theory and research

We looked at some of the difficulties facing curriculum research at the end of Chapter 6 when we were concluding our review of evaluation theory. In particular, we noted the unavoidable limitations to the scope of that research if, at the national level, it is to be confined to the collection of data about pupil performance and the effectiveness of teaching approaches, and if individual teachers evaluating their own work in their own classrooms are at liberty to adjust only their methods and are not permitted to modify either the content or the goals of their teaching, whatever their own evaluative activities indicate to them.

The implications of these moves for the continued development of curriculum theory are serious and far-reaching. It will be clear that those understandings we have explored in the earlier chapters of this book are placed at risk by current policies, which, as we have seen, ignore, reject without explanation or even vilify them. Curriculum theory is one of the chief targets of the anti-intellectual, even de-intellectualizing, process we referred to in Chapter 7 as a salient feature of current policies for the schooling system.

It will also be apparent, however, that most, perhaps all, of these insights into the complexities of education and the many facets of curriculum planning are the results of research, both empirical and conceptual, which has been conducted in a context free of the constraints of direct political controls, and especially free of controls based on a limited view of education and an unwillingness to permit it to become anything other than a national economic investment and/or training system. We have referred constantly throughout this book to the work of the Schools Council; and it was claimed in Chapter 5 that most of those major advances we listed earlier received a great boost from its work. The freedom of the Schools Council to conduct, always of course with the full approval of all concerned, experiments in curriculum design and, above all, to encourage free and open debate of all forms of curriculum issue by teachers and others, in the full knowledge that ideas which seemed, or even proved, successful and worthwhile might be put into practice, had an inevitable influence on the growth of our understanding of all aspects of that multifaceted phenomenon we saw in Chapter 1 the educational curriculum to be.

Nor is it only national agencies like the Schools Council which have used the freedom schools and teachers have hitherto enjoyed to develop new approaches to the school curriculum. The schools themselves and individual teachers within them, especially in the primary sector and even more specifically in the infant/first schools, where they have been less constrained even by those indirect pressures we noted in Chapter 7, have used that freedom to develop work of a most interesting and imaginative kind. It is not long since people travelled from far and wide to see the English primary school. For in some schools in this sector was to be seen an approach to education and the curriculum of a kind unmatched elsewhere. From this source too, then, many understandings have been generated and much theoretical speculation promoted (Blenkin and Kelly, 1981, 1987, 1996).

Opportunities for this kind of free experimentation and for the more speculative and reflective theorizing to which it gave rise no longer exist. Major national research projects are politically vetted and have important limitations placed on their scope. The 1988 Education Act does permit certain schools to experiment with their curricula outside the National Curriculum, but only after the Secretary of State has given his or her approval and on condition that regular reports are made to him or her. There is little or no scope, therefore, for anything that goes beyond the officially approved orthodoxy. And, while one might argue that it was precisely that transgression of the accepted orthodoxy which gave rise to the events and problems of the William Tyndale School, which we noted in Chapter 7, one has also to acknowledge that it has led to many advances and developments of which it would be difficult for anyone to disapprove. Freedom will always lead to some abuse; but this must always be measured against the advances it makes possible. Freedom to succeed must imply freedom to fail. However, as John Stuart Mill pointed out in his essay, *On Liberty*, without the clash of contrary opinions there can be no advance towards truth of any kind, and even the true opinion is held with greater conviction if it has been measured against contrary views.

This clash of contrary opinions is not now permitted, at least at the practical level, in matters of the school curriculum.

What does this imply, then, for curriculum theory? First of all, it must be stressed that we must strive to maintain the understandings we have achieved. No one who has read this book can have failed to recognize and acknowledge the complexities of the educational process and of the activity of curriculum planning which it reveals. And it would be difficult for anyone having appreciated those complexities to argue that it is legitimate, rational or even moral to ignore them in planning the curriculum. It is important that knowledge and understandings gained in any field should not be lost.

Secondly, it is important that knowledge and understanding gained should not be lost merely because it has been decided by those at any one time in a position to enforce their decision that they will not be used at that particular point in the development of the human race. This is important not least in order to ensure that they continue to be available both to make clear to those who come after that there is a wider range of available options than that currently on display, and to provide a theoretical base for any planners who might subsequently decide they wish to do things differently. It would be a great pity if, after all the progress that has been made in our understanding of the ramifications, both theoretical and practical, of more democratic, egalitarian and individual approaches to educational provision, we were to find ourselves starting from scratch if and when a future decision were made to move in this direction or to return to this kind of educational philosophy.

Maintaining these understandings, then, is important. It will not be easy in a context in which teachers will increasingly find them irrelevant to their practice, but every attempt must be made to maintain their presence in the consciousness of as many teachers as possible, not in order to press a particular view of education but to ensure continued awareness of the wider range of possibilities which exists for schooling.

Continued advance and development will be even more difficult to ensure, however. The present system places no bar, nor could it, on our thinking about education, however much it may seek to control our practice and even our research. At the conceptual level, therefore, there is no barrier to the continuation of those exercises in conceptual research, in clarification of concepts, in explication of the implications of different ideologies and practices, which have, as we have seen, made important contributions to the development of our knowledge and understanding of curriculum planning.

There is little scope now, however, to back these up with empirical research, study or experimentation. And it is impossible to tell how far theorizing about education can go without the backing of practical experience. Theory unrelated to practice has long been a target for criticism both within and outside the teaching profession; indeed, the disregard of theory by most teachers has done as much as any other factor to make it easy for the politicians and their aides to dismiss the findings of educational research and thus to de-intellectualize educational practice. It is difficult, therefore, to predict that theorizing about education and in particular the curriculum, of the kind this book has attempted to explicate, can advance very far in the absence of all real practical reference. If there is one general lesson to be learned from the experiences of recent years, it is that in education, and probably in all other spheres too, theory and practice must go hand in hand and side by side if either is to benefit in any significant way.

Nor, as we saw in Chapter 6, must we be misled into accepting generalized accounts of Ofsted inspections as any kind of valid research, since these are no more than summaries of findings derived from a closely hedged, political activity; and they either have no acknowledged theoretical frame or do not embrace any kind of research into this. Whatever their actual value, the political roots and allegiances of Ofsted and its new inspectorate must render all of its reports, both individual and general, professionally and intellectually suspect.

Finally, the lack of any kind of theoretical underpinning to the National Curriculum and its attendant policies and practices is a major weakness – one can think of no other field in which such sweeping prescriptions could, or would, be made with no research base of any kind – and its rejection of the need for such constitutes the main threat to both the maintenance and the continued advance of curriculum theory.

It also, perhaps more seriously, constitutes a major threat to the future of democracy. This has been apparent since the policies focused on the National Curriculum were first adumbrated. The extent of that threat has become clearer through the practices which have been adopted to implement those policies. These have been noted throughout. It will provide a suitable culmination to this book if we end by identifying them more clearly.

Democratic imperatives

I have argued elsewhere (Kelly, 1995) that democracy is more than a political system; it is also and above all a moral system. It is a political system which is characterized not by particular procedures, such as regular elections of government, but primarily by being based on certain fundamental moral principles. In a genuinely democratic society, the government's policy must accord with those principles. And, furthermore, all social institutions, including, and perhaps especially the education system, must also be established and conducted within the same moral framework.

I have also argued (1995) that the major elements of that moral framework, its first principles, are equality, freedom and, binding these together, respect for the rights of the individual. These, then are the concerns which should be at the root of all social policy and practice in any society which purports to be democratic. And these are the criteria by which curriculum policies and practices must be evaluated in a democratic context.

It is not necessary to say much more about the degree to which that process of politicization which we have traced has taken us further away from the attainment of these moral ideals in the last two decades or so. It has to be seen as a part of that 'conservative restoration' which Michael Apple (1990) has identified in the educational scene in the USA. 'The public debate on education, and all things social, has shifted profoundly to the right' (1990:378). Nor is this surprising when we consider what we have noted throughout – the ever-growing influence of the New Right and those elitist ideologies which Denis Lawton (1989, 1994) has outlined.

What we must note here is that such ideologies are not merely at odds with the ideology of the 'comprehensive planner'; they are also incompatible with the fundamental principles of democratic living. For democracy is not about privilege; it is about equality. And equality in education cannot be achieved unless we provide an appropriate curriculum, planned and implemented in such a way as to combat privilege and promote equity for all, regardless of social or ethnic origin. This has to be recognized as a basic democratic right. As Wilf Carr (1991:185) has said, 'the primary role of education in a democracy is to provide all its future members with the opportunity to develop those intellectual and moral qualities which meaningful participation in democratic life requires'. Enough has perhaps been said to demonstrate that the National Curriculum is far from being such a curriculum.

Furthermore, we drew attention at the end of Chapter 7 to the fact that the politicization process which has unfolded has been characterized by an ever-increasing loss of freedom at every level. Academic freedom is now a remote memory; teacher autonomy, however relative, is a thing of the past; parents may have the right (at least on paper) of selecting the school their offspring will attend, but this is a poor sort of freedom when the curriculum of all schools is virtually identical – unless of course they can afford to send them to schools in the private sector which are not subject to these constraints; and the pupils themselves now have little freedom to plan and negotiate their own learning activities. Yet, as Paulo Freire has said, in a democratic context education is 'the practice of freedom' (1976) rather than 'the pedagogy of the oppressed' (1972).

Perhaps more serious in the long term has been that process of de-intellectualization which we noted in Chapter 7 and again in this chapter. Openness in the face of knowledge is crucial for continued development. The form of political organization which is the opposite of democracy is totalitarianism. That form is characterized especially by its concern to maintain its *status quo*, and this it does primarily through control of the distribution of knowledge, discouragement of open debate and other forms of censorship, often in a covert form.

All that has been said about curriculum theory in earlier chapters is fundamentally a case for freedom of knowledge, thought, opinion, expression, and speech. And to deny the force of that theory is to deny these essential features of democracy and thus to deny democracy itself.

For a central feature of democracy, as John Dewey was at pains to stress, is that it provides a context in which knowledge can change, evolve, develop precisely because it is free of constraints of this kind. This is well encapsulated in the words of Winter (1991:468).

> The rational development of knowledge and the effective operation of democracy *both* depend on the existence of an informed and critical community, i.e. a community which has been 'educated' in the analytical skills which will enable them to evaluate and compare rival sets of assertions, arguments and 'facts'.

The introduction of constraints on this freedom, therefore, represents a major step away from genuine democratic forms. Yet again we have seen that current policies and practices seek seriously to limit the degree to which such evaluative and comparative activity can be pursued, even to the extent of comparing current policies with what they have replaced. The curriculum, as we have seen, is controlled and policed by methods which are not open to debate or discussion, and certainly not to modification or change by democratic processes, and schools and their teachers are evaluated according to criteria they have had little hand in establishing. 'Consultancy' is another word which has come to have a new meaning within the current discourse and rhetoric. For it now refers to a process of informing people of changes that are about to be made before they are actually implemented, so that they have time to comment, even though their comments are unlikely to be taken account of.

We have thus reached a situation in which freedom, equality and the democratic rights of teachers, pupils and parents have been compromised to a degree which renders current policies and practices highly vulnerable to the charge of being undemocratic.

What, then, would be the key features of a democratic national curriculum?

The key features of a democratic national curriculum

There are two main points which must be stressed in addressing the question of an appropriate national curriculum for a democratic society.

First, the curriculum itself must be such as to promote equality of empowerment. It must be geared towards the development of capacities and capabilities which will support every individual in developing as an autonomous member of a free and genuinely self-governing community. And it must do this in such a way as neither to favour the privileged nor to further disadvantage the under-privileged.

We have perhaps said enough already in this chapter to suggest that such a curriculum will not be found through a continuation of current policies and practices which are seriously flawed as well as being simplistic in conception and design. The solution must lie in further exploration of the alternative which the chapter has adumbrated – a curriculum based not on common knowledge-content but on common procedural principles, guidelines, even 'areas of experience' – a national curriculum which is adjectival rather than substantive, and thus descriptive rather than prescriptive (Edwards and Kelly, 1998).

Such a curriculum of course, as has been pointed out, will depend for its effectiveness on the professional judgement, interpretation and implementation of the individual teacher. And this brings us to the second major feature of a democratic national curriculum. It must be planned not by the politicians and their aides, but by those who actually understand curriculum, albeit working in a context of proper democratic control and accountability. We have seen throughout this book the degree of expertise and understanding of education and curriculum which has been built up over many years. We have also seen the extent to which the National Curriculum has been planned by people who have no awareness of the insights such knowledge and understanding can offer and no inclination to consult with those who do. Hence, their curriculum is seriously inadequate for the democratic context for which it is intended. The creation of an effective national curriculum depends crucially on there being a major input from the professionals.

The role of the professional in a democratic society is an interesting subject for debate, although one we cannot pursue at any length here. To allow any professional to dictate policy in his/her area of expertise is clearly unacceptable in view of the implications this has for the freedom of others. However, to marginalize the professional simply because of the threat of such dictation, as has been done in the planning of current educational policies for England and Wales, is unbelievably crass, since it is tantamount to saying that policies should be constructed by those who by definition lack the understanding to frame them intelligently and expertly. The solution has to be found in a policy of extensive consultation betwen policy-makers and professionals, to enable the input of professional expertise while guarding against its possible dominance. What is needed is considerably more than the tokenism of inviting into the policy-making process a few 'tame' professionals and academics, those who are known to be ready to toe the official line. For this does not give that 'clash of contrary opinions' which, as we saw, John Stuart Mill saw as essential to the emergence of anything like the 'truth'.

One is pleased, and, indeed, surprised, to note this happening elsewhere. In Ireland, for example, the first step which the government seems to take in any planned initiative is to set up a consultancy body which will bring together all interested parties, including the professionals and the academics. How long is it since a Minister of Education in the UK was able to preface the published record of a symposium on 'Philosophical Issues in Educational Policy' with comments like 'the symposium . . . is a particularly worthwhile and enriching contribution to the debate and, indeed, to the refinement of my own thinking in this area', 'these arguments leave no room for complacency', 'these papers . . . raise disturbing questions', 'the papers not only defy complacency, but also offer vision' and 'we may disagree with the conclusions but we cannot criticise the energy, vigour and strength of the arguments' (Hogan, 1995:iii and iv)? There is a model here for the role of the academic and the professional in any educational planning. Such involvement must be seen as a *sine qua non* of educational planning in and for a democratic society.

An appropriate curriculum for a democratic society, then, would be one which allowed for the continuing development of knowledge and understanding, which provided proper opportunities for young people to develop their powers of autonomous thinking and offered them social and intellectual empowerment and which provided teachers with the scope to achieve these goals through the exercise of their own judgement as professionals. This judgement would be exercised within a democratic system of accountability – accountability to their peers as well as to the wider community. And the framework for their work, a national curriculum framed in terms of guidelines and principles rather than subject-content would be planned, implemented and continuously reviewed by a body made up of professionals, academics, policy-makers and lay members – a General Teaching Council of the kind teachers and educationists have long been pressing for.

My friend and colleague, Gwyn Edwards, and I recently edited a book which was subtitled *Towards an Alternative National Curriculum*, and we concluded that book with a list of 'emergent principles for an alternative national curriculum'. Since these were predicated on the kind of democratic principles we have been discussing, it will provide a good conclusion to this section – and perhaps also the chapter and, indeed, the book – to quote some of the more significant of these here.

> The school curriculum is an essential element in the safeguarding of democracy, so that it cannot properly be framed or controlled by the representatives of any one political ideology, especially those who support a non-democratic ideology.

> Education is the responsibility of society as a whole, and, as such, should be under the direction of intelligent and committed lay-persons working closely, and in genuine collaboration, with informed, expert and caring professionals. The establishment of a democratically formed Teaching Council is long overdue.

> In a democratic society schools exist to provide an education for life, so that education must be planned as human development and not merely in terms of the acquisition of knowledge – as developmental rather than incremental, as a process rather than as a product.

> The essentials of such an education for life are personal enrichment, political empowerment and personal/social/moral adjustment and responsibility.

> The assumption has to be made (although it must be carefully monitored) that this is also the most effective route to economic success – for society as a whole as well as for each individual.

> All subject/knowledge-content is politically loaded, so that, even if the selection of curriculum content must always be ideologically driven, the manner of its presentation must be such as to invite challenge, questioning, critique, debate rather than mere assimilation and regurgitation.

Democratic education must be recognized as essentially a collaborative rather than a competitive activity.

The curriculum must be framed, therefore, not primarily in terms of its content but as a set of guidelines delineating the democratic entitlement of every young citizen.

A curriculum so framed cannot be operated by remote control or through a system of external testing and the application of sanctions. Its implementation must involve greater professional freedom and scope for the exercise of professional judgment by teachers.

The training of teachers (both initial and in-service) must again become the **education** of teachers, and must regain its former focus on the development of an understanding of young people, a recognition of the importance of caring for them and the acquisition of appropriate powers of professional judgment.

(Edwards and Kelly, 1998:199–200)

The present National Curriculum for England and Wales, satisfies none of these criteria, nor do its associated policies and practices. It is revealed, therefore, as not only flawed in the many ways which we have identified but also as inappropriate for a democratic society. And, in a fundamental sense, it stands outside the curriculum debate we have been overviewing throughout this book, since it neither accepts the value positions which are basic to that debate (e.g. a concept of *education*, an acceptance of democratic principles and a commitment to translating these into curricular realities) nor, as a result, does it pay any heed to the insights and understandings generated by the activities of those who are committed to those value positions and who thus have come to recognize some of the many complexities (and indeed possibilities) of planning a curriculum for education in the full sense. Indeed, there is no longer any basis for debate between those who take these issues seriously and the proponents of current policies and practices, since there is no common ground between them, no shared value system.

Hence, in updating this book it has not been possible to trace developments in our understanding of curriculum during the intervening years since the last edition, but merely to record and trace the processes of politicization by which that understanding has not only been discredited but has been replaced by a totally different culture, one that, as we have just seen, is impossible to reconcile with the democratic context it purports to inhabit.

The implementation of current policies has been a very expensive exercise, in terms not only of money but also of the toll it has taken, and continues to take, of conscientious and committed teachers at every level of the education system. And one can only end as one did in 1989 by wondering what progress might have been made if the same money, time and energy had been devoted to supporting the development of the curriculum and the raising of teacher quality by means other than the mere tightening of external controls. It is far from self-evident that negative measures are the best devices for securing positive ends. And there can be no more positive end than that of devising the most effective curriculum possible for developing the capacities and the potential of all the nation's children.

The story has been not only of what is but also of what might have been.

Key issues raised by this chapter

1) To what extent, if at all, can a subject-based or knowledge-based curriculum be appropriate in a democratic society?
2) How important is the teacher's professional freedom in the realization of an appropriate democratic curriculum for all children?
3) How can or should the exercise of that professional freedom be monitored?

Suggested further reading

Edwards, G. and Kelly, A. V. (eds.) (1998) *Experience and Education: Towards an Alternative National Curriculum*, London, Chapman.

Kelly, A. V. (1994) *The National Curriculum: A Critical Review* (updated version), London: Chapman.

Kelly, A. V. (1995) *Education and Democracy: Principles and Practices*, London, Chapman.

Ross, A. (1997) *Curriculum, Construction and Critique*, London: Falmer.

Bibliography

(All Harper & Row (London) titles are now published by Paul Chapman Publishing, London.)

Alexander, R. J. (1984) *Primary Teaching*, London and New York: Holt, Rinehart and Winston.

Apple, M. W. (1990) The politics of official knowledge in the United States of America, *Journal of Curriculum Studies*, 22(4):377–383.

Archambault, R. D. (ed.) (1965) *Philosophical Analysis and Education*, London: Routledge & Kegan Paul.

Arnold, M. (1908) *Reports on Elementary Schools*, London: HMSO.

Atkin, J. M. (1979) Educational accountability in the United States, in L. Stenhouse (ed.) (1979) *Educational Analysis*, 1(1), Falmer: Lewes.

Ball, E. (1981) *School Focused Curriculum Development: Constraints and Possibilities*, unpublished MA thesis, University of London.

Ball, E. (1983a) An approach to school based curriculum development, in Blenkin and Kelly (eds.) (1983) *The Primary Curriculum in Action*, London: Harper and Row. pp.183–199.

Ball, E. (1983b) Supporting curriculum development: case study of a school-focused support scheme, in Blenkin and Kelly (eds.) (1983) *The Primary Curriculum in Action*, London: Harper and Row.

Ball, S. J. (1984a) Facing up to falling roles; becoming a comprehensive school, in Ball, S. J. (ed.) (1984b) *Comprehensive Schooling; A Reader*, Lewes: Falmer.

Ball, S. J. (ed.) (1984b) *Comprehensive Schooling: A Reader*, Lewes: Falmer.

Ball, S. J. (1987) *The Micro-Politics of the School*, London: Methuen.

Ball, S. J. (1990) *Politics and Policy Making in Education: Exploration in Policy Sociology*, London: Routledge.

Ball, S. J. (1996) Recreating policy through quantitative research: a trajectory analysis, American Education Research Association Annual Conference, New York, 8–12 April.

Barker, B. (1987) Prevocationalism and schooling, in Holt, M. (ed.) (1987b) *Skills and Vocationalism: The Easy Answer*, Milton Keynes: Open University Press.

Becher, A. and Maclure, S. (1978) *The Politics of Curriculum Change*, London: Hutchinson.

Bennett, N. (1976) *Teaching Styles and Pupil Progress*, London: Open Books.

Bennett, N., Desforges, C., Cockburn, A. and Wilkinson, E. (1984) *The Quality of Pupil Learning Experiences*, London: Erlbaum.

Bennis, W. G., Benne, K. D. and Chin, R. (1969) *The Planning of Change*, 2nd edn, London and New York: Holt, Rinehart and Winston.

Bernstein, B. (1967) Open schools, open society?, *New Society*, 14 Sept.

Bernstein, B. (1971) On the classification and framing of educational knowledge, in Young, M. F. D. (ed.) (1971) *Knowledge and Control*, London: Collier MacMillan.

Bernstein, B. (1996) *Pedagogy, Symbolic Control and Identity: Theory, Research, Critique*, London: Taylor and Francis.

Black, P. (1993) The Shifting Scenery of the National Curriculum, in O'Hear and White (eds.) (1993) *Assessing the National Curriculum*, London: Paul Chapman.

Blenkin, G. M. (1980) The influence of initial styles of curriculum development, in Kelly, A. V. (ed.) (1980) *Curriculum Context*, London: Harper and Row.

Blenkin, G. M. (1988) Education and development: some implications for the curriculum in the early years, in Blyth, W. A. L. (ed.) (1988) *Informal Primary Education Today: Essays and Studies*, London: Falmer.

Blenkin, G. M., Edwards, G. and Kelly, A. V. (1992) *Change and the Curriculum*, London: Paul Chapman.

Blenkin, G. M. and Kelly, A. V. (1981; 2nd edn 1987) *The Primary Curriculum*, London: Harper & Row.

Blenkin, G. M. and Kelly, A. V. (eds.) (1983) *The Primary Curriculum in Action*, London: Harper & Row.

Blenkin, G. M. and Kelly, A. V. (1988a) Education as development, in Blenkin, G. M. and Kelly, A. V. (eds.) (1988b) *Early Childhood Education: A Developmental Curriculum*, London: Paul Chapman.

Blenkin, G. M. and Kelly, A. V. (eds.) (1988b) *Early Childhood Education: A Developmental Curriculum* (second edition 1996), London: Paul Chapman.

Blenkin, G. M. and Kelly, A. V. (eds.) (1992) *Assessment in Early Childhood Education*, London: Paul Chapman.

Blenkin, G. M. and Kelly, A. V. (eds.) (1997) *Principles into Practice in Early Childhood Education*, London: Paul Chapman.

Block, J. H. (ed.) (1971) *Mastery Learning: Theory and Practice*, New York, Chicago, San Francisco, Atlanta, Dallas, Montreal, Toronto, London, Sydney: Holt, Rinehart and Winston.

Bloom, B. S. *et al.* (1956) *Taxonomy of Educational Objectives. 1: Cognitive Domain*, London: Longman.

Bloom, B. S. (1971) Mastery learning, in Block, J. H. (ed.) (1971), *Mastery Learning: Theory and Practice*, New York, Chicago, San Francisco, Atlanta, Dallas, Montreal, Toronto, London, Sydney: Holt, Rinehart and Winston.

Blyth, W. A. L. (1974) One development project's awkward thinking about objectives, *Journal of Curriculum Studies*, 6:99–111.

Blyth, W. A. L. (1984) *Development, Experience, and Curriculum in Primary Education*, London: Croom Helm.

Blyth, W. A. L. (ed.) (1988) *Informal Primary Education Today: Essays and Studies*, London: Falmer.

Bobbitt, F. (1918) *The Curriculum*, Boston: Houghton Mifflin.

Boyne, R. and Rattansi, A. (eds.) (1990) *Postmodernism and Society*, London: Macmillan.

Brennan, W. K. (1979) *Shaping the Education of Slow Learners*, London: Routledge.

Broadfoot, P. (1996) *Education, Assessment and Society*, Buckingham: Open University.

Bruner, J. and Haste, H. (eds.) (1987) *Making Sense. The Child's Construction of the World*, London: Methuen.

Campbell, R. J. (ed.) (1993) *Breadth and Balance in the Primary Curriculum*, London and Washington, DC: Falmer.

Carr, W. (1991) Education for democracy? A philosophical analysis of the National Curriculum, *Journal of Philosophy of Education*, 25(2):183–191.

Carr, W. (1995) *For Education: Towards Critical Educational Enquiry*, Buckingham, Philadelphia: Open University Press.

Carter, D. S. G. and O'Neill, M. H. O. (eds.) (1995) *International Perspectives on Educational Reform and Policy Implementation*, London: Falmer.

Charters, W. W. (1924) *Curriculum Construction*, New York: Macmillan.

Cherryholmes, C. H. (1987) A social project for curriculum: poststructural perspectives, *Journal of Curriculum Studies*, 19(4):295–316.

Childs, J. L. (1956) *American Pragmatism and Education*, New York: Holt.

Chitty, C. (1990) Central control of the school curriculum, 1944–1987, in Moon, B. (ed.) *New Curriculum – National Curriculum*, London: Hodder and Stoughton.

Chitty, C. (1997) The school effectiveness movement: origins, shortcomings and future possibilities, *The Curriculum Journal*, 8(1):45–62.

Connolly, K. and Bruner, J. (eds.) (1974) *The Growth of Competence*, London: Academic Press.

Cooksey, G. (1972) Stantonbury Campus – Milton Keynes, *Ideas*, 23:28–33.

Cooksey, G. (1976a) The scope of education and its opportunities in the 80s, in Kelly, A. V. (ed.) (1976) *The Scope of Education. Opportunities for the Teacher*, Conference Report, London: Goldsmiths' College.

Cooksey, G. (1976b) Stantonbury Campus: the idea develops – December 1975, *Ideas*, 32: 58–63.

Cornbleth, C. (1990) *Curriculum in Context*, London: Falmer.

Cox, C. B. and Dyson, A.E. (eds.) (1969a) *Fight for Education: A Black Paper*, Manchester: Critical Quarterly Society.

Cox, C. B. and Dyson, A. E. (eds.) (1969b) *Black Paper Two: The Crisis in Education*, Manchester: Critical Quarterly Society.

Curtis, S. J. (1948) *History of Education in Great Britain*, London: University Tutorial Press.

Davies, I. K. (1976) *Objectives in Curriculum Design*, Maidenhead: McGraw-Hill.

Davies, L. (1994) *Beyond Authoritarian School Management*, Ticknell: Education Now Books.

Dearden, R. F. (1968) *The Philosophy of Primary Education*, London:Routledge.

Dearden, R. F. (1976) *Problems in Primary Education*, London: Routledge.

Dewey, J. (1902) *The Child and the Curriculum*, Chicago: University of Chicago Press.

Dewey, J. (1916) *Democracy and Education*, New York: Macmillan (page references are to 1961 edn).

Dewey, J. (1938) *Experience and Education*, New York: Collier-Macmillan.

Doll, W. E. (1989) Foundations for a post-modern curriculum, *Journal of Curriculum Studies*, 21(3):243–253.

Doll, W. E. (1993) *A Post-Modern Perspective on Curriculum*, New York: Teachers College Press.

Donaldson, M. (1978) *Children's Minds*, Glasgow: Fontana/Collins.

Donaldson, M. (1992) *Human Minds: an exploration*, London: Penguin.

Donaldson, M., Grieve, R. and Pratt, C. (eds.) (1983) *Early Childhood Development and Education*, Oxford: Blackwell.

Downey, M. E. and Kelly, A. V. (1979) *Theory and Practice of Education: An Introduction*, 2nd edn (revised 3rd edn 1986), London: Harper and Row.

Ebbutt, D. (1983) *Educational Action Research: Some General Concerns and Specific Quibbles* (mimeo), Cambridge Institute of Education.

Edwards, G. and Kelly, A. V. (1998a) Education as development through experience, in Edwards, G. and Kelly, A. V. (eds.) (1998b) *Experience and Education: Towards an Alternative National Curriculum*, London: Paul Chapman.

Edwards, G. and Kelly, A. V. (eds.) (1998b) *Experience and Education: Towards an Alternative National Curriculum*, London: Paul Chapman.

Eisner, E. W. (1969) Instructional and expressive educational objectives: their formulation and use in curriculum, in Popham, W. J., Eisner, E. W., Sullivan, H. J. and Tyler, L. L. (1969), *Instructional Objectives*, American Educational Research Association Monograph Series on Curriculum Evaluation No.3, Chicago: Rand McNally.

Eisner, E. W. (1982) *Cognition and Curriculum*, New York and London: Longman.

Eisner, E. W. (1985) *The Art of Educational Evaluation: A Personal View*, London and Philadelphia: Falmer.

Eisner, E. W. (1993) Reshaping assessment in education: some criteria in search of practice, *Journal of Curriculum Studies*, 25(30):219–234.

Eisner, E. (1996) *Cognition and Curriculum Reconsidered*, London: Chapman.

Elliott, G. (1981) *School Self-Evaluation – The Way Forward* (mimeo), University of Hull.

Elliott, J. (1976) Preparing teachers for classroom accountability, *Education for Teaching*, 100:49–71.

Elliott, J. (1981) *Action Research: A Framework for Self-Evaluation in Schools*, Cambridge Institute of Education.

Elliott, J. (1991) *Action Research for Educational Change*, Milton Keynes: Open University Press.

Elliott, J. (1996) School effectiveness research and its critics: alternative visions of schooling, *Cambridge Journal of Education*, 26(2):199–224.

Elliott, J. (1998) *The Curriculum Experiment: Meeting the Challenge of Social Change*, Buckingham: Open University Press.

Elliott, J. and Adelman, C. (1973) Reflecting where the action is, *Education for Teaching*, 92:8–20.

Esland, G. M. (1971) Teaching and learning as the organisation of knowledge, in Young, M. F. D. (ed.) (1971) *Knowledge and Control*, London: Collier-Macmillan.

Featherstone, M. (1988) In pursuit of the postmodern: an introduction, *Theory, Culture and Society*, 5,:195–215, London, Newbury Park, Beverly Hills and New Delhi: Sage.

Feinberg, W. (1975) *Reason and Rhetoric: the intellectual foundations of twentieth-century liberal education policy*, New York: Wiley.

Fielding, M. (1997) Beyond school effectiveness and school improvement: lighting the slow fuse of possibility, *The Curriculum Journal*, 8(1):7–27.

Foucault, M. (1979) *The History of Sexuality. Volume 1: An Introduction* (trans. Robert Hurley), London: Allen Lane.

Freire, P. (1972) *Pedagogy of the Oppressed*, Harmondsworth: Penguin.

Freire, P. (1976) *Education: The Practice of Freedom*, London: Writers and Readers Cooperative.

Fullan, M. (1993) *Change Forces: probing the depths of educational reform*, London: Falmer.

Galton, M. and Moon, B. (eds.) (1983) *Changing Schools . . . Changing Curriculum*, London: Harper and Row.

Galton, M., Simon, B. and Croll, P. (1980) *Inside the Primary Classroom*, London: Routledge.

Gipps, C. (1994) *Beyond Testing: Towards a Theory of Educational Assessment*, London: Falmer.

Goddard, A. (1983) Processes in special education, in Blenkin, G. M. and Kelly, A. V. (eds.) (1983) *The Primary Curriculum in Action*, London: Harper and Row.

Goddard, D. (1985) Assessing teachers: a critical response to the government's proposals, *Journal of Evaluation in Education*, 8:35–8.

Goodson, I. F. (1981) Becoming an academic subject: patterns of explanation and evolution, *British Journal of Sociology of Education*, 2(2):163–80.

Goodson, I. F. (1983) *School Subjects and Curriculum Change*, Beckenham: Croom Helm.

Goodson, I. F. (1985a) Subjects for study, in Goodson, I. F. (ed.) (1985b) *Social Histories of the Secondary Curriculum: Subjects for Study*, London and Philadelphia: Falmer.

Goodson, I. F. (ed.) (1985b) *Social Histories of the Secondary Curriculum: Subjects for Study*, London and Philadelphia: Falmer.

Goodson, I. F. and Ball, S. J. (eds.) (1984) *Defining the Curriculum: Histories and Ethnographies*, London and Philadelphia: Falmer.

Gross, N., Giacquinta, J. B. and Bernstein, M. (1971) *Implementing Organizational Innovations: A Sociological Analysis of Planned Change*, New York: Harper & Row.

Grundy, S. (1987) *Curriculum: Product or Praxis?*, London: Falmer.

Habermas, J. (1972) *Knowledge and Human Interests* (tr. J. Shapiro). London: Heinemann.

Haldane, J., (ed.) (1992) *Education, Values and Culture: the Victor Cook Memorial Lectures*, St. Andrews: University of St.Andrews.

Halpin, A. W. (1966) *Theory and Research in Educational Administration*, New York: Macmillan.

Halpin, A. W. (1967) Change and organizational climate, *Journal of Educational Administration*, 5.

Hamilton, D. (1976) *Curriculum Evaluation*, London: Open Books.

Hargreaves, A. (1989) *Curriculum and Assessment Reform*, Milton Keynes: Open University Press.

Harris, K. (1979) *Education and Knowledge: the structured misrepresentation of reality*, London: Routledge.

Havelock, R. G. (1971) *Planning for Innovation through the Dissemination and Utilization of Knowledge*, Ann Arbor, Michigan: Centre for Research and Utilization of Knowledge.

Hirst, P. H. (1965) Liberal education and the nature of knowledge, in Archambault, R. D. (ed.) (1965) *Philosophical Analysis and Education*, London: Routledge. Also in Peters, R. S. (ed.) (1973b) *The Philosophy of Education*, Oxford: Oxford University Press.

Hirst, P. H. (1969) The logic of the curriculum, *Journal of Curriculum Studies*, 1:142–58. Also in Hooper, R. (ed.) (1971) *The Curriculum: Context, Design and Development*, Edinburgh: Oliver and Boyd in association with the Open University Press. pp.232–250

Hirst, P. H. (1974) *Knowledge and the Curriculum*, London: Routledge.

Hirst, P. H. (1975) The curriculum and its objectives – a defence of piecemeal rational planning, in *Studies in Education 2. The Curriculum. The Doris Lee Lectures*, London: University of London Institute of Education.

Hirst, P. H. and Peters, R. S. (1970) *The Logic of Education*, London: Routledge.

Hobhouse, L. T. (1918) *The Metaphysical Theory of the State*, London: Allen and Unwin.

Hogan, P. (ed.) (1995) *Partnership and the Benefits of Learning*, Maynooth College: Educational Studies Association of Ireland.

Hogben, D. (1972) The behavioural objectives approach: some problems and some dangers, *Journal of Curriculum Studies*, 4(1):42–50.

Hoggart, R. (1992) *An Imagined Life (Life and Times Volume III: 1959–91)*, London: Chatto and Windus.

Hollins, T. H. B. (ed.) (1964) *Aims in Education: The Philosophic Approach*, Manchester University Press.

Holmes, E. (1911) *What Is and What Might Be*, London: Constable and Co. Ltd.

Holt, M. (1981) *Evaluating the Evaluators*, London: Hodder.

Holt, M. (1987a) *Judgement, Planning and Educational Change*, London: Harper and Row.

Holt, M. (ed.) (1987b) *Skills and Vocationalism: The Easy Answer*, Milton Keynes: Open University Press.

Hooper, R. (ed.) (1971) *The Curriculum: Context, Design and Development*, Edinburgh: Oliver and Boyd in association with the Open University Press.

House, E. R. (1974) *The Politics of Educational Innovation*, Berkeley: McCutchan.

Hoyle, E. (1969a) How does the curriculum change? 1. A proposal for inquiries, *Journal of Curriculum Studies*, 1(2):132–41. Also in Hooper, R. (ed.) (1971) *The Curriculum: Context, Design and Development*, Edinburgh: Oliver and Boyd in association with the Open University Press.

Hoyle, E. (1969b) How does the curriculum change? 2. Systems and strategies, *Journal of Curriculum Studies*, 1(3):230–9. Also in Hooper, R. (ed.) (1971) *The Curriculum: Context, Design and Development*, Edinburgh: Oliver and Boyd in association with the Open University Press.

Illich, I. D. (1971) *Deschooling Society*, London: Calder.

James, C. M. (1968) *Young Lives at Stake*, London: Collins.

Jeffcoate, R. (1984) *Ethnic Minorities and Education*, London: Harper and Row.

Jeffrey, R. and Woods, P. (1998) *Testing Teachers*, London: Falmer.

Keddie, N. (1971) Classroom knowledge, in Young, M. F. D. (ed.) (1971), *Knowledge and Control*. London: Collier-Macmillan.

Kelly, A. V. (ed.) (1976) *The Scope of Education: Opportunities for the Teacher*, Report of a Conference, London: Goldsmiths' College.

Kelly, A. V. (ed.) (1980) *Curriculum Context*, London: Harper and Row.

Kelly, A. V. (1980a) Ideological constraints on curriculum planning, in Kelly, A. V. (ed.) (1980b) *Curriculum Context*, London: Harper and Row, pp. 7–30.

Kelly, A. V. (1980b) *Curriculum Context*, London: Harper and Row.

Kelly, A. V. (1981) Research and the primary curriculum, *Journal of Curriculum Studies*, 13(3):215–25.

Kelly, A. V. (1986) *Knowledge and Curriculum Planning*, London: Harper and Row.

Kelly, A. V. (1987) The Assessment of Performance Unit and the school curriculum, *Curriculum*, 8(1):19–28.

Kelly, A. V. (1990) *The National Curriculum: A Critical Review* (updated edition 1994), London: Paul Chapman.

Kelly, A. V. (1992) Concepts of assessment: an overview, in Blenkin, G. M. and Kelly, A. V. (eds.) *Assessment in Early Childhood Education*, London: Paul Chapman.

Kelly, A. V. (1995) *Education and Democracy*, London: Paul Chapman.

Kelly, A. V. (1998) Personal, social and moral education in a democratic society, in Edwards, G. and Kelly, A. V. (eds.) (1998b) *Experience and Education: Towards an Alternative National Curriculum*, London: Paul Chapman.

Kelly, A. V. and Blenkin, G. M. (1993) Never mind the quality: feel the breadth and balance, in Campbell, R. J. (ed.) (1993) *Breadth and Balance in the Primary Curriculum*, London and Washington, DC: Falmer.

Kelly, P. J. (1973) Nuffield 'A' level biological science project, in Schools Council (1973) *Evaluation in Curriculum Development: Twelve Case Studies*, Schools Council Research Studies. London: Macmillan Education for the Schools Council.

Kennedy, K. J. (1995) An analysis of the policy contexts of recent curriculum reform efforts in Australia, Great Britain and the US, in Carter, D. S. G. and O'Neill, M. H. O. (eds.) *International Perspectives on Educational Reform and Policy Implementation*, London: Falmer.

Kerr, J. F. (ed.) (1968) *Changing the Curriculum*, London: University of London Press.

Kogan, M. (1978) *The Politics of Educational Change*, London: Fontana.

Kohlberg, L. and Mayer, R. (1972) Development as the aim of education, *Harvard Educational Review*, 4:449–96.

Kratwohl, D. R. (1965) Stating objectives appropriately for program, for curriculum, and for instructional materials development, *Journal of Teacher Education*, 16:83–92.

Kratwohl, D. R. *et al.* (1964) *Taxonomy of Educational Objectives. 11. Affective Domain*, London: Longman.

Lawn, M. (1990) From responsibility to competency: a new context for curriculum studies in England and Wales, *Journal of Curriculum Studies*, 22(4):388–392.

Lawton, D. (1969) The idea of an integrated curriculum, *University of London Institute of Education Bulletin*, 19:5–11.

Lawton, D. (1973) *Social Change, Educational Theory and Curriculum Planning*, London: University of London Press.

Lawton, D. (1975) *Class, Culture and the Curriculum*, London: Routledge.

Lawton, D. (1980) *The Politics of the School Curriculum*, London: Routledge.

Lawton, D. (1989) *Education, Culture and the National Curriculum*, London, Sydney, Auckland and Toronto: Hodder and Stoughton.

Lawton, D. (1992) *Education and Politics in the 1990s: Conflict or Consensus*, London and Washington, DC: Falmer.

Lawton, D. (1994) *The Tory Mind on Education 1979–94*, London: Falmer.

Lawton, D. and Chitty, C. (eds.) (1988) *The National Curriculum*. Bedford Way Papers 33, London: University of London Institute of Education.

Leeming, K., Swann, W., Coupe, J. and Mittler, P. (1979) *Teaching Language and Communication to the Mentally Handicapped*, London: Evans/Methuen Educational for the Schools Council.

Lyotard, J-F. (1984) *The Postmodern Condition: A Report on Knowledge*, Minneapolis: University of Minnesota Press.

MacDonald, B. (1973) Humanities Curriculum Project, in Schools Council (1973) *Evaluation in Curriculum Development: Twelve Case Studies*. Schools Council Research Studies. London: Macmillan Education for the Schools Council.

MacDonald, B. (1975) Evaluation and the control of education, in Tawney, D. (ed.) (1975) *Curriculum Evaluation Today: Trends and Implications*, Schools Council Research Studies. London: Macmillan Education for the Schools Council.

MacDonald, B. and Rudduck, J. (1971) Curriculum research and development projects: barriers to success, *British Journal of Educational Psychology*, 41:148–54.

MacDonald, B. and Walker, R. (1976) *Changing the Curriculum*, London: Open Books.

MacIntyre, A. C. (1964) Against utilitarianism, in Hollins, T. H. B. (ed.) (1964) *Aims in Education: The Philosophic Approach*, Manchester: Manchester University Press.

Maclure, S. (1968) *Curriculum Innovation in Practice: Canada, England and Wales, United States*, London: HMSO.

Mager, R. F. (1962) *Preparing Instructional Objectives*, Palo Alto, California: Fearon.

Maw, J. (1985) Curriculum control and cultural norms: change and conflict in a British context, *The New Era*, 22(4):95–98.

McMurtry, J. (1991) Education and the market model, *Journal of Philosophy of Education*, 25(2):209–217.

Metz, M. (1988, 1996) The development of mathematical understanding, in Blenkin, G. M. and Kelly, A. V. (eds.) (1988b) (2nd edn 1996) *Early Childhood Education: A Developmental Curriculum*, London: Paul Chapman.

Money, T. (1988) Early literacy, in Blenkin, G. M. and Kelly, A. V. (eds.) (1988b) *Early Childhood Education: A Developmental Curriculum*, London: Paul Chapman.

Moutsios, S. (1998) State curriculum control in Greece and England: a comparative study, Ph.D. thesis, London: University of London Institute of Education.

Murphy, R. and Torrance, H. (1988) *The Changing Face of Educational Assessment*, Milton Keynes: Open University Press.

Norris, N. (1990) *Understanding Educational Evaluation*, London: Falmer.

Nunn, T. P. (1920) *Education: Its Data and First Principles*, London: Arnold.

Nuttall, D. (1989) National assessment: complacency or misinterpretation?, in Lawton, D. (ed.) *The Education Reform Act: Choice and Control*, London: Hodder.

O'Hear, A. (1992) The Victor Cook memorial lectures, in Haldane, J. (ed.) (1992) *Education, Value and Culture: the Victor Cook Memorial Lectures*. St Andrews: University of St Andrews.

O'Hear, P. and White, J. (eds.) (1993) *Assessing the National Curriculum*, London: Paul Chapman.

Ortony, A. (ed.) (1979) *Metaphor and Thought*, Cambridge: Cambridge University Press.

Parlett, M. and Hamilton, D. (1975) Evaluation as illumination, in Tawney, D. (ed.) (1975) *Curriculum Evaluation Today: Trends and Implications*. Schools Council Research Studies. London: Macmillan Education for the Schools Council.

Peters, R. S. (1965) Education as initiation, in Archambault, R. D. (ed.) (1965) *Phiosophical Analysis and Education*, London: Routledge.

Peters, R. S. (1966) *Ethics and Education*, London: Allen & Unwin.

Peters, R. S. (1973a) Aims of education: a conceptual inquiry, in Peters, R. S. (ed.) (1973b) *The Philosophy of Education*, Oxford: Oxford University Press.

Peters, R. S. (1973b) *The Philosophy of Education*, Oxford: Oxford University Press.

Petter, G. S. V. (1970) Coherent secondary education, *Trends in Education*, 19:38–43.

Phenix, P. H. (1964) *Realms of Meaning*, New York: McGraw-Hill.

Piaget, J. (1969) *Science of Education and the Psychology of the Child* (1971 edn), London: Longman.

Pirsig, R. (1974) *Zen and the Art of Motorcycle Maintenance*, London: Bodley Head.

Plant, R. (1997) *Hegel*, London: Phoenix.

Popham, W. J. (1969) Objectives and instruction, in Popham *et al.* (1969) *Instructional Objectives*, American Educational Research Association Monograph Series on Curriculum Evaluation No.3. Chicago: Rand McNally.

Popham, W. J., Eisner, E. W., Sullivan, H. J. and Tyler, L. L. (1969) *Instructional Objectives*, American Educational Research Association Monograph Series on Curriculum Evaluation No.3, Chicago: Rand McNally.

Popper, K. (1945) *The Open Society and Its Enemies*, London: Routledge.

Powell, E. (1985) A modern barbarism, *The Times Educational Supplement* 4, January.

Quinton, A. (1978) *The Politics of Imperfection: The Religious and Secular Traditions of Conservative Thought in England from Hooker to Oakeshott*, London: Faber and Faber.

Reid, W. A. (1978) *Thinking about the Curriculum*, London: Routledge.

Rodger, I. A. and Richardson, J. A. S. (1985) *Self-Evaluation for Primary Schools*, London: Hodder and Stoughton.

Ross, A. (1997) *Curriculum, Construction and Critique*, London: Falmer.

Russell, B. (1950) *Unpopular Essays*, London: Allen and Unwin.

Rutter, M. , Maughan, B., Mortimore, P. and Ouston, J. (1979) *Fifteen Thousand Hours: secondary schools and their effects on children*. London: Open Books.

Sammons, P., Hillman, J. and Mortimore, P. (1995) *Key Characteristics of Effective Schools: A Review of School Effectiveness Research*, London: University of London Institute of Education and OFSTED.

Schon, D. A. (1971) *Beyond the Stable State*, London: Temple-Smith.

Schools Council (1967) *Society and the Young School Leaver*, Working Paper 11, London: HMSO.

Schools Council (1970) *The Humanities Project: An Introduction*, London: Heinemann.

Schools Council (1971a) *A Common System of Examining at 16+*, Examinations Bulletin 23, London: Evans/Methuen Educational for the Schools Council.

Schools Council (1971b) *Choosing a Curriculum for the Young School Leaver*, Working Paper 33, London: Evans/Methuen Educational for the Schools Council.

Schools Council (1973) *Evaluation in Curriculum Development: Twelve Case Studies*, Schools Council Research Studies, London: Macmillan Education for the Schools Council.

Schools Council (1974a) *Social Education: An Experiment in Four Secondary Schools*, Working Paper 51, London: Evans/Methuen Educational for the Schools Council.

Schools Council (1974b) *Dissemination and In-service Training: Report of the Schools Council Working Party on Dissemination (1972–1973)*, Schools Council Pamphlet 14, London: Schools Council.

Schools Council (1975a) *The Whole Curriculum 13–16*, Working Paper 53, London: Evans/Methuen Educational for the Schools Council.

Schools Council (1975b) *Examinations at 16+: Proposals for the Future*, Examination Bulletin 23, London: Evans/Methuen Educational for the Schools Council.

Schools Council (1975c) *The Curriculum in the Middle Years*, Working Paper 55, London: Evans/Methuen Educational for the Schools Council.

Schools Council (1978) *Impact and Take-up Project. A First Interim Report*, London: Schools Council.

Schools Council (1980) *Impact and Take-up Project. A Condensed Interim Report on Secondary Schools*, London: Schools Council.

Scriven, M. (1967) The methodology of evaluation, in Stake, R. E. (ed.) (1967) *Perspectives of Curriculum Evaluation*, American Educational Research Association, Monograph Series on Curriculum Evaluation No.1, Chicago: Rand McNally.

Shipman, M. D. (1971) Curriculum for inequality?, in Hooper, R. (ed.) (1971) *The Curriculum: Context, Design and Development*, Edinburgh: Oliver and Boyd in association with the Open University Press.

Shipman, M. D. (1972) Contrasting views of a curriculum project, *Journal of Curriculum Studies*, 4: 145–53.

Shipman, M. D. (1973) The impact of a curriculum project, *Journal of Curriculum Studies*, 5:47–57.

Sholle, D. (1992) Authority on the left: critical pedagogy, postmodernism and vital strategies, *Cultural Studies*, 6(2):271–289.

Simon, B. (1985) *Does Education Matter?*, London: Lawrence and Wishart.

Skilbeck, M. (1976) School-based curriculum development, in Open University Course 203, Unit 26, Milton Keynes: Open University Press.

Skinner, B. F. (1964) Education in 1984, *New Scientist* 21/5/1964.

Sockett, H. (1976a) *Designing the Curriculum*, London: Open Books.

Sockett, H. (1976b) Teacher accountability, *Proceedings of the Philosophy of Education Society*, July:34–57.

Stake, R. E. (ed.) (1967) *Perspectives of Curriculum Evaluation*, American Educational Research Association, Monograph Series on Curriculum Evaluation No.1, Chicago: Rand McNally.

Stake, R. (1972) Analysis and portrayal, paper originally written for AERA Annual Meeting presentation 1972, republished as 'Responsive Education' in *New Trends in Education*, No.35 (1975) Göteborg: Institute of Education, University of Göteborg.

Stenhouse, L. (1970) Some limitations of the use of objectives in curriculum research and planning, *Paedagogica Europaea*, 6:73–83.

Stenhouse, L. (1975) *An Introduction to Curriculum Research and Development*, London: Heinemann.

Stenhouse, L. (ed.) (1979) *Educational Analysis*, 1(1).

Stenhouse, L. (1980a) Reflections, in Stenhouse, L. (ed.) (1980b) *Curriculum Research and Development in Action*, London: Heinemann.

Stenhouse, L. (ed.) (1980b) *Curriculum Research and Development in Action*, London: Heinemann.

Stenhouse, L. (1983) The legacy of the curriculum movement, in Galton, M. and Moon, B. (eds.) (1983) *Changing Schools . . . Changing Curriculum*, London: Harper and Row.

Swann, W. (1981) *The Practice of Special Education*, London: Blackwell in association with Open University Press.

Taba, H. (1962) *Curriculum Development: Theory and Practice*, New York: Harcourt, Brace and World.

Tawney, D. (1973) Evaluation and curriculum development, in Schools Council (1973) *Evaluation in Curriculum Development: Twelve Case Studies*, Schools Council Research Studies. London: Macmillan Education for the Schools Council.

Tawney, D. (ed.) (1975) *Curriculum Evaluation Today: Trends and Implications*, Schools Council Research Studies, London: Macmillan Education for the Schools Council.

Thompson, K. and White, J. (1975) *Curriculum Development: A Dialogue*, London: Pitman.

Tizard, B. and Hughes, M. (1984) *Young Children Learning: Talking and Thinking at Home and at School*, London: Fontana.

Torrance, H. (1989) Theory, practice and politics in the development of assessment, *Cambridge Journal of Education*, 19(2):183–190.

Turner, B. (ed.) (1990) *Theories of Modernity and Postmodernity*, London: Sage.

Tyler, R. W. (1932) The construction of examinations in botany and zoology. Service Studies in Higher Education, Ohio State University, Bureau of Educational Research Monographs, 15:49–50.

Tyler, R. W. (1949) *Basic Principles of Curriculum and Instruction*, Chicago: University of Chicago Press.

Warnock, M. (1977) *Schools of Thought*, London: Faber.

Weiler, H. N. (1990) Comparative perspectives on educational decentralisation: an exercise in contradiction?, *Educational Evaluation and Policy Analysis*, 12(4):433–448.

Weiss, R. S. and Rein, M. (1969) The evaluation of broad aim programmes: a cautionary tale and a moral, *Annals of the American Academy of Political and Social Science*, 385:133–42.

Wellington, J. J. (1981) Determining a core curriculum: the limitations of transcendental deductions, *Journal of Curriculum Studies*, 13(1):17–24.

Wells, G. (1981a) Becoming a communicator, in Wells, G. (ed.) (1981b) *Learning through Interaction: The Study of Language Development*, Cambridge: Cambridge University Press.

Wheeler, D. K. (1967) *Curriculum Process*, London: University of London Press.

White, J. P. (1968) Education in obedience, *New Society*, 2 May.

White, J. P. (1971) The concept of curriculum evaluation, *Journal of Curriculum Studies*, 3:101–12.

White, J. P. (1973) *Towards a Compulsory Curriculum*, London: Routledge.

White, J. P. (1975) The end of the compulsory curriculum, in *The Curriculum – The Doris Lee Lectures 1975*, London: University of London Institute of Education.

White, J. P. (1988) An unconstitutional national curriculum, in Lawton, D. and Chitty, C. (eds.) (1988) *The National Curriculum*, Bedford Way Papers 33. London: University of London Institute of Education.

Whitty, G. and Young, M. F. D. (eds.) (1976) *Explorations in the Politics of School Knowledge*, Nafferton: Nafferton Books.

Williams, R. (1961) *The Long Revolution*, London: Chatto (also Penguin 1961).

Wilson, P. S. (1971) *Interest and Discipline in Education*, London: Routledge.

Winter, R. (1991) Post-modern sociology as a democratic educational practice? Some suggestions, *British Journal of Sociology of Education*, 12(4): 467–481.

Wittgenstein, L. (1980) *Culture and Value*, (edited von Wright, G. H. in collaboration with Nyman, H. tr. Winch, P.) Oxford: Blackwell.

Young, M. F. D. (ed.) (1971) *Knowledge and Control*, London: Collier-Macmillan.

Young, M. F. D. (1976) The rhetoric of curriculum development, in Whitty, G. and Young, M. F. D. (eds) (1976) *Explorations in the Politics of School Knowledge*, Nafferton: Nafferton Books.

Government reports and other official publications referred to in the text

Board of Education (1926) *The Education of the Adolescent* (the Hadow Report on Secondary Education), London: HMSO.

Board of Education (1931) *Primary Education* (the Hadow Report on Primary Education), London: HMSO.

Board of Education (1933) *Infant and Nursery Schools* (the Hadow Report on Infant and Nursery Schools), London: HMSO.

Board of Education (1938) *Secondary Education with Special Reference to Grammar Schools and Technical High Schools* (The Spens Report), London: HMSO.

Board of Education (1943) *Report of the Committee of the Secondary Schools Examinations Council: Curriculum and Examinations in Secondary Schools* (the Norwood Report), London: HMSO.

Central Advisory Council For Education (1959) *15 to 18* (the Crowther Report), London: HMSO.

Central Advisory Council for Education (1963) *Half Our Future* (the Newsom Report), London: HMSO.

Central Advisory Council for Education (1967) *Children and Their Primary Schools* (the Plowden Report), London: HMSO.

Department for Education and Employment (1992) *Choice and Diversity: A New Framework for Schools*, London: HMSO.

Department for Education and Employment in conjunction with the School Curriculum and Assessment Authority (SCAA) (1996) *Desirable Outcomes for Children's Learning on Entering Compulsory Education*: London: SCAA.

Department of Education and Science (1975) *A Language for Life* (the Bullock Report), London: HMSO.

Department of Education and Science (1977a) *A New Partnership for our Schools* (the Taylor Report), London: HMSO.

Department of Education and Science and the Welsh Office (1977b) *Education in Schools: A Consultative Document* (Green Paper), cmnd. 6869, London: HMSO.

Department of Education and Science (1977c) *Curriculum 11–16*, London: HMSO.

Department of Education and Science (1977c) *Curriculum 11–16*, London: HMSO.

Department of Education and Science (1978) *Primary Education in England: A Survey by HM Inspectors of Schools*, London: HMSO.

Department of Education and Science (1979) *Aspects of Secondary Education in England: A Survey by HM Inspectors of Schools*, London: HMSO.

Department of Education and Science (1980a) *A View of the Curriculum*, HMI Series, *Matters for Discussion*, no. 11, London: HMSO.

Department of Education and Science and the Welsh Office (1980b) *A Framework for the School Curriculum*, London: HMSO.

Department of Education and Science (1980c) *Special Needs in Education* (the Warnock Report), London: HMSO.

Department of Education and Science and the Welsh Office (1981) *The School Curriculum*, London: HMSO.

Department of Education and Science (1984a) *English from 5 to 16. Curriculum Matters 1*, London: HMSO.

Department of Education and Science (1984b) *Curriculum 11–16: towards a statement of entitlement*, London: HMSO.

Department of Education and Science (1985a) *The Curriculum from 5 to 16. Curriculum Matters 2*, London: HMSO.

Department of Education and Science (1985b) *Mathematics from 5 to 16. Curriculum Matters 3*, London: HMSO.

Department of Education and Science (1985c) *Music from 5 to 16. Curriculum Matters 4*, London: HMSO.

Department of Education and Science (1985d) *Home Economics from 5 to 16. Curriculum Matters 5*, London: HMSO.

Department of Education and Science (1986a) *Health Education from 5 to 16. Curriculum Matters 6*, London: HMSO.

Department of Education and Science (1986b) *Geography from 5 to 16. Curriculum Matters 7*, London: HMSO.

Department of Education and Science (1987a) *The National Curriculum 5–16: a consultative document*, London: HMSO.

Department of Education and Science (1987b) *Modern Foreign Languages to 16. Curriculum Matters 8*, London: HMSO.

Department of Education and Science (1987c) *Craft, design and technology from 5 to 16. Curriculum Matters 9*, London: HMSO.

Department of Education and Science (1988) *National Curriculum: Task Group on Assessment and Testing: A Report*, London: HMSO.

Department of Education and Science (1989) *National Curriculum: from Policy to Practice*. London:HMSO.

House of Commons Expenditure Committee (1976) *Policy-Making in the DES*, London: HMSO.

Office for Standards in Education (1995) *The OFSTED Handbook: Guidance on the Inspection of Nursery and Primary Schools*. London: HMSO.

Report of the Commission appointed to enquire into the state of popular education in England (the Newcastle Report) (1861).

Report of the Schools Inquiry Commission (the Taunton Report) (1868).

School Curriculum and Assessment Authority (SCAA) (1993) *The National Curriculum and its Assessment, Final Report* (the Dearing Report), London: SCAA.

School Curriculum and Assessment Authority (SCAA) (1997a) *Looking at Children's Learning: Desirable Outcomes for Children's Learning on Entering Compulsory Education*, London: SCAA.

School Curriculum and Assessment Authority (SCAA) (1997b) *Teacher Assessment in Key Stage 2*, London: SCAA.

Secondary Schools Examinations Council (1960) *Secondary School Examinations other than the GCE* (the Beloe Report), London: HMSO.

Index of names

Index of subjects